Real Security

SUNY Series, Global Conflict and Peace

Betty A. Reardon, editor

Real Security

Converting the Defense Economy and Building Peace

edited by
Kevin J. Cassidy and Gregory A. Bischak

State University of New York Press

Published by
State University of New York Press, Albany

Printed in the United States of America

For information, address State University of New York Press, State University Plaza, Albany, N.Y., 12246

Production by Dana Foote
Marketing by Bernadette LaManna

Library of Congress Cataloging in Publication Data

Real security: converting the defense economy and building peace /
edited by Kevin J. Cassidy and Gregory A. Bischak.
p. cm.—(SUNY series, global conflict and peace)
Includes bibliographical references (p.) and index.
ISBN 0–7914–1607–0 (hc : acid free).—ISBN 0–7914–1608–9 (pb : acid free)
1. Disarmament—Economic aspects. 2. Economic conversion.
3. National security. 4. Peace. I. Cassidy, Kevin J.
II. Bischak, Gregory, 1950– . III. Series.
HC79.D4R43 1993
338.4'76234—dc20 92–32011
CIP

10 9 8 7 6 5 4 3 2 1

This volume is dedicated to Seymour Melman for his pioneering research on economic conversion of the military-industrial complex and to Kevin Bean for his leadership in conversion work on the state and local levels.

CONTENTS

Part Two
The Making of Conversion Policy

FOREWORD

There is no single issue that opens all the areas of human security as does conversion. As can be seen from this rich collection edited by Kevin Cassidy and Greg Bischak with a view to a systematic synthesis, conversion raises all the crucial questions. Economic conversion is but the center of the many-faceted task of reconstituting world politics. It can be the main dynamic in rechanneling human energies from a concentration on the capacities to control and destroy to a focus on construction and development. It forces us to confront questions of fundamental social values by asking, "How we will use our resources; to what purposes and for whose benefit?" Having lived through decades of an exhausting arms race that benefited only those few who feared the evolution of authentic democracy, we need to prepare ourselves to exploit the opportunities presented by a world system that is rapidly changing. This volume is a vehicle for such preparation.

These essays challenge us to reflect upon multiple aspects of change and raise questions about the costs the military production imposes not only on our productive capacities, and social and economic infrastructures, but also on the political system and the very culture itself. While the arms race had devastating economic and political effects on most world regions, it may have had its most destructive impact on the degree to which it stalled, even reversed, the "American Dream." Only in the election campaign of 1992 could we again use the term without embarrassment, as the United States came to face what had been done to our visions of social equality, economic equity, and synthetic democracy by political and economic processes determined by the goal of military superiority. The authors Cassidy and Bischak have invited us to examine the various aspects of conversion and they provide us with information about these consequences, but more importantly they offer possibilities for alternatives.

The postulation and assessment of alternatives is a fundamental component of peace education. Now is the time for us to exercise the capacity to conceptualize other ways to conduct economic enterprise, assure national security, and resolve conflict. Cassidy's and Bischak's volume is a tool for the development of that capacity, and thus a significant contribution to peace education.

Betty A. Reardon
Series Editor

INTRODUCTION AND OVERVIEW

Kevin J. Cassidy

With the end of the Cold War and the dissolution of the Soviet Union, an unparalleled opportunity exists to reexamine the military and foreign policies of the United States. Events in the former Soviet Union and Eastern Europe have made it clear that U.S. security needs no longer require the same massive arsenal. Military spending is being cut, adversely affecting workers in many regions of the country. The Gulf War didn't change this. The war was a military victory, but it didn't answer the question that was an issue before it began: how should national security be established now that the Cold War is over? Answering that question will require a new way of thinking about the nation's security needs.

For contemporary Americans, real security also includes regular employment and affordable housing, sound banks and a reduced national deficit, a clean environment, and freedom from crime and drug-related violence. These needs cannot be met without a prosperous economy based on resurgent American industries able to hold their own in the world marketplace. National security then is not only military strength; it's a holistic response to a wide range of human needs. Meeting these needs at a time of recession and tight budgets would seem to be all but impossible without resources as yet undiscovered. Americans will have to find a new way of thinking about their country's domestic needs just as they have begun the process of reinventing the nation's foreign policy.

The link between these two dimensions of national security is economic conversion: the planned transformation of excess military production to civilian purposes. There is now abundant research indicating that the conversion process is entirely doable, that the obstacles are not technical or economic. The real barrier is the commitment to business as usual in American defense policy as well as in American economic practice. This attitude must be overcome before the particulars of conversion can be considered and implemented. Conversion advocates need to demonstrate that there are realistic alternatives to the militarism that has guided American defense policy and to the style of capitalism that has contributed to the nation's recent economic decline. Presenting these new alternatives is the role of the first four chapters, which make up part 1 of the book. Part 2 then treats conversion in more detailed terms, examining particular efforts in the United States and the former Soviet Union as well as a host of new approaches currently being developed.

Chapter 1 sketches an outline for a new defense policy for the United States. Written by Gregory A. Bischak, executive director of the National Commission on Economic Conversion and Disarmament, this essay points out that disarmament, and especially nuclear disarmament, was a major theme in American thinking until the Cold War pushed it into obscurity. Bischak argues that the end of the Cold War has created the opportunity to redefine disarmament goals and he describes the international structures and processes necessary to realize these goals in an era of nuclear proliferation. "It is a matter of inventing new institutions," he suggests, "rather than disinventing the bomb."

But the control of nuclear weaponry is just one aspect of the larger task of establishing international security. This can be achieved, Bischak points out, without the huge arsenals of the superpowers. He outlines the principles of "common security," advocated by a variety of contemporary thinkers, that would permit the United States to reduce military spending far more than is currently planned. Common security rejects the zero-sum game of traditional superpower rivalry and substitutes a recognition by each of the major powers of the others' legitimate security needs. This makes possible a strictly defensive alignment of all military forces instead of the war-making, first-strike capability each is still burdened with. This restructuring of forces would mean substantial reductions of weaponry and military personnel as well as the curtailing of nuclear modernization programs. Common security also envisions the development of stronger international and regional peacekeeping mechanisms as alternatives to superpower intervention in underdeveloped countries.

The extensive disarmament that such an approach would make possible will create economic upheaval in the numerous defense-dependent communities across the country. In chapter 2 Joel Yudken of the Project on Regional and Industrial Economics at Rutgers University addresses this problem by considering the conversion of defense facilities, not as a separate, unique task, but as a part of the larger goal of revitalizing America's entire industrial base. The nation now faces a series of daunting economic tasks: restoring the competitiveness of its civilian industry; renewing its infrastructure; providing good education, housing, and health care; as well as cleaning up the environment. What is required is a new national industrial and technological policy to prioritize production needs, a national needs agenda to redirect the resources of the United States.

Yudken points out that America's civilian manufacturing has been handicapped by the nation's huge investment in military production. Over the past forty years the military budget has actually exceeded the monetary value of all civilian industry's facilities and the nation's public infrastructure combined! In reality the country *has* had an industrial policy during these years, but it has been disguised as defense policy and therefore never evaluated in appropriate terms. The task now is to create an effective industrial policy and integrate economic conversion as a component of it.

If the United States has paid a high economic price for its involvement in the arms race, the nation's environment has also been penalized heavily for these defense policies. In fact, the penalty has been far harsher than Americans realize. This is the message of chapter 3 by Michael Renner of the Worldwatch Institute. Renner points out that the Department of Defense holds land roughly equivalent in area to the state of Virginia and has also attempted to add an area bigger than Connecticut and Rhode Island combined. Military maneuvers, war games, and weapons testing create severe degradation to this land and to the surrounding communities. Already ninety-six military bases across the United States are so badly polluted that they are on the Superfund National Priorities List. The contamination from nuclear weapons alone will cost between $100 billion and $300 billion to clean up. Other deleterious effects include military-generated air pollution and ozone depletion, along with the gargantuan consumption of fuels and energy. Renner also systematically documents the environmental catastrophe created by the Gulf War.

All of this makes disarmament even more compelling. Renner suggests a program for cleaning up the military's pollution and argues the case for conversion. He cautions, however, that not everything civilian is ecologically sound. It is necessary to have an environmental awareness beyond simply converting from military production. Without such an attitude we may be merely exchanging one form of pollution for another.

The real difficulty in redefining national security is not in setting out the themes of common security, economic revitalization, and environmental integrity, but in grappling with those who oppose this vision because they have a vested interest in the status quo. In chapter 4 Bischak names these interests including the corporations that produce the arsenals for the military, the labor force employed in the defense plants, and those representing these groups in Congress who promote new weapons systems in every military budget. Bischak points out that this system of "military corporatism" also includes the physical science and engineering professions, which benefit from high levels of government support for military research, as well as government managerial elites, which preside over the expanding bureaucracies. Key representatives from these vested interests comprise a rigid hierarchy that shapes national security policy. Bischak explains the historical development of this power as these groups have consistently increased their influence both inside and outside the government.

Economic conversion is an opportunity to undercut this military corporatism. By providing defense contractors and their work force with alternative, civilian products, conversion could begin to reduce the need these groups feel to pressure Congress for more weapons contracts. Especially through the broader industrial planning prescribed in chapter 2, conversion would permit the country to redeploy its scientific and technical personnel in the civilian sector where it is crucially needed. Part 2 of this book examines conversion efforts and what they can offer for the future.

Bischak and Yudken open part 2 with an examination of the myths that create obstacles to conversion planning. The authors begin with a consideration of the argument that normal economic growth can take care of the broad impact that the reduction in defense production is now having. They also examine the limits of private investment in responding to a defense downturn on the local level, as well as what can be expected from job-training programs. Finally, they address the argument of conversion opponents that conversion simply doesn't work. They point out that the evidence tells a far more complex story and that opposition to conversion is often an ideological reaction by those opposed to any positive role for government. In that respect the conversion debate is very much related to the broader question of the respective roles of the public and private sectors that is reflected in each facet of the conversion issue. Bischak and Yudken also examine the current slowdown in military production and demonstrate that it will be fundamentally different than the reductions following previous wars. This situation and the lessons learned from previous conversion efforts indicate that successful conversion planning will require a major coordinating role from the federal government.

The efforts to develop a federal conversion policy are described in chapter 6 by Maggie Bierwirth, a legislative aide to Congressman Sam Gejdenson (D-CT). Gejdenson's district is one of the most defense-dependent in the nation and Bierwirth has coordinated Gejdenson's efforts to respond to the needs of the tens of thousands of defense workers—and, indeed, the whole economy of eastern Connecticut. Bierwirth first sets out the three approaches considered to date by Congress. These range from the traditional response of making assistance available to unemployed workers, to the contemporary approach of providing diversification assistance to defense-dependent local economies, to the more direct plan of requiring defense contractors to set up alternative-use committees in their plants to do conversion planning.

Bierwirth provides a discussion of the political problems of each approach and an effort to find a compromise among the three. In the process she makes clear the particular problems of policy making in Congress, and especially the influence of the Pentagon on that branch of government. Ultimately, she concludes, conversion policy needs to be recognized and formulated as part of the larger issue of the economic redevelopment of the United States.

The difficulty of achieving conversion without a comprehensive national policy is made especially clear in chapter 7. This study, conducted by Catherine Hill, Sabina Dietrick, and Anne Markusen, represents the most comprehensive effort yet to analyze what happens when site conversion is attempted. The examples included here are: Quincy Shipyards, a division of General Dynamics, making military ships in Massachusetts; Blaw-Knox foundry, a subsidiary of White Consolidated Industries, making tanks in Indiana; the Long Beach plant of McDonnell-Douglas, manufacturing military aircraft in California; Lockheed Shipyards, Marine Division, outside Seattle; Philadelphia Naval Yards, repairing and overhauling military ships, and a Unisys Corporation plant in Minneapolis producing military computer systems for the Navy.

What is evident in these case studies is the extraordinary complexity of the conversion process. While technical in nature, it also involves countless other factors including the planning prerogatives of management, labor-management relations, the involvement of the local community, and the response of local and state elected officials, as well as the Pentagon and related federal agencies. It becomes clear that site conversion is technically doable but that defense contractors are often opposed to the process despite the downturn in military contracting. Their opposition may soften with a more dramatic downturn in defense spending. While the labor and community efforts chronicled here have not achieved success they are, nonetheless, important. They have demonstrated the broad-based support that exists for conversion, they have been catalysts for planning efforts at all levels of government, and they have highlighted a number of non-production problems (e.g., marketing) that need to be addressed.

For Michael Closson, director of the Center for Economic Conversion, the term *conversion* is not simply the process of transitioning workers from the defense industry into civilian manufacturing. In chapter 8 he discusses both conversion and diversification, explaining the latter as an opportunity for citizens in a defense-dependent area to redirect their economy to meet the needs of the community. In this respect diversification is first a democratic planning process in which the community assesses its resources, including the skills of workers at the defense plants, and determines how these resources can be used to produce a local peace economy. The focus is not on site conversion but on redeveloping the local economy in a civilian-oriented and environmentally sustainable way. This process, Closson emphasizes, is one that best includes not only management and labor but also the variety of groups that make up local community life. With these criteria in mind Closson evaluates a host of diversification projects including responses to military base closings in New Jersey, Texas, California, and New Hampshire as well as a varied set of community planning efforts in response to defense plant cutbacks in St. Louis, San Diego, Los Angeles County, Maine, and Vermont. This chapter also surveys the policies by municipal and state governments to encourage the economic development advocated by Closson.

An international approach is added by David W. McFadden in chapter 9 as he examines the state of the conversion movement in the former Soviet Union. A scholar of Russian and Soviet history who has also been involved in conversion efforts in this country, McFadden is in a unique position to analyze the situation in Russia and the other former Soviet republics. He explains the enormity of the Soviet military-industrial complex and its impact on the Soviet economy, where military production played an even more significant role in the economy than it has in the United States. McFadden describes the conversion program promoted by Mikhail Gorbachev, its acceptance as policy by the Soviet government, the formidable and largely successful obstacles placed in its way by the military-industrial bureaucracy, and the legacy inherited by Boris Yeltsin and his advisors.

But with the decentralization achieved through the dissolution of the Soviet state and the acceptance of free-market economics, the opposition to conversion by the bureaucratic elite is no longer as important a factor. The centralized economic system is now being overtaken in many areas by local and regional cooperatives able to attract managers and skilled workers ordinarily committed to industries associated with military production. Moreover, some of the most promising conversion efforts are happening through the participation of foreign companies in Russian economic development. McFadden chronicles these new international efforts which may ultimately prove to be the most influential factors in the conversion process there.

Chapter 10 recapitulates the major themes in the book and discusses them in the broader context of their contribution to democratic life in America. There has long been a concern over the lack of democratic participation in the making of public policy and nowhere is this more evident than in the formulation of national security policy. Military corporatism, as described by Bischak, has dominated this discussion to the virtual exclusion of alternative approaches such as common security. Military interests have been the major obstacle, as Bierwirth has pointed out, to comprehensive congressional policy on conversion as well as a dominant force against those who, like Yudken and Renner, have called for the transformation of American (military) industrial policy into one designed to meet civilian and environmental needs. Conversion can help democratize national policy making by restructuring military corporatism and, in so doing, reduce the pressure in Washington for a militaristic national security policy. This may open the policy-making process to the numerous individuals and groups who are committed to the kinds of alternatives addressed in this volume.

On the grass-roots level the myriad of conversion and conversion-related organizations cited throughout these chapters is testimony to the active group life that is at the heart of a truly democratic society. Moreover, the conversion case studies presented by Hill, Dietrick, and Markusen, and the diversification projects described by Closson, show how these groups have expanded the meaning of democracy by taking its values beyond strictly political institutions and into the economic realm itself. Chapter 10 uses two concepts, workplace democracy and "anticipatory" democracy, to explain the significance of this extension of democracy into the economic sector. The question of economic democracy invariably brings up another, related question: what is the role of government, and especially public planning, in the economy? Obviously this question is central to the conversion cases themselves and support for this type of public planning is explored here in terms of contemporary democratic theory as well as in the arguments of economists.

Such planning has to be focused on the goal of meeting so many fundamental social needs that have been ignored throughout the years of the arms race. Modern democratic political thought, as discussed in this chapter, has often made such positive material outcomes central to the meaning of democratic life. Conversion, especially at this extraordinary point in the nation's history, can contribute to this vision of a genuinely humane and participatory society.

Part One

Real Security and Economic Conversion

1

Cooperative Security, Disarmament and the Construction of International Peacekeeping Institutions

Gregory A. Bischak

Introduction

The disengagement from the Cold War by the United States and the former Soviet Union presents both nations with an unparalleled opportunity to develop an entirely new basis for ensuring peace and international security. With the collapse of the Soviet Union and the Warsaw Pact, the political rivalry which formed the raison d'être of the Cold War has virtually expired. Both nations have compelling reasons for drastically curtailing their respective military burdens because each country faces enormous financial and social deficits. In this context, a debate is unfolding within each country about the alternative approaches to domestic and international security.[1] Most discussions in the United States, however, focus on how to reduce and restructure the military consistent with the lower level of threats in the new international environment. The emphasis in this approach is on matching existing resources to the defensive needs of the country and its interests. Less discussion has been devoted to understanding how a common security framework coupled with a disarmament process and the construction of international peacekeeping institutions could improve international and domestic security while bringing an end to the arms race.

In this chapter I will investigate the real alternatives to the Cold War military system which have not been widely discussed and debated in the United States. In addition, I will review the current proposals that have originated from within the military establishment and contrast these proposals with others that call for a reduced and restructured U.S. military, examining their implications for the nation and the international order.

In place of the existing military system one can postulate four possible trajectories for the United States' role in the international security system. First, the entrenched adherents of the national security state have propounded and advanced what might be termed a "global power projection" framework for the post-Cold War order. While it has many variants it generally involves a scaled-down Pentagon oriented to limited power projection, but retaining substantial conventional forces and a nuclear force of perhaps 3,000 to 4,000 nuclear weapons.[2] I will argue that this global power projection model seeks to maintain U.S. military superiority even though it presupposes greater military cooperation among the northern industrialized powers.

A second security framework, which has evolved during the many years of the Cold War, is founded upon the doctrine of "common security." This common-security doctrine holds that in an interdependent world, a nation's security increasingly depends upon recognizing the security requirements of its neighboring nations in order to maintain and guarantee the political, economic, and environmental conditions of international stability. Under this common-security approach, the United States would require a far more limited military force geared to territorial defense, one which is noninterventionary, nonprovocative, and far less nuclear-dependent, possessing perhaps only 1,000 to 2,000 nuclear weapons. The reduction in military expenditures would require a corresponding increase in other expenditures to improve political, economic, and environmental conditions which currently threaten international security.[3]

A third approach envisions a truly international system of peacekeeping founded on the construction of international institutions to secure the peace through a standing international peacekeeping force, the formation of a permanent international inspectorate, and the development of international means to resolve disputes through international mediation and legal procedures. At the center of such an approach stands the United Nations, which would have to be reformed to reflect the end of the Cold War and the beginning of a new era of international peacekeeping and governance.[4]

A fourth approach, the most radical, envisions the development of a general and comprehensive disarmament process (GCD). This GCD framework builds upon proposals actually developed through negotiations between the United States and the Soviet Union during the Cold War. It sets forth a three-staged, verifiable process for the gradual elimination of weaponry among the leading industrialized powers, as well as the rest of the world. While often viewed as a utopian proposition, it will be argued here that GCD has had a pervasive practical influence on the regulation of international relations through various arms control and reduction treaties that have incorporated many of the institutional proposals first developed under the GCD framework.[5] Furthermore, it will be argued that the GCD framework has much to offer to post-Cold War policy debates.

Each of these alternative security frameworks is examined to show its respective assumptions about the objectives and the military and institutional requirements necessary to achieve these objectives. In addition, the likely budgetary implications of each approach are analyzed. Since each approach would involve major reductions in military forces and procurement, the economic implications are briefly discussed to introduce the role of economic conversion planning for avoiding and mitigating the negative economic repercussions of these reductions. Finally, a comparison of these different approaches is made to show how each framework may complement or conflict with the others. On the basis of this review, the author offers his own conclusions about the best direction for a post-Cold War international security order.

Prospects for a Post-Cold War U.S. Security Policy

With the breakup of the Cold War order, the United States can begin to reexamine the assumptions and costs of its military system and reshape its foreign and military policies. Halting steps in this direction have begun in Congress; however, there remains a tremendous amount of Cold War baggage that must be jettisoned if a fundamentally new approach to domestic and international security is to be crafted. Indeed, despite the dramatic changes in the Soviet Union and Eastern Europe, policy-makers have been slow to change their thinking.

A limited but significant change in U.S. military policy was signaled by the unilateral arms reductions proposed by President Bush on September 27, 1991, and the response by former President Gorbachev.[6] The Bush initiative called for about 3,000 tactical nuclear weapons to be dismantled and about 4,000 tactical and strategic weapons to be withdrawn, stored, or taken off alert status. The Gorbachev proposal went further by eliminating 1,000 more strategic missiles than called for by the recently signed START Treaty, and proposing a permanent nuclear test ban.[7] These Gorbachev proposals have subsequently been endorsed in principle by the Commonwealth Republics that have succeeded the Soviet Union. While these initiatives are commendable, they are overdue and will leave in place formidable military forces in each country. Indeed, these gestures may serve to disguise the true trajectory of events in the realm of international security. In particular, the Pentagon's long-range security plan suggests that the current administration seeks to ensure U.S. military supremacy into the next century.

There are powerful sources of resistance to cutting the military budget and restructuring our foreign and military policies. Internal forces continue to hold together the U.S. military system, and many of these bureaucratic, economic, and technological forces were reinforced by the dubious benefits of the victory in the Persian Gulf War. Within the Pentagon bureaucracy, military threat assessments have been readily adapted from the manifold global confrontation with the Soviet Union to a more complex set of "probable threats" from: Third World dictators, nuclear proliferation, instability in Eastern Europe, and narcotics terrorism.[8] Meanwhile the logic of nuclear deterrence continues to be used to justify a vast strategic nuclear force, which even the START treaty leaves mostly intact with an arsenal approximately as large as that which was deployed in 1982.[9] However, while the START treaty permits modernization of these strategic forces, recently there has been some effort to curb these programs.

Lying behind these strategic and technological changes are those bureaucratic and economic interests which have had a historical stake in the continuance of the arms race. Prior to the end of the Cold War confrontation, these military interests were embarking on a new military strategy that would make war more readily an instrument of foreign policy, which would spawn a new generation of weaponry to keep the military contractors in business.

Global Power Projection in the Post-Cold War Order: Deterrence and the Persistence of Memory

From Nicaragua to Panama to Iraq, the sliding scale of military power has been applied in the name of U.S. interests with varying degrees of force to match the objective. Yet, there are few within the military establishment who would argue that the United States should literally police the world. Rather, the military doctrines that have evolved over the last decade suggest the U.S. military has developed a capacity to selectively apply power only in those areas of the world where vital economic or political interests are threatened. Moreover, the use of increasingly lethal and controlled high-tech non-nuclear weaponry reflects the trend toward selective intervention, because the use of conventional weapons permits large-scale military action without the political and radioactive fallout from the use of even tactical nuclear weapons.

Military plans for selective global power projection in the post-Cold War era are founded on a revision of the old strategic concepts that have guided military planners for decades. The basic concept of deterrence holds that threat of massive retaliation against an adversary's potential aggression should deter it from such actions. In the nuclear era, however, this threat carried with it the prospect of mutual nuclear annihilation, making the threat of escalation from a conventional war to a strategic nuclear war a deadly game of potentially catastrophic dimensions. Indeed, despite elaborate war-making plans by strategic planners, political and military leaders came to realize that they had reached an impasse with the strategic nuclear arms race: they could threaten, but dared not use their most powerful weapons. This meant that the nuclear threat had become less credible.

Out of this dilemma came the recognition by military planners that the combination of increasingly lethal conventional munitions with precision-guided delivery systems could yield a measure of deterrence against potential adversaries. This idea of a more flexible, non-nuclear deterrence has come to be dubbed a "discriminant deterrent." Meanwhile, some strategic planners began to conclude that a smaller arsenal of nuclear weapons might be less risky and still capable of accomplishing its alleged mission of deterring the use of nuclear weapons. This latter notion, called "minimum deterrence" has become particularly attractive to many planners with the demise of the Soviet Union. Yet the idea actually had its origins in the early 1960s, on the eve of the strategic missile buildup.

However, the minimum-deterrence doctrine failed to win the day, and instead gave way to a massive nuclear arms race.

Today, these two notions of deterrence are increasingly shaping the mainstream debate within the national security establishment about the nature of the United States' role in the post-Cold War security order. In one sense the discriminant-deterrence concept is a more comprehensive doctrine that presupposes the adoption of a minimum deterrent nuclear force as part and parcel of an overall strategy to preserve U.S. military superiority. But in order to further understand the implications of these two doctrines, let us examine each in more detail.

The Discriminant-Deterrence Doctrine

The lineage of this new order can be traced to a report of the Commission on Integrated Long-Term Strategy entitled *Discriminate Deterrence,* published in January 1988.[10] This report, authored by several prominent veterans of the national security state, recommends that the United States integrate its strategies "for a wide range of conflicts: from the most confined, lowest intensity and highest probability to the most widespread, apocalyptic and least likely."[11] It further asserts that the credibility of the policy depends on assuring potential adversaries that "military aggression at any level of violence against our important interests will be opposed by military force."[12]

The war with Iraq was only the latest demonstration of this doctrine. It suggests that the war had less to do with a noble search for peace than with protecting American leverage on the world stage through military means. Indeed, the Cold War order appears to have been supplanted by a new arrangement of power among the United States, Europe, and Japan to broker the future economic order and security of the world.

By fighting the Gulf War the United States positioned itself to become the guarantor, into the next century, of the flow of oil and trade upon which the world economy depends. While the United States is far less dependent on the flow of Middle Eastern oil than Western Europe and Japan, the American economy still critically depends on this flow of nonrenewable energy. Nonetheless, the American geo-strategic interest in the Middle East is driven more by European and Japanese oil dependency than by our own. In this high-stakes game, U.S. military power becomes the trump card to be played in future negotiations over the terms of international finance and trade with our chief economic competitors.

These geo-strategic objectives require a military with a large navy, a highly mobile ground force, a tactical air force capable of delivering precision-guided conventional munitions, and large air- and sea-lift capability to rapidly move troops and materiél. These requirements differ from the Cold War military posture, which was geared to fighting two and one-half conventional wars simultaneously, while still fielding a strategic nuclear force. By contrast, a post-Cold War military force geared to more limited geo-strategic objectives does not necessarily require a large strategic or tactical nuclear force. Nor does it require huge standing forces for a conventional standoff with the Soviet Union in Central Europe. Instead, military planners are designing a somewhat smaller force that is more mobile and discriminate in its firepower and configured for a minimum nuclear deterrence.

The Minimum-Deterrence Doctrine

With the demise of the Soviet Union, the Cold War rationale for maintaining large strategic nuclear forces expired, leading many policy-makers to seek ways to dramatically reduce the United States' dependence on large nuclear forces. Indeed, two studies published by the National Academy of Sciences[13] and the Congressional Budget Office[14] suggest that the international environment has changed so fundamentally that it is now possible to consider a policy of "minimum nuclear deterrence." Minimum deterrence is a strategy that seeks to maintain the minimum number of strategic nuclear weapons required to inflict unacceptably large damage on one's adversary after one's nation has suffered a nuclear attack.[15]

This idea has been around since the early 1960s when President Kennedy's science advisor, Jerome Wiesner, argued that a few hundred survivable nuclear weapons would be sufficient to deter nuclear attack. Yet, this incisive insight into the logic of deterrence theory was put aside in favor of developing a large counterforce capability—a nuclear force designed for targeting the adversary's strategic forces so as to minimize subsequent damage from retaliation.[16] This counterforce strategy led to a massive buildup of the U.S. strategic missile force, rather than the adoption of a minimum-deterrence strategy by the Kennedy Administration.

Decades later the idea of minimum deterrence is being revived to reduce the tremendous strategic nuclear arsenals to levels that would not threaten the survival of the planet if a nuclear exchange were to take place. The National Academy of Sciences (NAS) postulates two different scenarios for a post-Cold War nuclear arsenal. Both assume continued progress in international relations between the United States and the reconstituted Soviet governments and postulate a post-START Treaty framework for further reductions in strategic forces. The first scenario would reduce the number of strategic warheads to between 3,000 and 4,000 and would prohibit the deployment of strategic defenses—although research would continue. The second scenario envisions a reduction to 1,000 to 2,000 nuclear weapons.

The emphasis in both scenarios would be on developing nuclear forces that would be reliable, available, and survivable, and therefore capable of ensuring a "stable deterrent." In essence, the NAS approach to deterrence shifts from a counterforce nuclear doctrine to one of "assured destruction," with military industry, ports and air bases, and command and control centers being the principal targets. The NAS study argues that a pure countercity targeting strategy could be avoided with this minimum deterrent; but the implications of such a doctrine are recognized obliquely at the end of the study, where it is acknowledged that most of these strategic targets are either in or near cities.[17] Thus, even a minimum deterrent of this size holds both nations at risk of near-total catastrophe. Indeed, the Congressional Budget Office (CBO) study on minimum deterrence notes that just 600 missiles would be adequate to functionally destroy the Soviet Union.[18]

However such a minimum deterrent might be justified from a political, military, or moral standpoint, from an economic point of view it would be far less expensive than the force currently deployed. Indeed, even after the START Treaty is implemented, according to the CBO, the United States will still spend about $50 billion annually to modernize and operate its nuclear arsenal.[19] Adopting a minimum-deterrent strategic policy would yield substantial savings. CBO considers two minimum-deterrent options: one with only 3,000 strategic warheads permitted for each side and a ban on strategic defenses would save $15.5 billion annually; another where only 1,000 strategic warheads are permitted and strategic defenses are banned would save $17.4 billion annually.[20]

Cost considerations together with the profoundly changed international environment will undoubtedly lead many political leaders to consider a minimum-deterrence policy for the United States. Yet, even the scenarios considered here would leave in place a terrifying potential for mass destruction. In addition, with the breakup of the Soviet Union, there is the prospect of several more nuclear powers emerging under independent governments. Meanwhile, nuclear proliferation will be made more difficult to control as aspiring nations emulate the nuclear powers. Some would argue that in order to move beyond the competitive military rivalry fostered by minimum deterrence and the pursuit of technological advantage, the world must look back to the dawn of the nuclear age when the international control of nuclear power was first considered within the United Nations framework.

The Military Budget and Force Planning

These plans for a more discriminating and minimum nuclear deterrent predate the breakup of the Soviet Union and the onset of the domestic budget crisis of the early 1990s. Nonetheless, the requirements for a smaller, more mobile but less nuclear dependent force dovetails well with the first Pentagon plan of the so-called post-Cold War era. It was, however, the budget crisis and the subsequent budget agreement to cap military and domestic spending which forced the Pentagon to begin recasting its budget priorities in concert with its new strategic objectives. The six-year defense budget plan introduced by Defense Secretary Richard Cheney in February 1991 reflects these budget constraints, as total defense spending will decline by 18 percent by 1996 from 1991 levels, after adjusting for inflation.[21] Military personnel levels are forecast to decline by 25 percent by 1996 from 1990 levels, with the Army and Air Force experiencing the biggest reductions. A few major procurement programs have also been terminated early under the Cheney six-year plan, including the MX missile, the Trident submarine, the F-16 aircraft, and the Navy's advanced tactical fighter, although much remains in the procurement pipeline. But the pressure for further reductions is being registered by internal Pentagon assessments that outline alternative budget options, including cutting spending to $240 billion by 1995 and active-duty forces to 1.3 million.[22]

These cutbacks serve three purposes for the Pentagon. First, they help counter criticisms that the Department of Defense (DoD) is still spending money on Cold War weapon systems that are no longer needed for the Soviet threat. Second, by saving money from these accounts the Pentagon can finance the next phase of high-tech weaponry geared to waging a wide range of conflicts and to securing access to geo-strategic regions of the world. Finally, this budget plan is consistent with that outlined in the DoD's *Discriminate Deterrence,* which argued that "we should turn to faster prototyping and testing of systems that would make our forces more versatile and discriminate. Furthermore, this approach recommends that "instead of buying various types of large 'platforms,' we should seek continued improvements in the sensors and command, control, and intelligence systems which can multiply the effectiveness of our ships and aircraft."[23] The U.S. military's success in the Gulf War has only strengthened these conclusions among military planners, although there is probably less "pressure" to accelerate these innovations since the collapse of the Soviet Union.

Despite these planned reductions, the Cheney plan is still predominantly driven by the "Soviet threat," with most conventional and strategic forces still focused on it. Moreover, the plan continues funding many strategic Cold War weapon systems such as the B-2 Stealth bomber, the Trident II D-5 missile, and the Strategic Defense Initiative. While Congress will probably eventually put an end to the B-2 bomber sometime in fiscal year 1993, congressional funding for the development of a ground-based strategic defense system to be deployed by 1996 raises the prospect of the possible withdrawal of the United States from the Anti-Ballistic Missile (ABM) Treaty of 1972.[24] These facts, together with the size and composition of forces provided for in the Pentagon plan, clearly imply the pursuit of military superiority and the continued capacity for global force projection.

Indeed, Congress is still deeply mired in Cold War thinking and has perpetuated many Cold War related procurement programs in classic pork-barrel style. The process has become so entrenched that even when the Pentagon wishes to terminate obsolete programs, Congress continues to fund them in order to provide jobs for constituents. In the Defense Authorization Act for Fiscal 1993, Congress saved the V-22 Osprey and the F-16 aircraft programs from termination, and continued funding upgrade programs for the M1A tank, the Bradley fighting vehicle, and the Apache AH-64 helicopter.[25]

Yet a day of reckoning is near, as the fiscal crisis of the federal government has forced all parties to review the Pentagon's plans. In an era of budgetary austerity at the federal, state, and local government levels it has become abundantly apparent that the nation cannot afford guns and butter. These factors have given rise to calls from all corners of society for deep cuts in military spending. As a result, Congress has joined the search for an alternative security policy that is both less costly and geared to the new international realities.

Cooperative Security and Northern Hemispheric Hegemony

Perhaps the most notable set of proposals for restructuring and reducing the military budget has come from William W. Kaufmann and John D. Steinbruner of the Brookings Institution.[26] These veterans of the Cold War have advanced different scenarios for reshaping and reducing the size and missions of the U.S. military and for cutting the military budget nearly in half by the year 2001. Given the collapse of the Soviet Union and the Warsaw Pact, the authors believe that military spending can be reduced by a far greater amount than the Cheney six-year plan. Furthermore, these authors propose that the United States go beyond simply reducing its military and instead forge a new cooperative security system that would depend upon joint action by the northern industrialized nations of the world in maintaining peace and security.

The authors first propose a less innovative approach that postulates a "low option" for reducing military spending over the 1993–2001 period. They compare their proposal to the Cheney plan, but see the Cheney plan extending in one of two directions after 1996: either spending will level off at the 1996 level in inflation-adjusted terms, or it will begin to grow to accommodate the deployment of the new generation of weapon systems now in the procurement pipeline. Against these two paths for the Cheney plan they measure the savings of their budget proposal. Under the low-option plan, they propose for spending to decline to $169.2 billion (in 1992 dollars) by the year 2001. This plan would realize cumulative savings of $315 billion as compared to the lower Cheney scenario. But if the Cheney plan implies more spending after 1996 for modernization, then savings could total $600 billion by 2001.

Under the low-option plan, strategic forces would be cut to 5,430 nuclear weapons, including land- and sea-based missiles and bombers—a number far exceeding a minimum-deterrent nuclear force. Moreover, this plan calls for eighteen Trident submarines to be deployed with the Trident II D-5 missile, which seems to imply that the Soviets must deploy more mobile land-based missiles in order to maintain a "stable" deterrent. Perhaps more disturbing, this plan calls for strategic defenses to be deployed with a limited ground-based system allowed under the ABM Treaty, thus laying the basis for the next phase of the arms race. Meanwhile, multiple-warhead, land-based missiles would be retired and replaced by the single-warhead Midgetman missile, assuming that in exchange the Soviets retire the "dreaded" SS-18 silo-based heavy missile.

This strategic forces plan is fraught with difficulties because it would likely generate another round of strategic modernization as each side seeks a new equilibrium for a "stable" deterrent. Another major problem is that the Commonwealth which succeeded the Soviet government faces a profound fiscal crisis that probably precludes any expenditures required for the compensating modernization implied by this scenario. Thus, if this plan were adopted it would either foment another round of modernization or leave the United States with an unambiguous strategic advantage.

With regard to conventional forces, the low option would seriously reduce the size and missions of U.S. ground forces by trimming the number of Army divisions from the eighteen proposed by Cheney to eleven by 2001. But Marine divisions would remain intact and the number of air wings would remain unaltered. Naval carrier battle groups would take the biggest hit, cut from twelve to six. Nonetheless, this would leave a formidable force capable of other Iraq-scale interventions. Indeed, the authors assert that except for the halving of aircraft-carrier battle groups, this force could meet the Desert Storm test because it possesses roughly twice the capacity needed to deal with the Iraq conflict. Thus, the implicit planning assumption is that the United States must be able to meet two major contingencies at once.

On the procurement balance sheet, several big-ticket systems would be terminated, including the B-2 bomber, Seawolf attack submarine, the C-17A jet transport, and two aircraft carriers. In addition, many next generation systems would be held at the R&D stage, with full-scale procurement and deployment deferred. Nonetheless, much would be left in the procurement pipeline that could reasonably be cut, particularly the ground-based strategic defense system. Moreover, the continued funding of many R&D programs such as Star Wars as an "insurance policy" would undoubtedly cultivate new constituencies for future procurement programs.

Cooperative Security Proposal

In an attempt to move beyond the unregulated national competition of the Cold War era, Kaufmann and Steinbruner propose a second option, a cooperative security arrangement that would include the western powers plus a reconstituted Soviet government and China. This security organization would regulate the size and composition of all member military establishments to reduce spending, increase efficiency, and curb proliferation, and would cooperatively manage international conflicts. This northern industrialized "military cartel" would, presumably, operate outside of the confines of the United Nations, and would seek to maintain international order by virtue of its collective power and wisdom.

This approach would only generate modest savings over the low option the authors propose, amounting to an additional $107.9 billion over ten years, and $424 billion when compared to the Cheney budget baseline. The force structure would be reduced to 3,000 strategic warheads, five fewer active air wings, and four fewer reserve air wings. In addition, no ground-based strategic defense would be deployed, although research would continue.

While Kaufmann and Steinbruner's proposals move some distance from the Cold War military footing of the Cheney plan, they still carry considerable Cold War baggage. In particular, their cooperative security proposal reveals telling assumptions. First, their plan assumes that a military cartel operating outside the United Nations can legitimately impose its will on the rest of the world. Second, they assume that this military cartel could realistically permit the maintenance of very large conventional and strategic national forces and still provide a manageable basis for cooperation among cartel members, let alone the rest of the world. Third, they argue that the arms trade can go forward while being successfully regulated through export controls and end-use inspections for those outside the supplier cartel. Finally, neither of their scenarios considers how phased disarmament might achieve more reliable and efficient results, especially if conducted on a more equitable basis between the North and South.

Despite these shortcomings the Kaufmann and Steinbruner proposals do provide a critical framework to assess the planning assumptions of the Pentagon and to consider alternative approaches. However, the maintenance of a very high level of strategic weaponry, coupled with continued research on strategic defenses, raises further questions about the adherence to old nuclear planning doctrines. Moreover, the continued reliance on a large-scale interventionary capability to meet at least two major contingencies raises questions as to whether this is the most efficient way to maintain international security. Indeed, the proposal to build a northern militarized cartel under their cooperative security plan threatens the world with a new hemispheric divide between North and South. A more far-reaching approach might seek to replace this interventionist military posture advanced by Kaufmann and Steinbruner with a more coherent approach that seeks to restructure U.S. military forces into a less provocative, less nuclear dependent, and noninterventionary force.

Principles of a Common Security Framework

In the later stages of the Cold War a wide variety of proposals were developed to replace the dominant, one-sided national security strategy with a concept of common security.[27] Over the years, numerous disarmament and arms-control experts have developed these proposals as a response to the destabilizing nature of the arms race.[28] Advocates of a common security policy have advanced several key principles that define and shape these policy recommendations.

First, they recognize that security ultimately depends on acknowledging the security needs of one's opponent in one's own security calculations. Neither side can gain a military advantage without elevating the risk to the other side. This, in turn, raises the risk to one's own side due to the threat of recourse to nuclear war. Throughout the Cold War, the political rivalry between East and West and the technological dynamic of the arms race have continually introduced such instability into the deterrence relationship, thereby undermining any sense of *common* security. Thus, the development of a common and stable international security framework requires more than military means for defense. It requires multilateral arms-reduction agreements under the auspices of international institutions, measures that seek to halt modernization of weaponry, and new institutions to verify international agreements and to develop nonconfrontational conflict-resolution procedures.[29]

It is especially important to distinguish this common-security doctrine from the cooperative-security doctrine proposed by Kaufmann and Steinbruner. Common security presupposes that all nations work to promote the conditions of political, economic, and environmental stability, presumably through international institutions. By contrast, the Kaufmann and Steinbruner approach presumes that the most powerful nations can band together to dictate the terms of international security to the rest of the world.

A second principle follows from the first, namely that military defensive measures should be *nonprovocative* or truly defensive in character. Accordingly, weaponry and forces should be made defensive by virtue of limitations on their range, destructive capabilities, and mobility. In addition, forces should be decentralized so that they don't invite preemptive first strikes by adversaries on large or threatening targets.[30]

Third, numerous experts and former high U.S. officials have suggested that mutual reduction of nuclear weaponry to the *minimum* levels necessary for a stable *deterrent* would curtail the nuclear arms race and eliminate the enormous investment in overkill capabilities. These same experts have developed such proposals and have observed that present verification capabilities make such an arrangement enforceable.[31] They argue that a restructuring of current nuclear arsenals could enhance stability by increasing reaction times, thus reducing the vulnerability of the smaller nuclear arsenal. In addition, it is argued that these actions would provide a powerful demonstration of the two major nuclear powers' commitment to reversing the nuclear arms race, and would act as a restraining influence on nuclear proliferation elsewhere in the world.[32] There are, however, some students of common security who argue that minimum deterrence could be viewed as a temporary stage, which would eventually give way to complete nuclear disarmament.[33]

Fourth, some have advocated the adoption of *noninterventionary* security agreements among the major powers, which would help to foster greater reliance on international peacekeeping institutions.[34] This would require the mutual withdrawal of forward-based forces stationed in client countries around the globe. Further, it would require greater international controls on arms transfers and the proliferation of weapons of mass destruction. In addition, it is argued that a progressive policy of economic engagement with middle- and low-income countries would more effectively address the root causes of regional instability. On the domestic front, changes in energy policies to encourage conservation and curtail dependence on oil imports would limit U.S. vulnerability to regional conflicts and lessen the reliance on military means to guarantee the flow of petroleum supplies.

Fifth, a central tenet of many common-security proponents is that the buildup of the United Nations and other international peacekeeping institutions would make a far greater contribution to regional security and conflict resolution than would the threat of intervention.[35]

Sixth, the implementation of multilateral, comprehensive test bans on nuclear weapons and missile flight testing would help curtail strategic arms modernization and inhibit the proliferation of these dangerous technologies to spread to other nations. In addition, the creation of international verification institutions would assist in enforcing these agreements and would promote greater trust and confidence among nations.[36]

The adoption of these principles in shaping future U.S. security policy would result in wide-ranging changes in U.S. military forces and budgets. In addition, it is argued that this integrated approach would define a rational process for reducing military spending, while building a broader security framework.

Economic Effect of a Common Security Policy

In a study of the economic effects of a common security policy entitled *Converting the American Economy,* these foregoing security principles were used as the basis for proposals on the restructuring and reduction of U.S. military forces.[37] The study proposed a series of phased reductions to be implemented over the 1991–1994 period.

It examined the impacts of a START II scenario that completely eliminated the next round of strategic modernization and reduced current strategic nuclear forces by 50 percent. Further, it argued for the complete elimination of the Star Wars program, together with negotiating new protocols for verifying an end to ABM research and to minimize the threat of a "breakout" from the ABM Treaty. In addition, it examined the savings accruing from deeper cuts in U.S. conventional ground and air forces and a halt to conventional force modernization. It advocated a multilateral agreement for establishing a new security regime in Northeast and East Asia, based on the settlement of disputes and the withdrawal of forward-based ground and air forces. Further, it called for the implementation of a noninterventionary policy for restructuring and reducing the interventionary potential of U.S. military forces. Finally, it examined the feasibility and impact of a bilateral agreement on large-scale reductions in the naval forces of the U.S. and the Soviet Union.

A rigorous verification regime is postulated to ensure compliance with these multilateral agreements. This would involve both baseline and challenge on-site inspections of weapons deployments, continuous monitoring of strategic production facilities, the establishment of sensing devices such as large seismic arrays and radar facilities to monitor test bans, and increased remote sensing capabilities through national technical means.[38] These approaches, which were pioneered by the Intermediate Range Nuclear Forces Treaty of 1987 and extended under the recently signed START Treaty, would help to reduce uncertainty about treaty compliance and therefore lower the risks associated with such an extensive disarmament process. There is increasing consensus about the feasibility and reliability of such intrusive verification technologies and institutional means.[39]

The study found that implementing these policy changes could yield savings averaging $70.5 billion per year over the 1991–1994 period. Savings would start at $34.5 billion in the first year and rise to about $105 billion by 1994. These were net savings, which included the costs of the additional verification requirements necessary to assure compliance with the arms-reduction agreements examined in this study. Savings would accrue faster under this approach than under the Kaufmann and Steinbruner approach, with more of the reductions taking place in the first five years.

The economic impact of these reductions was modeled using a computer simulation of the economy; it found that on average about 289,000 defense industry workers would be affected each year by these cutbacks in military spending over the 1991–1994 period. In addition, nearly 1.4 million other jobs would be annually affected by these cutbacks if no conversion program were put into place. However, the study also examined the benefits of shifting these savings to critical civilian needs, which were found to generate sufficient jobs to more than offset these losses. Yet there would still be substantial economic dislocation caused by this shift in federal priorities, which would require careful advance planning to minimize.

Regardless of the budgetary savings and economic impact of such an alternative security program, this policy merits consideration from a security standpoint because it goes beyond the force planning assumptions contained in the Cheney and the Brookings plans. Indeed, the more traditional plans seem excessive for the demands of a post-Cold War environment because they attempt to define a military force for numerous contingencies involving dubious risks to U.S. security. Indeed, the Pentagon has historically relied on worst-case scenarios to justify the deployment of forces for contingencies of relatively low probability—a point that Kaufmann and Steinbruner readily acknowledge, but fail to fully embrace in their own recommendations.[40]

The rationale for these more traditional planning assumptions is undermined by the fact that traditional military missions will be scaled back even under current plans because of increased reliance on bilateral and multilateral treaties and international peacekeeping operations. And while stalwart Cold Warriors retort by reminding us of the forty-five years of "peace" that our military investment and vigilance have won, these exponents conveniently overlook the fact that at least 20 million people have died in the numerous regional conflicts and proxy wars which were spawned by the Cold War rivalry. By contrast, the establishment of a noninterventionary and less nuclear-dependent posture would be less provocative than the current configuration of forces and therefore less likely to invite reciprocal armaments and deployment by potential adversaries. Perhaps more importantly, the creation of an ongoing verification process would ensure that risks were kept reasonably low through intrusive on-site inspections and continuous remote monitoring of treaty-regulated forces to ensure compliance with the multilateral arms-reduction process.

The Construction of International Peacekeeping Institutions

While general and complete disarmament may seem to be an abstract notion, the reality of international law and global government through the United Nations stands as a concrete reminder that the world has made some progress toward building an international peacekeeping system, albeit tentative and incomplete. Nonetheless, progress toward resolving many of the problems the world faces today will depend on greater cooperation among the peoples of the world. The post-Cold War era presents us with this opportunity.

Some have argued that concrete steps to build an alternative to war and conflict can be taken by reforming the United Nations and building up its peacekeeping potential.[41] This program involves several steps. First, an international inspectorate must be created that is capable of addressing problems of unconventional weapons and dual-use technologies currently beyond the purview of the International Atomic Energy Agency. Such an inspectorate must have the powers to police both the supplier countries in the industrialized north, as well as those in the developing world. Second, a standing international peacekeeping force must be established that is capable of a wide variety of peacekeeping missions, including enforcing the UN mandates and challenge inspections. Third, a standing verification capability is necessary to enable the United Nations to independently verify international treaties and the disposition of military forces. Fourth, international law must be developed to support the United Nation's peacekeeping operations and to provide an international process for dispute resolution and disarmament. Finally, the United Nation's charter must be reformed to eliminate the Cold War vestige of the five powers' veto rights in the Security Council.

This option, it is argued, could lay the foundation for a post-Cold War order that does not depend on the unilateral projection of U.S. military power or the joint action of the northern industrialized nations. Moreover, it could provide for more equitable relations between the North and the South by eliminating the one-way control of technology through suppliers' cartels among the developed nations. It could also provide a process and a capacity for addressing long-standing international disputes and conflicts not on the U.S. geo-strategic agenda. The buildup of such institutions would initially require the investment of several billion dollars annually by member nations. But in the longer run, these same nations could curtail their military expenditures as the international peacekeeping process becomes increasingly capable of guaranteeing security.

At the very beginning of the Cold War there were several far-reaching proposals that called for international control of nuclear weapons and technology, and for international peacekeeping mechanisms to ensure that nuclear proliferation and confrontation would not occur. Furthermore, there were proposals for a general and comprehensive disarmament (GCD), which grew up alongside the process of building the United Nations as the international forum to govern international relations. While Cold War strategic rivalry came to eclipse proposals for international nuclear and comprehensive disarmament, before the historic strategic confrontation completely took hold there were several major initiatives from the United States, the Soviet Union, and other nations. In many ways, these initiatives were far more influential than is often recognized. For these reasons it is important to review the history of nuclear and general disarmament proposals in order to evaluate their effect on history. Furthermore, there is much to be learned from these proposals about how to forge a post-Cold War international security order that would be more democratic and less militarized.

Disarmament and International Peacekeeping: Utopianism or Pragmatism?

The first use of nuclear weapons at Hiroshima and Nagasaki brought a sense of foreboding to the peace that followed the war. Recognizing the dangers of a nuclear arms race, many prominent scientists, especially the atomic scientists who organized the Federation of Atomic Scientists, joined with progressive political leaders, members of organized labor, and several civic groups to advance the idea of international control of nuclear power under the aegis of the newly formed United Nations. Indeed, the governments of both the United States and the Soviet Union felt morally and politically compelled to develop plans for implementing such international control and nuclear disarmament.[42]

In 1946, after much internal debate within the Truman Administration, the United States introduced the "Baruch Plan" to the United Nations. This plan called for all nations with nuclear potential to submit to continuous inspections by the United Nations before the United States would turn over its nuclear arsenal to UN control. Moreover, any nation found to be attempting to build a nuclear bomb would be subject to policing action by the United Nations, which could not be halted by veto in the Security Council. By contrast the Soviet plan, introduced by the Deputy Foreign Minister Andre Gromyko, called for all atomic weapons to be banned by the United Nations and demanded that existing weapons be destroyed. However, before either plan could be voted on, the United States cast a cloud over the proceedings by exploding atomic tests in the South Pacific.[43] This brought to an end constructive progress toward an international disarmament regime for controlling nuclear weapons.

In spite of this impasse the idea of nuclear disarmament was put on the international agenda, along with the revival of general and comprehensive disarmament. During the 1950s, two UN meetings occurred that laid out the general principles for a phased, verifiable general disarmament. The first was put forth in the United Nations Disarmament Subcommittee by Britain and France in June, 1954; it was outlined in "six principles" to guide the disarmament process, including nuclear disarmament.[44] While some progress was made in negotiating the general principles of a phased disarmament process, the negotiations bogged down in debates and disagreements over verification procedures and a lack of good faith.[45] However, these issues were revisited in the London meetings of the UN Disarmament Subcommittee in 1957, with some success in discussing conventional weapons reductions, but nuclear issues proved to be intractable.

Nothing tangible resulted from these talks, but they produced a general drift toward limiting the focus of discussion to partial measures rather than comprehensive disarmament initiatives. Indeed, the emphasis increasingly became one of arms control rather than disarmament, thus legitimizing the regulation of the arms race. But before the doctrine of arms control became fully installed as policy, the United States and the Soviet Union made one final serious effort at setting forth a general and comprehensive disarmament process.

General and Comprehensive Disarmament Plans, 1961–1962

Few Americans know that during the early 1960s, the United States government developed a plan for general and comprehensive disarmament. Under the Kennedy Administration, negotiations were conducted between the Soviets and the United States by Valerin Zorin and John Jay McCloy that led to an agreement of principles for general and complete disarmament, today known as the McCloy-Zorin agreement.[46] These principles were ratified by the United Nations General Assembly in 1961, which set the stage for further negotiations.

These principles culminated in the drafting by the Kennedy Administration of *Blueprint for the Peace Race: Outline of Basic Provisions of a Treaty on General and Complete Disarmament in a Peaceful World.*[47] This document outlined a three-stage plan for phased disarmament that included both nuclear and conventional weapons. During the first stage, which was to last three years, all categories of weapons were to be reduced by 30 percent. An International Disarmament Organization was to be established to ensure the verification of all aspects of the process. A system of zonal inspections was to be established for verification of the demobilization and destruction of weaponry. The production of fissionable materials would cease altogether during stage one. In the second stage, one-half of the remaining arsenals were to be destroyed over a three-year period. A United Nations Peace Force was to be set up to enforce the process and guarantee international security. During the second stage other nations were to be brought into the general disarmament process, once the commitment of the superpowers had been adequately demonstrated. Stage three was less well defined, but was to include all major military powers and was to be carried out as expeditiously as possible. Each nation would retain armaments for its police forces and would permit small arms.

The Soviets submitted a similar draft treaty, but its timetable was much more compressed, allowing only five years to accomplish all three stages.[48] Despite the great progress in drafting these plans, the international environment deteriorated as the Cold War heated up in Berlin and then Cuba. The Cuban missile crisis in 1962 marked the end of serious discussions of disarmament and led to an acceleration of the strategic arms race. Nonetheless, these discussions and the draft treaties left an important legacy.

Contemporary Issues of Disarmament

The draft treaties have had an enduring and pervasive influence upon the growth and development of collective security through international law and peacekeeping institutions. It can be argued that they laid the basis for many of the institutions that have been created over the last three decades for reducing weaponry and improving confidence in verification procedures. For instance, the Partial Test Ban Treaty, the Non-proliferation Treaty, and later arms-reduction agreements have employed ideas inspired by the general and comprehensive disarmament approach such as on-site inspections and challenge inspections, zonal inspections, declarations of weapons inventories, and the installation of on-site sensing equipment to verify treaties. These innovations have demonstrated that nonmilitary means can be created to guarantee security and bring the arms race to an end.[49]

Despite these contributions, the idea of general and comprehensive disarmament became a casualty of the Cold War. Many within the strategic establishment argued that the arms-control doctrine had eclipsed the notion of general and complete disarmament.[50] General and complete disarmament was increasingly dismissed as utopian because, it was argued, the world cannot disinvent nuclear power, and therefore must live with these weapons.

If nuclear proliferation is to be prevented, the world community must create institutions to ensure that these weapons do not spread further. The Non-Proliferation Treaty (NPT) and the International Atomic Energy Agency (IAEA) were created to carry out this objective. But the leading nuclear powers have not invested these institutions with the clout and autonomy necessary to ensure nonproliferation. Indeed, the unratified final document of the NPT review conference, which was not ratified by the United States, would have greatly expanded the powers of the IAEA, thereby allowing it to inspect both declared and undeclared facilities suspected of nuclear weapons production.[51] Furthermore, the major nuclear powers have undermined the nonproliferation process itself by encouraging the trade in critical nuclear and industrial technologies necessary for making these weapons. Moreover, the members of the "nuclear club" have not carried out their obligations under the NPT to end the reign of nuclear terror.

Obviously progress in addressing these problems must come from a commitment by the major powers to ending their nuclear monopoly, as called for by the NPT, and a commitment to confront the political and economic factors that produce nuclear proliferation. It is a matter of inventing new institutions, rather than disinventing the bomb. In this regard, the ideas and work that have been developed for a framework of general and comprehensive disarmament remain vital to the future security of the world.

Today, the framework of general and complete disarmament has been further developed by Marcus Raskin, a Distinguished Fellow of the Institute for Policy Studies Washington, D.C.[52] The architecture of the plan is basically similar to the Kennedy *Blueprint*, but the institutional details for settling disputes and adjudicating claims have been further worked out, together with much of the detail on the disarmament process itself. While the general public may be unaware of the general disarmament framework, policy-makers would be well advised to examine this approach for the solutions to the seemingly intractable problems of war and peace.

Each of these visions of international security and peacekeeping provide credible alternatives to the ossified Cold War thinking that continues to dominate public debate and discussion of post-Cold War security policy. However, they are not all interchangeable, although some are complementary and tend to reduce the reliance on military force. Nonetheless, these contending approaches should become the focal points of public debate so the citizens of this nation and the world can clearly make a choice among alternative futures.

Economic Conversion and Alternative Security Policies

Regardless of which security approach is taken, the disengagement from the Cold War will involve a large reallocation of resources. This winding down from the high levels of Cold War military expenditures will require careful planning in order to minimize the economic disruption and maximize the potential from reallocating our resources.

If our nation is to develop a post-Cold War security policy that is less reliant on military force, it must address the economic implications of this large-scale shift in resource use.[53] However, even the limited Pentagon plan has made abundantly clear that reductions in military spending will produce major economic disruption. Already, nearly 300,000 defense-industry workers have been laid off in 1990 and 1991.[54] Under Defense Secretary Cheney's six-year plan, over the 1992–1997 period active-duty troops will be reduced by 348,100; civilian DoD workers will be cut by 148,000; and defense-industry workers will be reduced by 813,600.[55] In the midst of a stagnant economy, further military reduction could worsen the situation. The solution of these problems lies in planning for economic conversion of military industry to civilian use, and in reallocating federal spending to dampen the shock during the transition to a peacetime economy.

Conclusion

Forging a post-Cold War security policy should involve all segments of our society in democratic debate over the merits of each alternative approach to security. To date, most of the discussion has focused on extensions of the deterrence doctrines that have their origins in the Cold War era. These traditional approaches to security threaten to continue the pursuit of military superiority as the means to guarantee international stability. Yet, those who would wager that America's superpower status can be secured by military power alone fail to appreciate the limits of this power. Forty-five years of Cold War spending has diverted critical resources from the kinds of productive investments necessary to build a sustainable economy.

Indeed, the recognition of limitations has led some proponents to suggest that the northern industrialized nations could effectively police the world together. Under such cooperative security schemes the United States would continue as the world's superpower, but would not have to bear the burden alone. But such a northern military cartel would abrogate the progress made in international governance and would erect new hemispheric divides between the north and south of the globe. These proposals represent a clear attempt to circumvent the United Nations as the proper forum for regulating international relations and resolving disputes. Moreover, such an approach would undermine any progress toward achieving a common security based upon the conditions of political, economic, and environmental stability.

In order to build the conditions of a truly "common security," we should examine the recommendations advanced by those voices less often heard in the debate. Indeed, this review of alternative security approaches suggests that the common security approach can be complemented and reinforced by implementing many of the proposals for building up international peacekeeping institutions. Furthermore, success in reducing instability and other threats to security may pave the way for more comprehensive disarmament approaches. However, the first clear steps for the United States should involve a restructuring of its military into a force that is non-interventionist and less nuclear dependent. In parallel, the United States should undertake to encourage the build up of international peacekeeping institutions under the auspices of the United Nations. The construction of international peacekeeping institutions will require the dismantling of many Cold War political arrangements within the United

Nations, especially within the Security Council. Finally, a disarmament and demilitarization process holds great promise in reducing the tensions that the Cold War has left behind, particularly the proliferation of nuclear and unconventional weaponry. These issues should be prominent elements in the debate over a post-Cold War security policy.

Now, as the Cold War era comes to a close, we cannot afford to miss this historic chance. Rather than simply advocating that our former adversaries disarm and convert to peacetime economies, we should take the initiative and demonstrate our commitment to building a post-Cold War security order.

Notes

1. In the United States the most prominent contribution to the debate comes from William W. Kaufmann and John Steinbruner of the Brookings Institution in their book, *Decisions for Defense, Prospects for a New Order* (Washington D.C.: The Brookings Institution, 1991). In the Soviet Union, the debate was ably summarized by Alexei Izyumov in an article entitled "The Monster, A Profile of the Soviet Military-Industrial Complex," appearing in *Moscow News* 8 (1991).

2. Such a substantial minimum deterrent is proposed by the National Academy of Sciences in their book, *The Future of U.S.-Soviet Nuclear Relations* (Washington D.C.: National Academy of Sciences, 1991). Also, the Congressional Budget Office proposes several scenarios for reducing strategic forces in its study *The START Treaty and Beyond* (Washington, D.C.: Congressional Budget Office, 1991). Other such proposals may be found in Harold Feivson, Richard Ullman, and Frank von Hippel, "Reducing U.S. and Soviet Nuclear Arsenals," *Bulletin of the Atomic Scientists*, August 1985: 144–150.

3. See M. Anderson, G. Bischak, and M. Oden, *Converting the American Economy, The Economic Effects of an Alternative Security Policy* (Lansing, Michigan: Employment Research Associates, 1991), 5–16 for the details of such a noninterventionary, nonprovocative defense scenario. The minimum deterrence scenario discussed here, however, is far less ambitious than the 500 postulated by Robert McNamara, *Blundering Towards Disaster* (New York: Pantheon, 1986), 122–23.

4. For an overview of this perspective see Harry Hollins, Averill Powers, and Mark Sommers, eds., *The Conquest of War: Alternative Strategies for Global Security* (Boulder, Colo.: Westview Press, 1989), chapter 3.

5. For a brief review of GCD proposals see Anthony DiFilippo, *Arms Control vs. Disarmament* (Washington D.C.: National Commission for Economic Conversion and Disarmament), Briefing Paper No. 6. Also see Hollins et al., *Conquest,* chapter 4.

6. See Jeffery Smith, "President Orders Sweeping Reductions in Strategic and Tactical Nuclear Arms," *Washington Post,* 28 Sept. 1991, A-23. Also see Serge Schemann, "Gorbachev Matches U.S. on Nuclear Cuts and Goes Further on Strategic Warheads," *New York Times,* 6 Oct. 1991, A-1.

7. Ibid.

8. See Department of Defense, *Secretary of Defense's Report to Congress for Fiscal Year 1992,* (Washington D.C.: February, 1991).

9. See Thomas Cochran, et al., *The Nuclear Weapons Databook, Vol. II,* (Cambridge, Mass.: Ballinger Books, 1987), table 1.5, p. 19.

10. See Long-Term Commission on Integrated Strategy, Department of Defense (DoD), *Discriminate Deterrence* (Washington D.C.: January, 1988).

11. Ibid., 64.

12. Ibid.

13. National Academy of Sciences, *Future.*

14. Congressional Budget Office, *START Treaty.*

15. Hollins et al., *Conquest,* 54–63.

16. See Fred Kaplan *The Wizards of Armageddon* (New York: Touchstone Books, 1988).

17. National Academy of Sciences, *Future,* 58, appendix B9.

18. Congressional Budget Office, *START Treaty,* xvii.

19. Ibid., 62.

20. Ibid., 62.

21. See Office of the Comptroller of the Department of Defense, *National Defense Budget Estimates, FY 1992,* March 1991, table 1–2, p. 5.

22. See Eric Schmitt, "Pentagon Making a List of Choices for Spending Cuts," *New York Times,* 24 Nov. 1991, A-1.

23. DoD, *Discriminate Deterrence,* 68.

24. See House of Representatives, *National Defense Authorization Act for Fiscal Year 1992 and 1993, Conference Report to Accompany H.R. 2100* (Washington D.C.: U.S. Government Printing Office, November 13, 1991), 34–39, especially 38–39.

25. Ibid.

26. Kaufmann and Steinbruner, *Decisions.*

27. This discussion is drawn from the author's earlier work, Anderson et al., *Converting the American Economy,* 5–6.

28. Hollins et al., *Conquest.* Also see Admiral Gene la Rocque, "What is Ours to Defend?," *Harpers* (July 1988) 39–50; and Richard Barnet, et al. *American Priorities in A New World Era* (New York: World Policy Institute, 1989), especially pp. 10–20 and the technical appendix. For an earlier version see Paul Walker, "A Post-Reagan Military Posture," in *Post-Reagan America* (New York: World Policy Institute, 1987).

29. For a discussion of the concept of common security see Stockholm International Peace Research Institute, *Policies for Common Security,* (London: Taylor & Francis, 1985), IV: 219–235.

30. For a discussion of the concept of nonprovocative defense see Hollins et al., *Conquest,* 78–87.

31. See note 2 for several noteworthy sources on this discussion.

32. A detailed proposal for a minimum-deterrence posture is set forth in Feivson et al., "Reducing Arsenals." Also see McNamara, *Blundering*.

33. See for example Marcus Raskin, *Essays of a Citizen* (Armonk, N.Y.: Sharpe 1991) chapter 11.

34. An examination of noninterventionary regimes is provided in Hollins et al., *Conquest,* 185–6.

35. See Hollins et al., *Conquest,* chapters 3 and 4.

36. For a detailed examination of these issues see Allan S. Krass, *Verification: How Much Is Enough?* (London: Taylor & Francis, 1985). Also see Steve Fetter, *Toward a Comprehensive Test Ban* (Cambridge, Mass.: Ballinger Books, 1988), especially chapters 4–6.

37. See Anderson et al., *Converting the American Economy,* 1–2, 5–16.

38. See Krass, *Verification,* for a review of the technologies and their reliability in verifying treaty compliance issues. Also see Fetter, *Comprehensive Test Ban,* for a discussion of the technical and institutional requirements for a comprehensive nuclear test ban.

39. See the Congressional Budget Office study, *U.S. Costs of Verification and Compliance Under Pending Arms Treaties* (Washington, D.C.: GPO, September 1990), for a thorough examination of the interrelationship between costs and risk reduction.

40. See especially discussion in Kaufmann and Steinbruner, *Decisions,* chapter 2 and compare those requirements to the extensive missions postulated on pages 55–66.

41. See Hollins et al., *Conquest,* chapter 3.

42. For a history of this public policy debate see Gregg Herkin, *The Winning Weapon* (Princeton: Princeton University Press, 1988), especially pp. 169–172. Also see Ronald W. Clark, *The Greatest Power on Earth* (New York: Harper and Row, 1980), 241–80. Another treatment is given in Charles R. Morris, *Iron Destinies, Lost Opportunities* (New York: Harper and Row, 1984). The official history is presented by Richard A. Hewlett and Oscar Anderson, *The New World, 1939–1946* (University Park: Pennsylvania State University, 1962), 499–530. Also see Richard Hewlett and Francis Duncan, *The Atomic Shield, 1947–1952* (University Park: Pennsylvania State University Press, 1969).

43. Clark, *Greatest Power.*

44. See DiFilippo, *Arms Control,* 5–7.

45. There is a great deal of disagreement about the reasons that caused these talks to fail. A good discussion is provided by Lawrence Weiler, who had held a post in the Eisenhower Administration during this period, in his article, "General Disarmament Proposals," *Arms Control Today* (July/August 1986).

46. DiFilippo, *Arms Control,* 8.

47. See U.S. Arms Control and Disarmament Agency, *Blueprint for the Peace Race: Outline of Basic Provisions of a Treaty on General and Complete Disarmament in a Peaceful World* (Washington D.C.: May 1962).

48. DiFilippo, *Arms Control.*

49. See Weiler, "General Disarmament."

50. See especially the collection of pieces by leading strategic thinkers of the 1960s in Donald Brennan, ed., *Arms Control, Disarmament and National Security* (New York: George Braziller, 1961).

51. See James Raffel, "Disarmament: Now More Than Ever," *The New Economy* 2, no. 9, (February 1991), 10–11.

52. See Raskin, *Essays.*

53. See David Alexander, *How Big is the Military Economy? Gross National Product vs. Real Resource Use* (Washington D.C.: National Commission for Economic Conversion and Disarmament, 1989).

54. See National Commission for Economic Conversion and Disarmament *National Defense Industry Layoffs for 1990* and *National Defense Industry Layoffs to date for 1991* (Washington D.C.: National Commission for Economic Conversion and Disarmament, 1991).

55. Active duty troop reductions from Secretary of Defense, *Annual Report to the President and Congress,* (January 1991), table B-1; Civilian DoD personnel reductions and defense industry work force reductions were estimated from Comptroller of the DoD, *National Defense Budget Estimates FY 1992,* (March 1991), table 7-7. The 1994–1996 period was estimated by using a two-year moving average of the percentage change in employment.

2

Economic Development, Technology, and Defense Conversion: A National Policy Perspective

Joel Yudken

Introduction—Barriers to Conversion

In the early eighties, aerospace giant McDonnell Douglas Corporation (MDC) was in a serious quandary. Its Douglas Aircraft plant in Long Beach, California, was operating at only 30 percent capacity and as many as 10,000 of its employees had been laid off. MDC is the product of a 1967 merger between the St. Louis-based McDonnell Aircraft Company, a highly successful builder of military fighter aircraft, and the California-based Douglas Aircraft Company, known mostly for its commercial jetliners (the DC-9 and DC-10). Cash-rich McDonnell had hoped to establish a counter-cyclical ballast for its boom-and-bust military business, while Douglas was looking to be bailed out of its financial woes. But the marriage failed to produce the desired results for either partner. Soft civilian aircraft markets, accidents involving its planes, mismanagement, and bungled sales all contributed to Douglas's predicament.

Bob Berghoff, president of United Auto Workers Local 148, was also worried. Most of the unemployed Douglas workers were members of his unit. With the aid of an economic adjustment specialist from the California Department of Economic and Business Development, and consultants from the Silicon Valley-based Midpeninsula Conversion Project (now the Center for Economic Conversion), Berghoff took the initiative. He succeeded in setting up a series of meetings with plant managers to explore alternative product options—mass-transit vehicles, commuter aircraft, and cogeneration equipment—for utilizing idle plant capacity and reemploying some of his workers.[1]

At the time, MDC had few other options. It was unsuccessful in finding a foreign or domestic partner to invest in a joint design and production agreement for making a new fuel-efficient, commercial widebody jetliner. The R&D costs alone for such a plane were estimated to be as high as $2 billion. The alternative was to invest monies out of its own pocket for the new product. The company also embarked on aggressive efforts to sell stretch versions of its MD-80 (the old DC-9 Super 80). While MDC eventually was somewhat successful with the MD-80s, these sales plus those of its KC-10 military tanker (a converted DC-10) and some navy trainers were not enough to offset the decline in Douglas's fortunes. In the end good business sense dictated yet another option. Despite signs of serious interest in the union-initiated proposal, MDC's upper management in St. Louis instead chose to militarize the Douglas plant. Douglas won a multi-billion R&D contract from the Air Force for the C-17 supercargo plane—with follow-on production contracts likely—flipping around its traditional 30/70 percent mix of military to civilian business to 70/30.

The MDC experience exemplifies some of the principal obstacles standing in the way of a successful economic conversion program for military-dependent firms, workers, and communities in the United States. One barrier is the "wall of separation" between military and civilian businesses.[2] Because military-dependent and civilian commercial firms operate in very different market environments, their respective organizational structures and cultures tend to diverge, as well as their engineering, design, and marketing practices. In the MDC case, for example, McDonnell's military-oriented top executives, mostly members of the founding McDonnell family, consistently clashed with the Douglas leadership, and made many mistakes in their commercial marketing efforts. Their solution was to turn Douglas into a predominantly military firm; this was a type of business they understood.

An equally important barrier—one, in fact, that defines the larger context that has fostered this wall of separation—is the lack of coherent national policies that provide incentives and markets for converting military facilities. Since World War II, the U.S. government has conducted a concerted military-led industrial policy that created a highly concentrated complex of military-dependent industries with substantial exit barriers institutionalized by government policies: the lack of effective markets for new alternative technologies and products; the lack of technical, marketing, and organizational experience and competence to produce and market these products; and the lack of incentives and supports for military firms to invest in ways to overcome these limitations. As the MDC case illustrates, military industrial companies will not be motivated to invest in new civilian technologies as long as powerful incentives remain in the military market, where both R&D and production costs are underwritten by the Pentagon.

The winding down of the Cold War and the growing competitiveness in global markets, however, present the United States with a new and very complex challenge for the 1990s: how can it most efficiently redirect the enormous economic, technological, and human resources tied to military production to needed civilian applications, simultaneously strengthening economic performance and improving the quality of life, while mitigating the economic hardship for military-dependent workers, businesses, and communities caused by the military reductions? In this chapter, it will be argued that to meet this challenge the tasks of converting military resources to civilian use and instituting new industrial policies for promoting economic development and meeting basic human needs must be linked in a common economic agenda implemented through a new national policy strategy.

First, the chapter examines the nature, roots, and costs of the military's industrial policy in the United States, which has favored the development of a select set of industries (aerospace, communications, and electronics equipment), while it neglected, ignored, or shortchanged others. By contrast, other advanced industrial nations have targeted civilian economic and social concerns for investment and technical development. Hence, European and Japanese companies enjoying the backing of their respective governments—through R&D subsidies, tax breaks, trade protections, and other institutional supports—have rapidly increased their share of civilian product markets in industry after industry. While U.S. companies lead the world in producing advanced military aircraft, missiles, and satellite systems, Airbus Industries—subsidized by four European governments—has been capturing wider and wider shares of the commercial aircraft market, even threatening the predominant position of

Boeing.[3] While U.S. electronics firms excel in producing a wide range of highly specialized electronic devices and components for military guidance, electronic warfare and command, control, and communications systems, Japanese and European firms—with help from their respective governments—have captured most of the consumer electronics and components markets, and are rapidly chipping away in the few remaining high-tech areas of U.S. commercial superiority (i.e., computers and semiconductors). Similar stories can be told for advanced materials, robotics and machine tools, supercomputers, and other critical technologies.[4]

Second, the chapter critically assesses an important new policy initiative, dubbed "dual-use technology policy," that has emerged in reaction to the failure of traditional laissez-faire, Cold War era policies of the Reagan and Bush administrations to reverse the decline in U.S. economic performance. Championed by a loose coalition of high-tech industrial, military, academic, and government officials, dual-use policy would give the government (particularly the Department of Defense) a more active role in supporting the development of specific areas of advanced technology considered useful for both military and civilian ends. Motivated largely by industrial concerns over the declining U.S. position in civilian manufacturing, and Pentagon worries about a comparable deterioration of the defense industrial base, it seeks to reconcile the increasingly divergent needs of military and civilian technology, to bolster simultaneously U.S. industrial competitiveness and military superiority. This proposal constitutes a new de facto industrial and economic conversion policy for the nation, which has garnered strong bipartisan support in Congress and, despite general White House opposition, even the backing of important Bush administration officials.

Third, the chapter evaluates the limits of both the traditional macroeconomic and dual-use policies, first, with respect to their stated objective of improving U.S. economic competitiveness, and then, more importantly, with respect to meeting broad national needs. It contends that laissez-faire policies, which rely solely on market forces, will be inadequate for stimulating new technical and economic progress in the coming decade, and the dual-use policy would perpetuate the influence of the military's industrial policy on U.S. technical development, creating too few demand inducements in the civilian sector to truly improve the nation's sagging economic performance.

Fourth, the chapter examines the prospects of economic conversion of military industry in light of this policy debate, arguing that neither the laissez-faire nor the dual-use policy fosters the necessary demand and supply supports for enabling a successful conversion of military technological and economic resources at the national, regional, or local levels. Nor do they make adequate provisions for short-term economic adjustment assistance. By the same token, conventional approaches to conversion and economic adjustment are also shown to be insufficient for either easing the pain of transition for military-dependent firms, workers, and communities, or making the shift to new productive activities and markets.

Finally, the chapter proposes an alternative policy strategy that links economic conversion and adjustment to new investments in science, technology, and economic development, keyed to critical civilian economic, social, and environmental needs. This strategy would seek to establish new national priorities—economic stability, the environment, and health—to replace the current emphases on national security and competitiveness. The new national goal areas would serve as the primary filters or "focusing devices"—using Stanford economist Nathan Rosenberg's term[5]—for guiding new public investments, new initiatives in science and technology, and economic adjustment and technical assistance programs. The chapter further claims that this policy strategy would be the most preferable and beneficial approach to economic development and industrial restructuring, while creating the optimal conditions for implementing effective economic conversion and adjustment policies at the national, regional, and local levels.

One, Two, Three Many Industrial Policies

Industrial policy has an even more controversial, if shorter, history than economic conversion. It has been defined generally as an "attempt by the government to guide or shape industrial trends through the use of tax incentives, subsidies, and loans."[6] Ann Markusen identifies several typical features of an industrial policy: the targeting of particular sectors as growth leaders; substantial support for R&D, through incentives or direct subsidies; provision of capital for plant, equipment, and operating expenses; encouragement for various forms of industrial collaboration and planning; the monitoring and shaping of competition, e.g., by spreading around business or providing emergency assistance to ailing firms whose survival is deemed critical; government-guaranteed markets for industry outputs, especially in the early stages of development, which helps to ensure volume for growth and cost recovery; trade policies that promote exports of the industries involved and protect them from the rigors of international competition; and adjustment assistance for firms, workers, and communities affected by the closing of facilities.[7]

The concept of industrial policy gained currency in the early 1980s. The Democrats made it a key platform in their 1984 campaign, pitching it as an antidote to the decimation of heartland industries—auto, steel, textiles—that had reached its highest levels in the beginning of the decade. Through a number of ploys, President Reagan successfully aborted this effort. In line with the deregulation and privatization movements of that period, White House laissez-faire ideologues argued strenuously against anything that smacked of "excessive" government intervention in the private sector. Their rallying cry was that government had no business "picking industrial winners and losers" in the marketplace.

In reality, this neoclassical hand wringing over industrial policy is something of a red herring, if not hypocritical, given the numerous ways the federal government historically has played an active role, often with the blessings of free marketeers and in partnership with the private sector, in guiding industrial development in the United States. Indeed, it can be argued that not only have there been several examples of direct federal intervention in promoting special industrial interests, but various types of industrial policy have been employed for many years by the federal government in pursuit of national political, economic, and social goals.

Over the years, many of the policy instruments mentioned above have been used to build up industries deemed important to the nation's well-being (usually those that had strong lobbies to champion their cause). An important early example was the creation in 1915 of the National Advisory Committee for Aeronautics (NACA), later absorbed into the National Aeronautics and Space Administration (NASA, created in 1958), to further the science and technology of aeronautics and advise the military and other government agencies on aeronautical research.[8] NACA was a response to the nation's perceived inadequacy in aviation research and production—by World War I the United States had only twenty-three aircraft compared to 1,400 in France and 1,000 in Germany.[9] It conducted and funded research on airframe and propulsion technologies, pioneered the construction and use of large wind tunnels, and served as an important source of performance and other test data in aeronautics. As David Mowery and Nathan Rosenberg point out, NACA (and its successor NASA) "did more than simply support research yielding results that were diffused widely within the industry; they underwrote a portion of the costs of the research infrastructure associated with innovation in airframes and engines."[10]

Linda Cohen and Roger Noll observe that every administration since World War II has pursued policies that directly benefitted select areas of industrial and technological development: the Roosevelt and Truman administrations funded the beginnings of the computer industry; the Eisenhower administration spawned the semiconductor and nuclear power industries; the Kennedy-Johnson administration gave the nation the Apollo program, the supersonic transport (SST), and the war on cancer; Nixon, Ford, and Carter spent billions of federal dollars on energy R&D in response to the 1970s energy crises. Even President Reagan, who came to power on the promise of reducing government's role in the economy, "supported programs to develop commercially attractive breeder reactors, nuclear fissions, orbital manufacturing facilities (Space Lab) and rocket planes (the Orient Express)."[11]

The federal government has also actively engaged industrial policy tools in the areas of health (medical R&D subsidies, market creation through Medicare), agriculture (land-grant colleges, R&D subsidies, experiment stations and technical extension services, crop subsidies), energy R&D subsidies and other measures to spin off a civilian nuclear power industry from the military's nuclear program, price regulation, subsidies for oil, coal, and gas); and space (the concerted national effort in the 1960s to put a man on the moon, building up U.S. rocket technology for both military and civilian purposes).

In each instance, government intervention helped to spawn and/or nurture a select set of industries and develop the science and technology and industrial base needed to pursue national objectives. Correspondingly, these policies have helped to shape specialized market and industrial structures, specific lines of science and technology development, and patterns of investment in these areas by the private as well as public sector, with specific social, economic, political, and cultural consequences. But, while these industrial policies molded activity in their respective arenas, none has been as comprehensive and vigorous, with as great an impact on economic, industrial, and science and technology development in the United States, as the military-led industrial policy pursued since World War II.

The Military's Closet Industrial Policy

Every element of Markusen's list above has been employed in the military's closet industrial policy. It is called a closet policy because it has rarely been acknowledged as an industrial policy, as it was pursued under the rubric of national security, and not as a means to stimulate economic activity. Since World War II, the Pentagon has actively nurtured an enormous industrial base, with a massive science and technology enterprise geared to the specialized needs of strategic and tactical warfare. This military-led industrial policy spawned a powerful aerospace, communications, and electronics (ACE) industrial complex and spun off several commercially important technical innovations and industries, which for many years contributed to U.S. technological advantage.[12] Not incidentally, the ACE industries are among the few in the U.S. manufacturing sector with a positive trade balance. Aerospace, for example, registered nearly $37 billion in exports in 1990, contributing $26 billion to the U.S. trade balance.[13]

Munitions and shipbuilding have also benefited from the military's largesse over the years, but ACE industries have consistently grabbed the lion's share. Aircraft, shipbuilding, missiles and spacecraft, ordnance, tanks, and communication equipment rank as the most defense-dependent industries; each obtained at least 40 percent of its sales from the military. In 1985, missiles ranked the highest in defense dependency; the industry got almost 100 percent of its business from the military. Shipbuilding and ordnance each got over 90 percent, while aircraft and communications received 79 percent and 60 percent, respectively. But, of the 40 percent of the military budget that goes to the manufacturing sector for production and R&D contracts, the aerospace, communications, and electronics equipment industries got 79 percent in 1990, or $62 billion of a total $78 billion in Department of Defense (DoD) outlays; this is far greater than the $11 billion received by shipbuilders.[14]

The ACE industries also both receive the largest portion of the government/DoD R&D spending and are the largest performers of industrial R&D.[15] The military has long been a dominant actor in U.S. science and technology. Since World War II technological superiority has been considered by military policy-makers to be key for maintaining military superiority. Providing more than 80 percent of all federal funds for R&D up through the early 1960s, the military currently accounts for nearly two-thirds of all federal R&D and about one-third of total public and private (and fully a third of all industrial) R&D spending. By the same token, private industry performs approximately two-thirds—$24.7 billion in 1990—of the Pentagon's R&D. In 1989, the aerospace industry ranked number one in R&D spending with $19.1 billion, accounting for more than a fifth of all manufacturing R&D. About 82 percent of these funds came from the federal government, primarily from the DoD and NASA. Electronics and communications, together, followed closely behind, with $18.5 billion in overall R&D expenditures. Of this, 43 percent came from federal sources. Not surprisingly, the combined ACE industries garnered over 80 percent of all federal R&D funding disbursed to all manufacturing firms in the U.S.[16]

Government policies have directly aided these industries in other ways, as well. This includes providing much of the capital for facilities and equipment used by defense contractors. In the early 1980s the Pentagon invested about $18 billion in plants and equipment, with a replacement value of $100 billion. The government's industrial holdings include 146 plants and a half million items of equipment, 60 percent of which were in the hands of contractors. It still owns a major portion of the facilities used by contractors, including most of the plant space and equipment in the munitions and strategic missiles industries and about one-third of that of the aircraft industry.

The government, furthermore, has not been adverse to giving special breaks to ACE firms when they get into trouble, ostensibly on the grounds of preserving the industrial base for national defense. Between 1958 and 1973 the government undertook some 3,652 rescue operations to help financially troubled firms. A major example in the early 1970s was the $350 million government loan guarantee given to Lockheed to help it stay in business, after getting into serious financial trouble over its C-5A military transport and commercial L-1011 jetliner projects.[17] Underlying such bailouts is a form of economic blackmail, aptly expressed in the quip by Congressman William Moorhead (D-PA) in 1970, in which he compared Lockheed's threat of bankruptcy to that of "an 80-ton dinosaur who comes to your door and says, 'If you don't feed me, I will die.' And what are you going to do with 80 tons of dead, stinking dinosaur in your yard?"[18]

The Pentagon also attempts to spread around its contracts to ensure the well-being of its principal contractors. James Kurth calls this practice the "follow-on imperative," in which the big companies get "turns" in being granted the latest contract in the sequence of new weapons systems.[19] Kurth recently predicted that Lockheed, which has been having financial difficulties, would be the next to receive a follow-on contract. In early 1990 the Lockheed-led team won the bid for the lucrative Advanced Tactical Fighter contract.[20]

In addition to these direct forms of aid, the Pentagon has provided trade supports to its favored industries for decades and operates a large

Foreign Military Sales program. The Export-Import Bank has also favored the commercial side of the aircraft business, perhaps more than most industries, with preferential financial packages for the export of aircraft comparable to those given by European governments. Up through 1971, for example, Boeing received $600 million in loan guarantees from the Export-Import Bank, which helped induce foreign airline purchases of its products.[21] The winding down of the Cold War and corresponding reductions in the defense budget have given foreign sales new importance for the military industrial sector. The Gulf War has given further impetus for U.S. military exports, which, as one aerospace executive has remarked, is "the only game in town right now."[22] Shortly after hostilities were over, the Bush administration asked Congress to appropriate $1 billion in loan guarantees for overseas customers of U.S. military contracts, to help the latter compete in an increasingly crowded market; it was the first such request for aid since the 1970s.[23]

In addition to building, subsidizing, and bailing out industries, the Pentagon has made modest efforts to alleviate the worst impacts of military cutbacks, particularly base closures, on defense-dependent workers and communities. The Office of Economic Adjustment (OEA), established by the DoD in 1961, has provided guidance and adjustment assistance to several communities in redeveloping closed bases, with mixed success. Overall, the extent and quality of the programs available to aid stricken communities and workers have not been, by and large, adequate to the task. Nevertheless, there is at least tacit recognition by the Pentagon of a responsibility to provide such aid.

Roots and Costs

Some of the roots of the military-led industrial policy can be traced to the first decades of the century; the role of NACA in nurturing this nascent aircraft industry was noted earlier. But a full-blown commitment by the Pentagon to build and foster a supporting industrial base was an outgrowth of World War II. The United States emerged out of the war as the premier military and economic power on the planet, with a new sense of its "manifest destiny" as the guardian (and promoter) of the capitalist "Free World." The federal government embarked on an aggressive program of building up its military arsenal to counter the rise of Soviet power and back its growing foreign commitments and interests in the postwar era. The war convinced policy-makers of the primacy of air power for carrying out the new U.S. military doctrine; later military doctrines would be built around missile capabilities, and even later, around achieving technological superiority.

To implement these doctrines the Pentagon recognized that it needed a compliant and robust industrial and technological base that it could mold to meet its specialized requirements. At the same time, an ailing aircraft industry lobbied hard in the late 1940s for direct forms of government support. Not coincidentally many of its top executives were in the forefront calling for an air-power-centered military force. Building on the successful collaborative experiences of the war, the convergent interests of military and industrial and other government policy-makers (not to mention many academic and labor leaders) subsequently cemented a new postwar partnership between government and the private sector, which spawned the emergent aerospace, electronics, communications, and computer industries.

Over the first postwar decades, this policy seemed to serve U.S. foreign and economic needs well. It bolstered U.S. corporate interests internationally, while providing direct stimulation for economic development domestically on the regional level, forging a prosperous "gunbelt"—described by Ann Markusen and Joel Yudken as "a patchwork of cities and towns strung out along an arc from Alaska to Boston, sweeping down through Seattle, Silicon Valley, and Los Angeles in the West, across the more southerly mountain and plains states, through Texas and Florida, and up to the eastern seaboard through Newport News and Long Island to Massachusetts and Connecticut."[24] Finally, direct-buys and spin-offs from the military-led industrial policy fueled the development of commercially significant high-technology products such as computers, jet planes, lasers, semiconductors, and robotics, and the industries that produced them.

But this early prosperity was also a product of certain advantages that the United States had over other industrial nations right after the war. While the U.S. industrial base was left largely intact—in fact, it was greatly stimulated and built up during the war—and benefitted from massive pent-up capacity and demand for consumer goods in the postwar era, the economies of most of the other combatant nations were badly damaged, if not shattered, and needed time to be rebuilt. In short, the United States was able to maintain its economic and military preeminence in the world during the first postwar decades mainly because, with the exception of the Soviet Union in the military sphere, there simply were no viable competitors.

The military's industrial policy has not been without its costs, however. One group of Pentagon critics, the "depletionists"—its best known proponents include Seymour Melman, John Ullmann, and Lloyd J. Dumas—has long contended that military spending is a major drain on the civilian economy, diverting vital capital, technical, and human resources away from productive uses. Critics of the depletionist view, such as Gordon Adams, director of the Washington-based Defense Budget Project, and former White House economic adviser Murray Weidenbaum, on the other hand, downplay these impacts primarily on aggregate economic grounds. They like to point out that the defense budget accounts for only 5–6 percent of the gross national product (GNP), for example.

There clearly is not space for a full discussion of this debate here. Markusen and Yudken present elsewhere in some depth a different set of arguments that shows how, as the U.S. military-industrial policy directly and indirectly built up certain sets of industries, regions, and occupations, others were shortchanged over the past forty years.[25] In short, while certainly not all the nation's economic ills can be blamed on the military economy, the actual pattern of U.S. economic development manifested locally, regionally, and nationally in the postwar era owes a great deal to Pentagon policies.

To a degree, there does indeed appear to be a diversion of resources, especially in the realm of science and technology, from the civilian to the military sector, as claimed by depletionist scholars. The greatest costs to the nation's economic and social well-being derive from the trade-offs among competing national priorities forced upon the nation by the military-industrial policy. The decision to build up the massive military-industrial system in the United States entailed significant opportunity costs in terms of various possible public and private investments in economic and social development that had to be foregone in the name of national security. Consider the illustrative example of steel. To make their industries competitive, European and Japanese firms and governments poured money into steel R&D, especially in the 1970s. In contrast, U.S. steel firms were cutting back, and the federal government preferred to concentrate its R&D resources on military industrial objectives. Hence, while the White House pushed the Strategic Defense Initiative (which has been bankrolled at the rate of $3–6 billion per year since the early 1980s), the steel industry was not able to get $15 *million* for its Leapfrog Technology initiative fully funded, despite support from President Reagan's science advisor George Keyworth.[26]

Unfortunately, measuring opportunity costs is very difficult, as it entails evaluating alternative futures that we cannot really know. On the other hand, the rise of European and Asian economic powers in the last couple of decades gives us another basis for comparison. The United States is no longer without major economic competitors. Its war-torn allies and former enemies—ironically, the latter have fared the best—are now fully recovered and modernized and pursuing aggressive industrial policies of their own, built, however, around civilian goals. It is increasingly apparent, even to many government, business, and academic leaders, that the U.S. military-led industrial policy is much less successful than the policies of its trading partners in generating technological innovation, productivity growth, and enhanced industrial performance—not to mention the country's lack of policies for addressing its environmental, health care, infrastructure and urban crises.

Out of the Closet—The Rise of Dual-Use Policy

The fundamental changes in international political and economic conditions over the past decade, especially in the last few years, have forced a reconsideration of military doctrine and force structure, and brought into question the efficacy (which some critics have always doubted) of the Cold War military-led industrial policy as the fountainhead of commercial technology development in the increasingly competitive global markets. This has begun to force the DoD's industrial policy out of the closet, with greater cries from both within and outside the Pentagon for a more explicit DoD role in shaping commercially important technology opportunities. Once on the leading edge, military technology has fallen behind commercial technology in many areas. In addition, the needs and requirements of military and civilian technology development have diverged significantly over the years.[27] Military planners have become concerned with the decline of the ability of U.S. high-tech firms to supply vital components and systems—a symptom of the general decline of the U.S. industrial base—which has resulted in ever greater reliance on foreign sources.[28]

The concern over the purported deterioration of the defense-industrial base echoes a parallel concern in the civilian sector over how to respond to the declining competitiveness of the nation's industries in the global marketplace. A primary issue in this controversy is the proper role of government in guiding economic and technological development. On one side of the divide are several industrial, academic, and political leaders who seek greater federal government involvement in strengthening the commercial sector. This group wants the government to take a leadership role in reversing the rapid decline of the U.S. market share, which has occurred in one industry after another since the 1970s. It is asking for, in effect, a new high-tech industrial policy, although it has cloaked its proposals with the rhetoric of "industry-led policy" and "technology policy" in an effort to appease free marketeers from whom the notion of "industrial policy" is ideologically abhorrent.

To achieve its goal of U.S. high-tech industry regaining the competitive edge, this group wants the government to employ several policy instruments, such as trade protections, R&D tax incentives, relaxation of anti-trust laws, reduced regulation, strengthened intellectual property rights and patent laws, and various macroeconomic measures. But its most controversial demand is for significant government investment *targeted* to the development of critical technologies relevant to commercial high-tech needs.

Principal opposition to this position has come primarily from powerful White House officials (in particular former White House Chief of Staff John Sununu, Office of Management and Budget Richard Darman, and Council of Economic Advisers chief Michael Boskin), who rightly perceive that these proposals—regardless of the appellations given them—would constitute an industrial policy. They are especially skeptical of federal programs that target specific industries and technologies for special treatment, on the grounds that this unduly interferes with the workings of the marketplace.

In efforts to circumvent the White House's opposition, the high tech policy proponents have sought help from the one governmental entity toward which every administration since World War II has turned a blind eye with respect to government intervention in private-sector activity: the military. A new convergence of interests has evolved in recent years between forward-thinking military R&D managers and commercial high-tech industrialists. Linking their interests is the doctrine of "dual-use" technology, which attempts to reconcile both military and commercial technical requirements.[29] Government and business would collaborate on R&D programs that give priority to those areas of science and technology development deemed important for both military and commercial ends.

Semiconductor manufacturing technology, high-definition display, high-performance computing, advanced materials, robotics, optoelectronics biotechnology, and advanced machine tools are examples of such technologies receiving significant military subsidy. The Pentagon's lead R&D agency, the Defense Advanced Research Projects Agency (DARPA) has been elected as the principal federal agency to manage this effort. DARPA officials in the late 1980s have proudly equated the role of their agency to that of Japan's Ministry of International Trade and Industry (MITI).[30] Already DARPA is the principal sponsor of dual-use projects within the commercial sector; it funds most of the technologies mentioned above. This includes providing $100 million yearly to Sematech, a consortium of semiconductor firms, and $50 million for the recently initiated precompetitive technologies program. The DoD, meanwhile, supports a large manufacturing technology program and even funds the Office of Science and Technology Policy's (OSTP) newly formed Critical Technologies Institute.[31]

From the military point of view, a virtue of this strategy is that it would tie commercial high-tech industry more closely to its needs. Military industry will keep on the cutting edge of advanced technology in the design of new generations of "smarter," more flexible, rapidly deployable conventional weaponry—the kinds that were employed against Iraq in early 1991—that are more suitable for the new role of the U.S. military as the world police. Dual-use policy will also strengthen the hand of Pentagon reformers in their efforts to overhaul the military design and procurement system, and tie it more directly to U.S. commercial industry. Military weapons producers would have greater incentive to incorporate domestically produced, off-the-shelf, state-of-the-art commercial components and subsystems into their designs. Theoretically, this would greatly cut the costs of new weapons systems while increasing their performance quality and reliability. At the same time, U.S. commercial high-tech producers would benefit, not only from supply-side subsidies for R&D, but from an expanded domestic demand (i.e., the DoD) for their new products, which also could be sold competitively in world markets.

Through the Back Door

The dual-use cause has not yet prevailed, as the firing of Craig Fields as DARPA director in 1990 for his entrepreneurial activities attests.[32] But the obvious need to do something about the nation's flagging industrial base and the intensifying restructuring of the U.S. military-industrial system will undoubtedly require some sort of accommodation between the dual-use and laissez-faire forces. To get around the Bush administration's flak, high-tech policy advocates have embarked on a more piecemeal, backdoor strategy, built around the notions of technology policy and critical technology lists, which has met with some success in Congress and even grudging acceptance from within the White House. With the backing of OSTP director D. Allan Bromley, the Bush administration has given back-door endorsements to so-called generic precompetitive technology R&D programs favored by the high-tech supporters, such as the multi-agency high-performance computing initiative and advanced manufacturing technology programs of the Commerce Department's National Institute for Standards and Technology (NIST). In 1990, the Commerce Department issued a report on emerging technologies with potential to advance "productivity and quality" and create a "multitude of new products and services."[33] Dual-use policy proponents have also taken heart from the report OSTP recently sent to Congress entitled "The U.S. Technology Policy." As leading dual-use advocate Lewis Branscomb, from Harvard's Kennedy School of Government, notes, "building a consensus in the White House for any document with the words 'technology policy' in the title was no small achievement."[34]

Nevertheless, the Bush administration's 1992 budget request asks for only minuscule levels of funding for civilian-based, commercially relevant technology programs, compared to those funnelled through the Department of Defense. Instead it proposes that basic civilian research and megabuck, pork-barrel "big science" projects (such as the Superconducting Super Collider, Space Station, Strategic Defense Initiative, and Human Genome project) receive substantial funding increases. National defense R&D programs, especially for large weapons systems development—although cut back from prior-year levels—will continue to receive the lion's share of the federal government's R&D largesse.

The pressure for a dual-use policy continues to intensify, nonetheless. New proposals for establishing a dual-use policy are being put forth by influential private-sector groups. The recently released report by the Carnegie Commission on Science, Technology, and Government, for example, urges a transformation of DARPA into a National Advanced Research Projects Agency (NARPA), which would still operate under the auspices of the Pentagon. NARPA would oversee the development of the national technology base that covers both military and civilian technology needs. The report also proposes changes in the roles of the National Security Council and other executive offices that would make technology policy a central concern of both national security and economic policy at the highest levels of the executive branch. Meanwhile, in a political end run in Congress, bipartisan backers of dual-use policy tagged a full-blown technology policy amendment onto the 1992–1993 Senate National Defense Authorization bill. This substantially institutionalizes the lead role of DoD/DARPA in both the government and the private sector in managing dual-use technology initiatives in the future.[35]

The Limits of Dual-Use Policy

The outcome of the dual-use technology debate will have profound consequences for the nation's economic health and international security. By the same token, it will shape the conditions that determine technology opportunities in economic conversion in the years to come. Both the dual-use and traditional macroeconomic approaches to technology and economic development therefore warrant a more critical examination than has thus far appeared in the literature. First, the historical and empirical evidence tends to belie the laissez-faire premise that market forces alone are sufficient for accounting for the direction and nature of technical change in the economy. Much of this evidence has been presented, in recent years, in the writings of economists and economic historians critical of traditional equilibrium models of technical innovation and economic change, such as those of Richard Nelson, Sidney Winter, Christopher Freeman, Giovanni Dosi, and Nathan Rosenberg, among others.[36]

According to this school of thought—which has roots in the earlier works of Joseph Schumpeter—market forces alone are not sufficient to explain the processes of technical innovation and diffusion and their impact on a nation's economic performance. Instead, technological developments are seen as both a product *and* cause of dynamic economic change. A complex set of economic, institutional, and social forces operate as selection and focusing mechanisms that shape the patterns of technical and industrial development.[37] Moreover, combined with these forces, the constraints of prior technical and organizational histories of firms and industries—what Dosi calls technological paradigms and trajectories[38]—historically have exercised as great an influence on the paths of technological and economic development as ordinary market mechanisms. Arguing that "the ordinary messages of the marketplace are general and not sufficiently specific," Rosenberg notes that "there have existed a variety of devices at different times and places which have served as powerful agents in formulating technical problems and in focusing attention upon them in a compelling way."[39]

In these terms, industrial policies such as those practiced by Japan and several Western European governments can be viewed as explicit forms of institutional focusing and selection, which attempt to affect both the supply and demand sides of technological change: in the former, inducements are provided in the form of R&D subsidies and incentives and other institutional mechanisms that attempt to guide the trajectories of science and technology problem solving according to specified political, social, and economic criteria; in the latter, selection pressures are applied through direct product purchases and regulatory restraints. In short, over the past few decades Japan and Western Europe have conducted policies that consciously sought to focus industrial technology trajectories and the development of new paradigms towards what they considered desirable social and commercial objectives (e.g., energy efficiency, advanced modes of transportation, enhanced manufacturing performance).

By contrast, the United States has followed a different set of industrial policies, guided by a different set of national goals—mostly dominated by concerns for national security and military power—and employing a different set of focusing and selection mechanisms. These, in turn, have fostered certain industrial and technological paradigms, while others have been ignored and neglected. As Dosi observes, in the United States "military and space programs operated . . . as a powerful focusing mechanism towards defined technological targets, while at the same time providing financial support to R&D and guaranteeing public procurement."[40]

Correspondingly, as we saw earlier, the economic fruits of the U.S. policies have been quite different compared to those borne from those employed by its economic competitors. On the plus side, Robert W. Rycroft and Don E. Kash cite the success stories of the medical, defense, and agricultural sectors where continuous policy support has been applied, which, they add, are also the"source of most technologies that produce large trade surpluses." They enumerate the gains of employing such focused policies:

> Five categories of agricultural products (cereals and grains, oilseeds, cotton, animal feed, and tobacco) have succeeded in large part because of government intervention with the explicit goal of capturing the international market. Defense successes have been in the areas of aircraft and spacecraft, computers and scientific/engineering instruments. The medical products which have been the major beneficiaries of government involvement are pharmaceutical preparations (e.g.,

prescription drugs), biological products (e.g., new vaccines) as well as medicinal chemicals.[41]

The roles government has played in innovation in each case illustrate some of the main types of institutional focusing devices: underwriting of high-risk, front-end R&D costs; serving as a "marriage broker" between government, industry, and universities to create the organizational context needed for undertaking continuous innovation; creating market demand through the procurement and use of new and improved products and processes.[42]

On the negative side in the industrial and civilian technological sectors in the United States that have not been favored by such institutional inducements—where no or relatively weak focusing devices have been employed—we have seen that industry after industry, from traditional manufacturing (steel, auto, and textiles) to high technology (consumer electronics, semiconductor chips) has suffered major losses in production capabilities and markets, while those nations with focused policies have rapidly gained ground in these same areas.[43]

The emergence of dual-use and other competitiveness initiatives in recent years indicates that at least a few sectors of the industrial and political elite have finally woken up to the reality of the contradictory policies of the United States; while the government conducts vigorous industrial policies in some arenas, it is forbidden to help guide private sector efforts in the economic areas most crucial to U.S. long-term industrial performance. In order to circumvent this quandary, dual-use technology policy seeks to establish institutional devices for focusing investment in militarily relevant commercial technology development, unencumbered by the constraints of military specifications. For example, advanced microchips designed and produced by civilian commercial vendors could also be used in military systems.

A virtue of the dual-use proposal is that it demands that the federal government take the lead in establishing better mechanisms for guiding the nation's future industrial development. It recognizes the centrality of mobilizing the nation's science and technology resources to the success of this venture. Given the military's predominance in the nation's science and technology affairs, dual-use policy also strives to direct federal R&D policies so that the science and technology needs of national security are at least made more compatible with those of the civilian economy.

Nevertheless, the dual-use technology strategy is deficient on two major grounds.[44] First, despite its best intentions, the continued centrality of military agencies in guiding the dual-use program will inevitably constrain the paths of technological development in directions that are not optimal either from an economic or societal perspective. Second, the military tie-in aside, the criterion of economic competitiveness will still unnecessarily limit the development of several economically and socially critical technologies. In short, dual-use policy does not address, and may even compete with, a number of critical national needs—such as the environment, public infrastructure, mass transportation, renewable energy, occupational health and safety, and education—that will require carefully tailored investments in science and technology for their solution.

Because the military's industrial policy would largely remain in force, the persistent role of the Pentagon as the principal federal sponsor of the high-tech industrial program may hinder technology transfer in precisely those areas of greatest commercial and national need. Not all critical areas of civilian science and technology meet the test of military relevancy. The difficulties of bridging the wide gap between military and civilian paradigms in technological development may be an underlying reason why, despite substantial, long-term DoD funding for dual-use technologies such as robotics, semiconductors, supercomputers, superconductors, airframes, advanced propulsion, and advanced ceramics, U.S. commercial firms in these areas continue to lose ground to Japanese competitors.

In the final analysis, DARPA, which leads the national dual-use effort, is a military agency, with a mandate to develop advanced technologies that meet military criteria. Its programs of necessity favor the needs of military over civilian users. More generally, the success of dual-use policy is predicated on a change in Pentagon procedures that would entail changing weapons parts specifications so dual-use commercial products can be used. But even Senator Sam Nunn (D-GA), head of the Senate Armed Services Committee, has expressed skepticism during recent hearings that anything could be done in this area. "How are you gong to do that?" he asked. "You're talking about changing the culture of military procurement. You have thousands and thousands of people over there writing military specifications."[45] In any event, the military's (primarily DARPA's) dual-use initiatives are only about 3 percent of the DoD's R&D budget. Thus, dual-use policy will not solve the fundamental problem that the military still consumes most federal R&D dollars, and crowds out investments in civilian research.

Dual-use policy will also continue to limit—in fact, it may even narrow further—participation in science and technology policy making to a small group of industrial, governmental, and professional interests. There are no provisions to involve other major stakeholders in society in the national S&T policy process, despite recognition, for example, that worker participation in technology decision making enhances industrial productivity. Hence, R&D managers have little incentive to incorporate broader social concerns into their agendas, such as the environmental or employment impacts of new production technologies. Using Dosi's terms, the lack of such inputs into the processes that guide technical innovation reinforces technological paradigms that either do not contribute, or are even antithetical to, social and environmental goals.

Moreover, a competitiveness agenda that targets only a handful of select technologies for investment, based on narrow economic criteria, will itself limit opportunities for developing other economically vital technologies. For example, although public investments in rebuilding the public infrastructure, developing renewable energy sources, and cleaning up the environment would be equally important for enhancing the nation's economic performance, stimulating broad new species of scientific and technical innovation, such programs would not be supported by dual-use policy. In fact, given the tightening federal budget constraints dual-use programs may very well compete with, if not preclude, public investments in these other critical areas of social and economic need. For example, manufacturing industries (such as steel and textiles) and industries that produce alternative energy and environmental products, which currently suffer from a dearth of R&D funding, are unlikely to be targeted in a dual-use industrial policy.

In addition, the targeting of generic technologies for supply-side support is alone not a sufficient means for enabling new technical paradigms to evolve. Demand-side inducements are also needed for promoting new directions for technical change. By signaling new market opportunities, government-created demands help to stimulate private-sector investment in new areas of technical development. This was particularly the case for the military-led industrial policy in the first postwar decades, which not only spawned new generations of sophisticated weapons technologies, but generated a number of commercially significant innovations. For example, Mowery and Rosenberg observe:

> The benefits that are sometimes perceived to flow from military R&D are in fact the product of military R&D plus frequently massive military procurement. The willingness of private industry to commit substantial resources to innovation

> in a particular sector has been dominated by awareness of the potentially large markets for military products of superior design and performance capability. Without the pull of defense procurement in such sectors as jet aircraft, integrated circuitry, and computers—especially in the critical early years of development of these technologies—the impact of military R&D spending alone would have been far smaller.[46]

Dual-use policy assumes that global market forces will provide the necessary demand-pull incentives for promoting commercial innovation in the United States, if only the federal government will help out on the supply side. Given the intensifying world competition in advanced technology products at a time of global recession and international instability, this seems a dubious premise. Without comparable demand-side public investments in civilian areas, such as alternative energy technologies and mass transportation, the military once again may become, by default, the demand creator of last resort for advanced technologies, as new and exotic intelligent weapons systems become increasingly reliant on sophisticated devices, software, and materials.

Economic Conversion Redefined

Another shortcoming of both the dual-use technology and laissez-faire policies is the scant attention paid to problems of economic adjustment, diversification, and conversion for workers and communities suffering dislocations due to military cutbacks. The conversion problem looms large at this time, not just because of the question of whether U.S. adjustment capacity is sufficient to handle the mounting military-induced dislocation, but because of the strategic importance of the military sector, despite its small share of total GNP, to the nation's industrial performance.

First, military industry is a much larger part of the nation's durable goods manufacturing sector than of the economy as a whole. Defense industry accounts for about 15–17 percent of the nation's manufacturing employment and an even greater share of these jobs in key industrial regions. In 1980, for example, *before* the 1980s buildup, defense-related jobs accounted for at least one-fifth of manufacturing employment in California's Santa Clara County according to an Office of Economic Adjustment-sponsored report prepared by SRI International.[47] Changes in military demand also have significant impacts on overall national and regional manufacturing outputs and exports in the United States.

Second, military spending dominates U.S. public investment priorities. Hence, it has precluded investments—in public infrastructure rebuilding, environmental controls, alternative energy sources, and commercial R&D—that have significant economic pay-offs for U.S. industries.

Third, the most direct way that the military impinges on U.S. civilian economic performance is its control over the major portion of the nation's vital science and technology resources. The military and commercial high-tech industrial sectors are increasingly in competition for many of the same scarce technical resources, a fact that gave rise to the dual-use policy discussed earlier.

Economic conversion can therefore be defined as the optimum reallocation of public and private economic assets, from the military to civilian industrial sectors, that enhances national economic performance and social well-being. A crucial criterion is that this be accomplished with minimal dislocation of workers and communities. Conversion of military facilities ideally would preserve the bulk of the jobs, reemploy much of the plant and equipment, and maintain as large a part of the local economic base as possible. Corporate diversification, in which a firm shuts down existing facilities while it buys into new product divisions, leaving workers and communities high and dry, clearly does not meet this criterion. Nor do community-initiated diversification efforts—including many high-tech development strategies—that do not aid local workers and businesses most directly affected by cutbacks and closures.

There have been several corporate and employee-community initiated conversion efforts in the United States since 1970. Among the most notable efforts of firms—notable mainly for their lack of success—are attempts by Boeing-Vertol, Grumman, and Rohr to shift military divisions to production of mass-transit vehicles (rail cars, buses) in the 1970s. On a smaller scale, Kaman Corp. and Frisby Airborne Hydraulics have achieved limited success in converting military-based technologies to commercializable products.[49]

The best known employee-community-led conversion projects in the 1980s involved Douglas Aircraft (see earlier), Blaw-Knox, Unisys, and General Dynamics' Quincy Shipyards.[50] Learning from their lack of success at the plant level—noting the lack of incentives and resources to assist conversion, especially by small- and medium-sized firms—community-worker groups have since turned much of their attention to promoting municipal and state conversion policies. Minnesota, for example, has one of the best state-initiated programs; it was first advanced by and includes extensive participation of labor and community conversion activists.

Critics point to the limited success of conversion as evidence that it lacks viability. In actuality, this is a classic "catch-22" situation. Inadequate government commitment and institutional support for conversion have been major reasons why it is both an unattractive option to corporate managements and very difficult to implement under current economic conditions. At the same time, the lack of conversion successes has been used to undermine political efforts to establish such mechanisms. Federal and state support might include assistance for: new product R&D; planning and feasibility studies; employee adjustment; retooling; finding new buyers; establishing employee stock ownership plans, worker buy-outs, and the like; and arranging financing. If such institutional aid had been available on a larger scale and in a more coordinated fashion—say, if the Defense Economic Adjustment bill sponsored year after year by Congressman Ted Weiss (D-NY) had been enacted—the conversion success rate might have been greater.

On the other hand, as the earlier McDonnell Douglas example illustrates, the problem of making conversion viable goes beyond providing economic adjustment and technical assistance. In general, many conversion advocates have tended to underestimate the significant institutional and deep structural economic factors that underlay the conversion failures to date. In practice, economic conversion is a very complex and difficult process. Conversion proponents and critics alike have noted the many barriers military-industrial firms confront when trying to shift to civilian pursuits, whether through diversification or conversion.

In the terms of the "neo-Schumpeterian" writers above, the conversion problem should be understood as a switch from one technological paradigm (military) to another (civilian). Military-related industry has evolved its own unique paradigms of technical and organizational development, which have been fostered and institutionalized—focused and selected—by the Pentagon's industrial policy for over forty years. A substantial divergence—a wall of separation—between military and civilian firms has emerged over time in their modes of operating, engineering, and marketing. These are the technical and organizational exit barriers that make it difficult for military firms to convert to civilian production. The reconversion from wartime to civilian production after World War II, which entailed primarily civilian firms switching back to the original modes of activity (in reality, somewhat reconfigured by their years of war work) was therefore a far easier task than the current problem of converting industries that have become increasingly entrenched in military-driven paradigms over the Cold War period.

While in theory it is possible to identify many civilian products and technologies to which military firms may be capable of switching their production activities—in fact, lists of such products have been developed in various studies and actual conversion efforts—the problems of technology transfer involved are formidable. As one corporate executive stated in response to a U.S. Senate questionnaire:

> Personally, I happen to question the ability of a company devoted solely to defense-space to succeed in the commercial field. They have a tendency to underrate the complexity of the problems and the capabilities of their future competitors.[52]

The Boeing-Vertol conversion experience supports this perception. Boeing officials admitted that they had failed to anticipate the engineering challenges presented in the project.[53] The requirements of civilian technical development generally are substantially different, even in similar production areas, such as aircraft, than those in the military industry. Over the Cold War period, the skills of military-dependent engineers and scientists have correspondingly diverged from those required in civilian industries. It is hard—though not impossible—for those trained in the design of military hardware and software, who are used to specialized military performance specifications, to transfer their experience to the civilian arena where cost or very different performance criteria are emphasized.

Successful conversion therefore requires long lead times and substantial planning, retooling, and retraining of many sectors of the work force, particularly managers and engineers, to enable firms to adjust to different cycles of technical innovation and product development.[54] Conversion legislation and policies would provide various forms of government assistance for these tasks. Support for R&D would also be needed, not only for short-term product development, but to help firms evolve new civilian-oriented paradigms of technology development over the long term.

Supply-side inducements such as these, which help companies over the hurdles of technology transfer, are necessary but not sufficient conditions for successful conversions. Success is also contingent on there being effective markets for products that plants can convert their production to. For example, it can be argued that the Boeing-Vertol experience was in reality not a total failure. The company had moved quite far along the learning curve in the design and production of transit cars. The primary problem was a lack of stable markets for their product to allow them to follow that curve further and actually begin to make a profit. Boeing officials themselves noted that a major obstacle was a lack of coherent national mass transportation policy. More generally, the comment of Boeing Chairman William M. Allen, in response to the Senate query, illustrates the corporate sensitivity to the market signals provided by government.

> The company has examined many of the civil systems markets during the past five years. These have included in-depth studies of surface transportation, water management, waste disposal and security systems. We find that each of these have elements consistent with our technical and systems management capabilities. However, we do not see either established national goals in these areas, consistent commitment to adequate funding, reasonable-size contracts of adequate duration, or contracting modes consistent with these (civilian markets).[55]

The general decline in U.S. civilian manufacturing performance, therefore, presents a serious obstacle to defense companies shifting their production to new areas, even if they do all the right things internally. As the United States loses ground in one civilian industrial arena after another, because of both a lack of technical competence and a loss of market share, military firms seeking to diversify into civilian markets confront a dilemma when contemplating the difficulties of converting their facilities. At the heart of this dilemma, note Markusen and Yudken, is the fact that no other product area offers the guarantee of federal commitment, public resources, and luxuriously long lead times that producing defense hardware did.[56]

But given the massive cuts in military hardware systems expected over the next few years, the problem devolves to: what kinds of new national focusing devices will be needed—or possible—to enable military firms to overcome exit barriers and smoothly move into new areas of civilian technology with minimum costs to the individuals, communities, and firms involved? It is obvious that neither the laissez-faire economic policies of the Bush administration nor the proposed dual-use technology policies will be able to do the job.

The former will do little to provide the kinds of targeted supply and demand inducements that would be needed. Moreover, an administration reluctant to extend unemployment benefits at the heart of a recession is unlikely to do much to bolster an already overburdened system for aiding displaced workers, much less target defense workers for special consideration. The latter is too narrowly focused on helping a limited number of technologies and industries. Only a few types of military-dependent firms, mainly high-tech component suppliers, would directly benefit from dual-use policy. In addition, dual-use policy will not create new civilian markets for military firms to convert into. As noted earlier, it even may not be successful in helping domestic commercial high-tech firms compete in existing markets.

Linking Economic Development to Human Needs

What is required is a different kind of strategy, one that links conversion of defense resources to rebuilding the nation's economic capacity and addressing pressing national needs. The nation will have to redirect vital technical and economic assets now locked into the military economy—the so-called peace dividend—towards these ends. The new strategy would include mechanisms that minimize the costs of adjustment for workers and communities. At the same time, it would make large-scale economic conversion and adjustment much more feasible undertakings.

What would this strategy actually look like? First, new national goals are needed that respond to the deeply felt needs and capture the imagination of the general populace. Markusen and Yudken maintain that three priorities should top the list: economic stability, the environment, and health.[57] These areas of national concern would guide public- and private-sector commitments in the coming decades, just as national security served as the number-one focus for U.S. industrial policy over the Cold War period. These are the principal elements for creating *real* security in the new era.

In effect, we need new industrial policies targeted to each area of national need. Each case implies a specific set of goals, criteria, and standards for the design and implementation of government policies, programs, and investments for focusing activity in the private sector, just as the overarching concern of defense conditioned how public spending helped shape industrial, scientific, and technological development in the past. Each is briefly discussed below, though all warrant more extensive discussion.

Economic Stability vs. Competitiveness

Policies that promote economic stability would build and maintain the economic well-being of communities and regions, while cushioning both against the displacement caused by military cutbacks, international competition, technological change, and other economic shocks. Economic stability does not mean stagnation. On the contrary, building community stability implies investing in activities that promote vigorous and diversified economic growth, create new and decent jobs, enhance the productivity of domestic industries and the quality of their goods and services, increase the standard of living, and revitalize moribund industries and local economies (e.g., inner-city areas).

At the same time, stabilization policies would attempt to regulate growth to preserve the economic and social integrity of communities and maximize job security for the local work force. All too often, Markusen and Yudken observe, "champions of the market and capital mobility ignore the destructive effects on workers, households, local governments, and regional businesses when a local economic environment changes."[58] but some dislocation in a vibrant economy is inevitable; Joseph Schumpeter's notion of "creative destruction" remains a force of economic evolution in capitalistic societies.[59] Hence, adequate economic adjustment assistance available to all categories of workers would be a mandatory component of any new economic development program.

It should be further noted that the targets of economic stability policy are not specific industries, but the economies of regions and communities. This implies that national policies would need to be developed and coordinated with those implemented at the state and local level, which in turn would be aided by and stimulated by the federal programs. These policies would necessarily emphasize creating the material conditions, such as infrastructural supports—mass transportation, communications, sewage systems, utilities, bridges, highways—that allow businesses and communities to function more efficiently and effectively on a day-to-day level.

The goal of economic stability must be distinguished from competitiveness, which is the current rage and principal goal of dual-use policy. As MIT economist Paul Krugman points out, "there is surprisingly little coherent discussion of what 'competitiveness' means." Businesses can be described by their competitive position, but for nations it is not a relevant notion. In fact, Krugman argues that "trade between countries is so much unlike competition between businesses that many economists regard the word 'competitiveness,' when applied to countries, as so misleading as to be essentially meaningless." A danger of competitiveness is that it raises once again the specter of nationalistic competition, particularly against Japan. It is "one of those issues," he observes, "like national defense, that can easily be used as a patriotic cloak for special interest politics." But it is not international competition that threatens to put the United States out of business, but low rates of savings and investment, low spending on R&D, and low quality basic education.[60]

Competitiveness, therefore, is not the real problem, but a symptom of the problem. What is needed is a new economic order in which firms, workers and communities have a common sense of where they are going. Policies that target economic stability—which also would improve the competitive position of domestic and local industries—along with the environment and health, could provide this common agenda.

Targeting the Environment

Most everybody is concerned about the mounting environmental problems: pollution of the air, water, and soil; toxics in our homes and workplaces; depletion of scarce natural resources; global warming and a depleting of the ozone layer; threats to the biosphere and species diversity on the planet. These are issues that transcend local, regional, and international boundaries. There is growing political support for government programs to invest in solutions, and to strengthen controls and regulations.

However, as most environmental problems derive from uncontrolled production practices, environmental standards are all too often pitted against economic necessity and interests. The jobs of loggers, for example, have allegedly been threatened by efforts to save wilderness areas and animal habitats. Environmental policies, therefore, need to do more than the target larger global environmental problems and strengthen the controls and regulation of waste emissions. They must also promote an environmental agenda that is compatible with and built into economic development.

The new strategy would stress a new rubric gaining popularity in recent years: sustainable development. According to Ken Geiser, professor of environmental policy at the University of Lowell, sustainable development refers to the integration of industrial and environmental needs into a single vision of industrial development. First emerging in regard to agriculture, sustainability is now being applied to manufacturing. "Sustainable farming," Geiser says "aims to lessen the need for chemical pesticides and fertilizers in favor of practices that work with natural ecological cycles to improve the soil and increase the pest resistance of plants."[61] Sustainable manufacturing would include the following features: appropriate technologies for the desired ends, safe and environmentally compatible materials, production processes that minimize waste products, energy efficiency, safe and skill-enhancing work environments, and resource conservation.

Sustainability shifts the emphasis of government policies from regulation, control, and treatment to prevention. Pollution reduction and resources preservation would be built into the design of production processes, technologies, and organizations, as well as products for consumers and other producers. Sustainability policy departs from conventional environmental regulation in that it attempts to more directly influence the decisions of private firms regarding the selection of materials and technologies. At the same time, it would benefit the private sector: by designing pollution-control and waste-reduction technologies into the front end of production, the back-end costs of pollution clean-up and waste management for firms—indeed, for society as a whole—would be substantially lessened, if not eliminated.

In a similar vein, sustainability needs to be applied to the production of public goods and services, such as in the design and placement of mass transit systems or highways, or of sewage treatment systems, where government policies can have the most direct impact—by setting environmental design standards in procurement contracts, for example. Minimizing the threats to worker health and safety in private- and public-sector production should be considered a concern of sustainability as well.

Revamping the Health-care System

Few would dispute that the health-care system in the United States is in a crisis. As medical costs escalate, more and more U.S. citizens lack access to adequate health-care insurance and medical services. How to revamp the health system is a monumental issue beyond the scope of this essay. It is encouraging, at least, that this problem has risen above the horizon of the average person's political concern, becoming an issue in the 1992 political campaigns and undoubtedly in future campaigns.

For many years, the United States has been conducting a medical industrial policy, which has created a medical-industrial-academic-government complex every bit as entrenched and in some ways more massive—medical care accounts for 12 percent of the GNP, twice the share of the military economy—than the military-industrial complex. This has garnered a powerful set of vested interests with a stake in maintaining the current system, including medical practitioners and their professional organizations (e.g., the American Medical Association), hospitals and clinics, suppliers of pharmaceutical and medical products, research centers at universities, hospitals, government, private firms, and last but not least, the insurance industry.

Certain paradigms of medical methods, procedures, technologies, and delivery have become entrenched, as well. In the United States, more than in other advanced nations, medical treatment has become reliant on increasingly expensive, baroque technologies—hardware and drugs—not unlike the growth of the modern exotic high-tech military arsenal. In what he aptly terms the "medical technology 'arms race,'" *New York Times* reporter Andrew Pollack reports that there is "a growing recognition that the uncontrolled use of high-technology medical equipment and procedures . . . helps drive the relentless increase in medical cost." Pollack observes that medical practitioners are rewarded more for using sophisticated treatments than for routine health care. Hence, there is a tendency to overuse advanced, expensive medical procedures. Bolstering this up is a "huge medical technology industry," which is "spewing out streams of innovations and marketing them heavily, with profit rather than social utility often its prime motivation."[62]

As with the environmental problem, the antidote is to put a much greater emphasis on prevention. A new health policy would tie public investments, health care, delivery programs, regulation, and scientific and technological development to new goals of preventative care, equal access to inexpensive high-quality medical care, and freedom from occupational and environmental threats to health and safety. Given that there are over 120 million working people in the United States, a preventative emphasis on reducing occupational health and safety hazards would receive a high priority, as would greatly expanding the availability of health insurance coverage through the workplace.

In addition to identifying new areas of national commitment, we need to identify the principal policy measures and instruments required for implementing this new agenda. These include new public investments, new initiatives in science and technology, and expanded supports for economic adjustment.

Public investments are needed in rebuilding the public infrastructure, environment protection, renewable energy sources, education, health care, mass transportation, affordable housing, and the like. It may seem counterintuitive to promote new government spending programs at a time that calls for serious budget restraint. The case for increasing public investment is being made, however, by a number of economists, on the basis that it will stimulate the productive base of our declining economy and put it back on track. Jeff Faux and Todd Schafer of the Economic Policy Institute, for example, note that "the United States could not have successfully developed a powerful private economy without large and sustained government outlays on transportation, education, and the generation of new technologies." The evidence indicates that government spending on public infrastructure, education, training, early childhood programs, and civilian research pays off in the growth of private investment, productivity, and profits. They point out that over the past years the United States has been investing less, while other advanced industrial nations have been investing more in these areas, "setting the stage for further declines in living standards and competitiveness." They calculate that the United States currently suffers an "investment deficit" of between \$60–125 billion each year.[63]

There are legitimate differences of view regarding the selection of specific types and amounts of investment; these would need to be hashed out in a national debate. Faux and Schafer present what they admit is a "narrow, conservative definition" of investment, limited to spending for human resources, non-defense physical capital (highways, bridges, pollution control, etc.), and non-defense R&D. Inclusive of these ends, the proposed economic development strategy suggests a slightly expanded range of investments. In any case, the goals, objectives, and criteria articulated in the discussion above, for the major areas of economic stability, the environment, and health, would set the principal parameters for guiding these investment choices.

Targeted science and technology initiatives are needed for building the civilian scientific and technological base for achieving the new goals. Public investments in areas of civilian need would create substantial demand forces for redirecting private-sector activity. Especially if coupled to demand-creating social programs, investments in civilian R&D are supply-side inducements that would also shift the patterns of U.S. technological development in directions compatible with producing socially needed goods and services. Although the proposed new science and technology agenda would probably overlap with the current national R&D agenda, it would also include many other R&D areas not currently funded or supported at lower levels.

In Dosi's terms, a R&D agenda emphasizing community stability, health, and the environment would promote new paradigms and trajectories of technical innovation and diffusion. It is likely that many of the so-called emerging or critical technologies such as those identified by the

Pentagon, the Commerce Department and the Office of Science and Technology Policy would also appear on the critical technologies list of the new economic development strategy. They cover a wide range, including advanced materials, microchip manufacturing, computer-aided manufacturing, high-performance computing, advanced propulsion, and biotechnology. At the same time, the demand-pulls of a human needs-centered investment program would tend to focus even these so-called generic technologies along different paths of development, and emphasize different kinds of cross-cutting synergies and clustering of innovations, than those driven by military and/or narrow high-tech commercial needs.[64]

The criteria for guiding the selection of critical technologies for national needs will be quite different from those of the military or high-tech industry. Rather than just economic efficiency (or cost), product performance, or marketability guiding technology choices, the new agenda suggests a larger set of social criteria and values, tied to concerns about the environment, energy efficiency, job security and skill enhancement, occupational and consumer health and safety, autonomy and participation, and the quality of public services. A machine-tool technology or agricultural process developed to optimize this set of criteria will differ from those designed according to military or narrow commercial objectives. New problems in scientific research would also be emphasized. In short, demand-driven criteria imply a new scientific and technological policy agenda for the United States.

The new agenda would require legislating new regulations and standards for production processes, products, and R&D protections concerning privacy, information access, and intellectual property rights; tax credits and incentives; among other measures. Most importantly, however, it would require a significant reordering of R&D spending priorities at all levels of government, and in the private sector. First, it would entail rethinking and redefining the missions of existing federal R&D agencies, such as the Department of Energy (DoE), NASA, the National Science Foundation, the National Institutes of Health, and even those of the DoD. This includes changing the mandates and priorities governing their in-house and extramural R&D programs. For example, if the DoE changes from its current primary emphasis on nuclear energy and weapons to promoting the development of alternative, renewable energy sources, the national laboratories under its direction—especially the weapons labs at Livermore, Sandia, and Los Alamos—would more easily be able to convert their research programs to the new agenda. Meanwhile, other agencies now at relatively low levels of R&D funding, such as the departments of Transportation, Commerce, Labor, and the Environmental Protection Agency, might find their R&D budgets beefed up. Proposals for creating new agencies, such as the National Institutes for the Environment promoted by ecologists and environments, or a civilian advanced-technology agency, also may have a better chance of success. Undoubtedly, the new agenda would result in a downplaying of DARPA's role in civilian technology. Although the agency would continue to emphasize dual-use technologies, it may no longer be the primary sponsor of research in these areas.

Many of our most important problems, however, are cross-disciplinary in nature and too complex to fall under the missions of a single agency. The OSTP's cross-agency Federal Coordinating Council on Science, Engineering, and Technology (FCCSET) has been surprisingly successful in pushing large-scale multi-agency, multi-disciplinary science and technology projects, most notably the High Performance Computing and Communications Program.[65] The new agenda, in particular, raises a number of significant cross-disciplinary problems in our society that would entail cooperation and coordination across agencies and institutions, involving federal, state, and local governments, business, labor, academia, and the public interest community in their solution. Suggested cross-cutting science and technology initiatives addressing areas that currently are not adequately supported by federal programs, but should be, are listed below. These can be thought of as new, grand challenges in science and technology—perhaps candidates for future FCCSET panels—similar in scope to our efforts to reach the moon, cure cancer, or produce a strategic defense system. Each would target for public investment a unique set of social, industrial, and R&D programs.

- *Sustainable industrial production*. Can we produce energy efficient, environmentally clean industrial technologies?
- *Human resource productiveness*. Can we design technologies that enhance job security and the quality of work life—health and safety, skill, participation, and autonomy in the workplace—while at the same time improve productivity and product quality?
- *Revitalizing the manufacturing base*. Can we introduce new flexible technologies, as well as incremental innovations and technical assistance, that, while satisfying the criteria of sustainability and human productiveness, both strengthen domestic high-tech manufacturing and revitalize traditional industries such as steel and textiles?

- *Transportation infrastructure.* Can we build, safe, efficient, environmentally benign large-scale transportation systems for both between and within major metropolitan areas?
- *Urban infrastructure development.* What technologies do we need to rebuild the transportation, communication, sewage, housing, and other public service systems of our metropolitan areas?
- *Sustainable agriculture.* Can we design energy-efficient, environmentally safe, sustainable agricultural technologies?

Economic adjustment and technical assistance policies are needed to aid communities, workers, and businesses affected by dislocation induced by military cutbacks, technological change, or international competition. An economic development strategy would emphasize substantially revamping, expanding, and improving the coordination of government economic adjustment programs, with greatly increased budgets for their implementation. It would also provide resources and technical assistance for helping workers, communities, and managements make effective plans to convert facilities and/or diversify local and regional economies. Legislation would be needed to institutionalize early-warning, rapid-response, labor-management cooperation and worker participation as key features of all economic assistance programs. In addition, there would need to be pressures and incentives for companies to work more supportively with worker/community initiated efforts to convert, diversify, buy out, provide adjustment assistance, and the like, when they decide to close a plant or make major layoffs. It needs to be stressed that such programs represent investments in the efficient reuse of economic resources as well as a means to reduce the costs to society of human hardship and not, as some would argue, drains on the economy.

Can We Get There From Here?

The downsizing and the restructuring of the military has given a new life to conversion and economic adjustment proposals. How the United States should shift its priorities and enormous capital, technical, and labor resources to meet the demands of the evolving new world economic and political order will dominate the nation's policy debate in the coming decade. There is therefore much opportunity for promoting a new economic development strategy, if the right critical mass of political, economic, and social interest groups in society can be brought together. There are a few necessary (but not sufficient) conditions for establishing this critical mass.

First, a strong argument needs to be made and presented to the public that this strategy would yield greater benefits to society and the economy than the current laissez-faire or dual-use economic policies; it would satisfy the needs and concerns of a broader cross-section of constituencies and interests in the nation. An underlying premise is that new public investments, coupled with targeted scientific and technological initiatives and economic assistance programs, would guide the private sector in shifting its resources into activities that result in significant economic and social payoffs.

Not only would it address pressing problems in the society and the environment—reducing so-called externality costs of environmental degradation, occupational and environmental illness and injuries, and unemployment—the proposed public investment strategy would directly stimulate both economic and technological progress and improve the economic performance of domestic industries. It would create and preserve jobs, strengthen the economies of communities and regions, and raise the standard of living, while meeting environmental, health, and quality-of-life needs. By linking economic development to national needs, powerful new focusing devices and inducements would be established in the national economy. These, in turn, would create effective markets and stimulate technical innovation, along trajectories that are mutually supporting and synergistic, in the production of goods and services that directly serve human needs. New "virtuous circles" would be created: as the private sector is induced to reorient its activities in response to the new government-provided market signals, it would increase its own investments in these same areas.

These initiatives and investments would consequently generate new classes of manufacturing technologies, capital goods, and consumer products; create new industries and types of high-skilled jobs; and stimulate new directions for scientific discoveries and new opportunities for technical innovation. Scientists, who are feeling the pinch of a zero-sum budget game and pork-barrel politics (which diverts funding towards large-scale science projects), would also gain, despite the goal-oriented nature of these programs. A national needs-driven strategy will actually diversify and expand their portfolios of funding sources, as new problems in basic science are defined within the science and technology initiatives. In addition, many of the so-called critical technologies for high-tech competitiveness will also be well supported. For example, new computing, advanced materials, and microelectronic technologies would find numerous applications in the science and technology initiatives listed above.[66]

A second condition for promoting the new strategy is to show how it would expand the democratic participation of broad sectors of society in economic, scientific, and technological policies and decisions in both the public and private sectors. This could take a number of forms, such as citizen involvement in R&D advisory boards, work-force participation in production management, state and local technical assistance programs, conversion/diversification planning boards, etc., all of which allow easier access to community and labor groups in vital decision processes. The participation of a broader range of interests in the society is a vital condition for crafting industrial policies that are both economically effective and socially equitable. Representation of labor unions, environmental organizations, or community groups in this process would lead to different criteria in the technology design and resource allocation processes than currently exists. A democratically determined, human-centered filter for focussing technical change would be created, stimulating new technology paradigms and trajectories, especially if the selection process is bolstered by new demand forces in socially desirable areas.

Third, active promotion by national, regional, and local grass-roots/public-interest constituencies would be essential for making the new economic strategy a serious political issue at the national level. As yet, the debate over industrial policy remains the province of a small political, economic, and technical elite, somewhat invisible to the general public. Only recently have there been signs of concern among public-interest, labor, and other grass-roots constituencies, particularly among those working on conversion, environmental, and work-place technology issues. This includes the emergence of community/labor/public-interest group-led initiatives to influence industrial, scientific, and technological policies, such as the Campaign for Responsible Technology, the 21st Century Project, the National Toxics Campaign, and the Federation for Industrial Renewal, and state and local conversion-diversification projects in Minnesota, Maine, Washington, and California, among others. Labor unions and technical professional societies have also begun to articulate their own concerns and agendas regarding these issues.[67]

The Campaign for Responsible Technology (CRT) is perhaps a leading representative of this genre. Comprised of community, environmental, and labor groups from around the nation concerned with environmental and occupational health issues in high-tech manufacturing, CRT has been able to get executives from the joint government/private-sector-funded Sematech consortium to meet with them about employment, community, and R&D issues. It has also been approaching congressional leaders to set up hearings that would explore broadening out Sematech's mandate to include broader social and environmental concerns.[68] Similarly, the 21st Century Project seeks to inject the objectives of the new economic development strategy into the political agendas of grass-roots constituencies, strengthening both their own efforts while giving teeth and direction to national policies.[69]

Conversion advocates have an especially large stake—and some have become directly involved, such as the National Commission on Economic Conversion and Disarmament—in seeing a strategy such as that described above implemented, as it would create the optimum conditions for an efficient conversion of the military's economic, scientific, and technological assets to civilian use, and efficient reemployment of displaced workers. National policies with new goals for guiding public investment and scientific and technological resources would create new markets for products, business opportunities, and provide new sources of capital, making both plant-site conversions and community diversification efforts more viable, and making adjustment for workers and communities easier.

The growth of grass-roots activism around issues of science and technology, economic conversion, and industrial development are encouraging indications that such concerns are finally beginning to be perceived as serious bread-and-butter problems that shouldn't be left in the hands of managerial elites and scientific or technical experts. Only time will tell if this new momentum will be able to grow into a force that can create the kinds of shifts needed at the level of national policy.

Notes

1. For a discussion and evaluation of this effort see Joel S. Yudken, "Conversion in the Aerospace Industry: The McDonnell-Douglas Project," in Suzanne Gordon and Dave McFadden, eds., *Economic Conversion, Revitalizing America's Economy* (Cambridge, Mass.: Ballinger Publishing, 1984), 130–143; and Catherine Hill, Sabina Deitrick, and Ann Markusen, "Converting the Military Industrial Economy," *Journal of Planning Education and Research* (1992).

2. For discussion of the "wall of separation," see Ann Markusen and Joel Yudken, *Dismantling the Cold War Economy* (New York: Basic Books, 1992), especially chapter 4.

3. Steven Greenhouse, "There's No Stopping Europe's Airbus Now," *New York Times,* 23 June, 1991, section 3: 1, 6.

4. For discussion of critical technologies, see *Report of the National Critical Technologies Panel* (Washington, D.C.: U.S. Government Printing Office, March 1991). Also, Council on Competitiveness, *Picking up the Pace: The Commercial Challenge of American Innovation* (Washington, D.C., 1988), and *Gaining New Ground, Technology Priorities for America's Future* (Washington, D.C., March 1991). In its reports the Council on Competitiveness, a private sector industry-labor coalition (not to be confused with the White House's Council on Competitiveness headed by Vice-President Dan Quayle), sounds the alarm over the decline in U.S. high-tech industrial competitiveness and argues for government policies to help bail out the economy.

5. Nathan Rosenberg, *Perspectives on Technology* (New York: Cambridge University Press, 1976), 123.

6. Kim Moody, "Industrial Policy," *Labor Notes,* July 27, 1983.

7. See Ann Markusen, "Defense Spending: A Successful Industrial Policy?" *International Journal of Urban and Regional Research* 10., no. 1 (1986): 105–22; and Markusen and Yudken, *Dismantling,* especially chapter 3.

8. Markusen and Yudken, *Dismantling,* 14.

9. Daniel S. Greenberg, *The Politics of Pure Science* (New York: New American Library, 1967), 8.

10. David C. Mowery and Nathan Rosenberg, *Technology and the Pursuit of Economic Growth* (New York: Cambridge University Press, 1991), 184.

11. Linda R. Cohen and Roger G. Noll, *The Technology Pork Barrel* (Washington, D.C.: The Brookings Institution, 1991), 1–2.

12. This point and the discussion below is elaborated in Markusen and Yudken, *Dismantling,* chapter 3.

13. Aerospace Industries Association of America," 1900 Year-End Review and Forecast—An Analysis," mimeographed (Washington D.C., December 12, 1990), table VI.

14. Markusen and Yudken, *Dismantling,* 35 and table 3.1.

15. Military industry R&D funding is highly concentrated among certain industries and firms, which in turn are much more R&D intensive than in the manufacturing sector as a whole. During the first Cold War buildup, by 1956, the federal government financed 87 percent of the aircraft and parts and 56 percent of the electrical equipment industries' R&D expenditures, while shares for scientific instruments and chemicals were 25 percent and 3 percent respectively. In the same year R&D spending accounted for almost 20 percent of the sales of the aircraft and parts industry, compared to only 3 percent for all U.S. industry; by 1960 this share rose to 30 percent. See Markusen and Yudken, *Dismantling,* especially chapters 3 and 5.

16. Ibid.

17. When Douglas was in serious trouble with its DC-8 and DC-9 in 1967 it got $75 million from the federal government. More recently, General Dynamics and others have benefited from similar government-supported recoveries. Markusen and Yudken, *Dismantling,* ch. 3.

18. Quoted in *The Washington Post,* 6 March 1970. Cited in Berkeley Rice, *The C-5A Scandal* (Boston: Houghton Mifflin Co., 1971), 183.

19. James R. Kurth, "Aerospace Production Lines and American Defense Spending," in Stephen Rosen, ed., *Testing the Theory of the Military-Industrial Complex* (Lexington, Mass.: D.C. Heath, 1973), 135–156;

20. James R. Kurth, "The Follow-On Imperative in American Weapons Procurement, 1960–1990," paper presented at the Conference on the Economics of Disarmament, Economists Against the Arms Race, University of Notre Dame (December 1, 1990).

21. Markusen and Yudken, *Dismantling,* 54. See also Daniel Todd and Jamie Simpson, *The World Aircraft Industry* (London: Croom Helm,

1986), 59, 187; Robert Reich, *Minding America's Business* (New York: Vintage, 1983), 236.

22. Quoted in Charles Lane et al., "Arms for Sale," *Newsweek,* 8 April 1991, 22–27.

23. Clyde Farnsworth, "White House Seeks to Revive Credits for Arms Exports," *New York Times,* 18 March 1991, D-6.

24. See Markusen and Yudken, *Dismantling,* chapter 6. The concept of a gunbelt was first developed and elaborated in in Ann Markusen, Peter Hall, Sabina Deitrick, and Scott Campbell, *The Rise of the Gunbelt* (New York: Oxford University Press, 1991).

25. See Markusen and Yudken, *Dismantling,* especially chapters 3–6.

26. For discussion on the steel industry see Ann Markusen, *Steel and Southeast Chicago: Reasons and Remedies for Industrial Renewal,* report to the Mayor's Task Force on Steel and Southeast Chicago, (Evanston: Center for Urban Affairs and Policy Research, Northwestern University, 1985) and "Planning for Communities in Decline: Lessons from Steel Communities," *Journal of Planning Education and Research* 7, no. 3 (1988): 173–184; Seymour Melman, *Profits without Production* (New York: Alfred Knopf, 1983), 188–199; Robert Reich, *Minding America's Business* (New York: Vintage, 1983), 155–168.

27. For discussion of this point see Jay Stowsky, "Beating Plowshares into Double-Edged Swords: The Impact of Pentagon Policies on the Commercialization of Advanced Technologies," (Berkeley, Calif.: Berkeley Roundtable on the International Economy [BRIE], April 1986); Leslie Bruechner and Michael Borrus, "Assessing the Commercial Impact of the VHSIC [Very High Speed Integrated Circuit] Program," BRIE working Paper (Berkeley, Calif.: BRIE, December 1984); Jacques S. Gansler, *Affording Defense* (Cambridge, Mass.: The MIT Press, 1989), 215–238 and endnotes.

28. For discussions about problems of the defense technology base, see U.S. Congress, Office of Technology Assessment, *The Defense Technology Base: Introduction and Overview—A Special Report,* OTA-ISC-374

(Washington, D.C.: U.S. Government Printing Office, March 1988), and Office of Technology Assessment, *Holding the Edge: Maintaining the Defense Technology Base,* OTA-ISC-420 (Washington, D.C.: U.S. Government Printing Office, April 1989).

29. See Lewis M. Branscomb, "The Case for a Dual-Use National Technology Policy," *The Aspen Quarterly* 2, no. 3 (Summer 1990): 33–52 and "Toward a U.S. Technology Policy," *Issues in Science and Technology* vol. VII, no. 4 (Summer 1991): 50–55.

30. Joel S. Yudken and Michael Black, "Targeting National Needs, A New Direction for Science and Technology Policy" 7, no. 2 *World Policy Journal* (Spring 1990): 263.

31. David P. Hamilton, "Technology Policy: Congress Takes the Reins," *Science* 250 (9 November 1990): 747.

32. See Eliot Marshall, "Beating Swords into . . . Chips?" (box in "U.S. Technology Strategy Emerges"), *Science* 252 (5 April 1991): 22; and William J. Broad, "Pentagon Wizards of the Technology Eye Wider Civilian Role," *New York Times,* 22 October 1991, C-1, C-11.

33. U.S. Department of Commerce, Technology Administration, *Emerging Technologies, A Survey of Technical and Economic Opportunities* (Washington, D.C., Spring 1990).

34. Branscomb, "Toward a U.S. Technology Policy," p. 51.

35. The recently passed bill includes appropriations of $281 million for manufacturing technology development and $60 million for a Critical Technologies Partnership under DARPA.

36. See, for example, Richard R. Nelson and Sidney G. Winter, *An Evolutionary Theory of Economic Change,* (Cambridge, Mass.: Belknap Press of Harvard University Press, 1982); Giovanni Dosi, *Technical Change and Industrial Transformation* (New York: St. Martin's Press, 1984; Mowery and Rosenberg, *Technology.*

37. Nelson and Winter present an evolutionary theory of how technical processes drive and are driven by economic change. They contend

that treating innovation "within an evolutionary model provides a far better basis for modeling economic growth fueled by technical advance than does the neoclassical model," even if the latter is modified to include variables representing technical change. In their theory, economic change is conceived as the product of a continual process of "search and selection": firms constantly "search" for new knowledge and technical know-how (including, but not limited to, R&D for making innovations in their production and organizational systems while market, institutional, and social processes "select" out, in an evolutionary sense, the most successful innovations and innovating firms. "Search and selection," they add, "are simultaneous, interacting aspects of the evolutionary process: the same prices that provide selection feedback also influence the directions of search. Through the joint action of search and selection, the firms evolve over time, with the condition of the industry in each period bearing the seeds of its conditions in the following periods." See Nelson and Winter, *An Evolutionary Theory,* 19. Rosenberg first presents his notion of a "focusing device" in Rosenberg, *Perspectives on Technology,* 123.

38. Dosi defines *technological paradigm* as a "model" or " 'pattern' of solution of *selected* technological problems, based on *selected* principles derived from natural sciences and on *selected* material technologies" and *technological trajectory* as "the pattern of 'normal' problem solving activity (i.e., 'progress') on the grounds of a technological paradigm." Giovanni Dosi, *Technical Change,* 15. He writes: "The identification of a technological paradigm relates to the generic task to which it is applied (e.g., amplifying and switching electrical signals), to the material technology it selects (e.g., semiconductors and more specifically silicon), to the physical/chemical properties it exploits (e.g., the 'transistor effect' and the 'field effect' of semiconductor materials), to the technological and economic dimensions and trade-offs it focuses upon (e.g., density of the circuits, speed, noise-immunity, dispersion, frequency range, unit costs, etc.).

39. Rosenberg, *Perspectives on Technology,* 110.

40. Giovanni Dosi, *Technical Change,* 18.

41. Robert W. Rycroft (Center for International Science and Technology Policy, George Washington Univ.) and Don E. Kash (Institute of Public Policy, George Mason Univ.), "Technology Policy Requires Pick-

ing Winners," paper presented at the Annual Meeting of the American Political Science Association (Washington, D.C., August 29–September 1, 1991), 16–17.

42. Ibid., 17.

43. See Markusen and Yudken, *Dismantling,* chapter 3, for further elaboration of the different economic costs and consequences of the U.S. military-led policy versus the costs and consequences of the civilian focusing policies of its economic competitors.

44. For a critical elaboration of the weaknesses of the high-tech "dual use" industrial policy, see Yudken and Black, "Targeting National Needs."

45. Quoted in David E. Rosenbaum, "Arms Makers and Military Face a Wrenching New Era," *New York Times,* 4 August 1991, 1, 34.

46. Mowery and Rosenberg, *Technology,* 144.

47. President's Economic Adjustment Committee, Office of Economic Adjustment, Office of the Assistant Secretary of Defense (Manpower, Reserve Affairs, and Logistics), *The Role of Defense in Santa Clara County's Economy* (Washington D.C.: The Pentagon, August 1980), 66.

49. For discussions of corporate conversion efforts, including Kaman, see Robert DeGrasse Jr., "Corporate Diversification and Conversion Experience," in John Lynch, ed., *Economic Adjustment and Conversion of Defense Industries* (Boulder, Colo.: Westview Press, 1987). For discussion on Frisby Airborne see M. Louise McNeilly, "Braving the New World," *Plowshare Press* 15, no. 1 (Winter 1990): 1, 6.

50. For overview of employee-community efforts see Hill, Deitrick, and Markusen, "Converting the Military Industrial Economy." See also Markusen and Yudken, *Dismantling,* chapter 8.

52. M. G. O'Neil, president of the General Tire and Rubber Company, in response to letter of inquiry by Senator Abraham Ribicoff (D-CT). Reported in U.S. Senate, Committee on Government Operations,

Subcommittee Executive Reorganization and Government Research, *National Economic Conversion Commission: Responses to Sucommittee Questionnaire,* (September 1970), 46. Quoted in President's Economic Adjustment Committee (PEAC) and the Office of Economic Adjustment (OEA), Office of the Assistant Secretary of Defense (Manpower, Installations and Logistics), "Previous Industrial Conversion Experience," (Prepared by Robert DeGrasse), *Economic Adjustment/Conversion, Appendices* (Washington, D.C.: The Pentagon, July 1985), M-4.

53. PEAC and OEA, *Adjustment/Conversion,* M-20.

54. For more detailed treatment of the problem of conversion of defense-dependent engineers and scientists see Joel Yudken and Ann Markusen, "The Labor Economics of Conversion for Military-Dependent Engineers and Scientists," in Martha Gilliland and Patricia MacCorquodale, eds., *Engineers and Economic Conversion* (Boulder, Colo.: Westview Press, in press). See also Markusen and Yudken, *Dismantling,* chapter 6, which also includes discussion of the conversion problem.

55. Committee on Government Operations, *National Economic Conversion,* 162. Cited in PEAC and OEA, *Adjustment/Conversion,* M-3.

56. Markusen and Yudken, *Dismantling,* 214.

57. See Markusen and Yudken, *Dismantling,* chapter 9.

58. Ibid.

59. See Joseph A. Schumpeter, *Capitalism, Socialism, and Democracy, 3rd Edition* (New York: Harpers, 1950) and *Business Cycles: A Theoretical, Historical, and Statistical Analysis of the Capitalist Process* (New York: McGraw Hill, 1939).

60. See Paul A. Krugman, "Myths and Realities of U.S. Competitiveness," *Science* 254 (November 8, 1991): 811–815.

61. Ken Geiser, "The Greening of America, Making the Transition to a Sustainable Economy," *Technology Review* 94, no. 6 (August/September 1991): 64–72.

62. Andrew Pollack, "Medical Technology 'Arms Race' Adds Billions to the Nation's Bills," *New York Times,* 29 April 1991.

63. Jeff Faux and Todd Schafer, "Increasing Public Investment, New Budget Priorities for Economic Growth in the Post-Cold War World," briefing paper for the Conference on Investing in America's Future, Washington, D.C., 21 Oct. 1991 (Washington, D.C.: Economic Policy Institute, October 1990). See also Jeff Faux, "Back to the Peace Dividend," *The New York Times,* 13 Sept. 1991, op-ed; Robert Kuttner, "Savings Alone Won't Jump-Start the Economy," *Business Week,* 21 Oct. 1991, 18; Robert Heilbroner, "Lifting the Silent Depression," *The New York Review of Books,* 24 Oct. 1991.

64. See *Report of the National Critical Technologies Panel,* and Council on Competitiveness, *Gaining New Ground.* The Council on Competitiveness report notes the substantial overlap between the U.S. government lists and those put out by Japan's MITI and the European Community. But, there are also several differences, reflecting the different goals and missions of the respective agencies or institutions that generated the lists. It is interesting that energy and environmental technologies are listed by the OSTP, the Europeans, and Japanese, but are not included in the DoD and Commerce lists. The OSTP is the only one that mentions surface transportation, however. The Japanese lists such items as human related technology and disaster prevention technology, which do not appear elsewhere. See pp. 65–68.

65. FCCSET panels have proven uniquely successful in guiding science and technology initiatives through the federal budget process. Aside from the High Performance Computing and Communications Program, FCCSET initiatives slated for large increases in the FY 1992 budget include the U.S. Global Change Research Program and a science and math education program. OSTP director Bromley plans to establish other FCCSET committees over the next couple of years. Joseph Palca, "It Ain't Broke, But Why Not FCCSET?" *Science* 251 (15 Feb. 1991): 736–737. See also "Science Initiatives in the 1992 Budget," *Science* 251 (25 Jan. 1991): 376–377.

66. See Yudken and Black, "Targeting National Needs," for elaboration of these points.

67. Labor unions such as the International Association of Machinists (IAM), United Autoworkers, and Communication Workers of America have long been concerned with technology and work problems. In the 1980s the IAM put forth their famous New Technology Bill of Rights, and tried (unsuccessfully) to get legislation passed in support of its provisions. They currently run a large educational center on the outskirts of Washington, D.C., to provide their members with information on technology and collective bargaining issues. Professional societies have only recently been engaged in trying to promote new research priorities, although groups like the Computer Professionals of Social Responsibility, and unorganized groups in the physics and mathematics disciplines have been active through the 1980s in trying to stop DoD's Strategic Defense Initiative and, more generally, have argued for less military dependency in their respective fields. In 1990 a group of representatives of major professional societies, such as the Association for Computing Machinery (ACM), American Physical Society, and Institute for Electrical and Electronic Engineers among several others in the physical, natural, and social sciences and engineering, got together in an attempt to create a new Coalition for Science & Technology in a New Era. The ACM itself put out a document in 1991 calling for new priorities based on national needs: see Barbara Simons, *On Building a Research Agenda for Computer Science*, IBM research report (RJ 8201 [75160] Computer Science) (Yorktown Heights, NY: IBM Research Division, 28 June 1991).

68. See CRT position papers: Lenny Siegel, Ted Smith, and Rand Wilson, "Sematech, Toxics, and U.S. Industrial Policy: Why We Are Concerned," (1990); and Rand Wilson, "From Day Care to DARPA: Bargaining for a New Industrial Policy," (1991), Campaign for Responsible Technology, 408 Highland Avenue, Somerville, MA 02144. See also Kirk Ladendorf, "Sematech pressed on environmental safety," *Austin American-Statesman,* 2 June 1990, C1–2.

69. See Michael Alexander, "Advocacy group pushes for shift in R&D funding," *Computerworld,* 11 November 1991. In the fall of 1991 the 21st Century Project received its first major grant of $100,000 from the Rockefeller Foundation.

3

Environmental Dimensions of Disarmament and Conversion

Michael Renner

Introduction: Toward a Peaceful and Sustainable Economy

The 1990s mark the beginnings of an era in which fundamental change occurs in two domains critical to the future of human existence. The first is the realm of national and international security. National security has been and still is invoked to justify the relentless pursuit of military prowess—the maintenance of large armed forces, the deployment of ever-deadlier weapons systems, and the frequent intervention in the affairs of weaker nations. But the end of the Cold War provides a unique opportunity to dismantle and convert to peaceful uses a large portion of national war-making capacities and to redirect society's priorities. The second area is the fate of the biosphere. The assault on the environment has reached crisis proportions, threatening to exhaust the earth's regenerative capacity. Humanity now stands at the threshold to irreversible degradation of many of the natural systems that underpin all of human life. At the same time, though, environmental awareness is soaring in many countries and the concept of ecological sustainability is gaining ground as an alternative approach to economic development, suggesting that the current destructive path may yet be abandoned.[1]

The themes of disarmament/conversion and environment/sustainable development may seem separate and unrelated. Yet they interact in many ways, and solving one set of problems while disregarding the other will prove difficult. Reversing ecological destruction cannot succeed without halting the military's onslaught against the environment. Conversely, in this age of profound environmental crisis, military conversion needs to aim beyond a search for civilian labels and to incorporate ecological guidelines into alternative-use proposals. Put simply, producing more cars instead of tanks, for example, will not be part of the solution, but part of the problem.

The costs of warfare and permanent war preparation—human, economic, and ecological—are often justified by vague references to national security requirements. Yet, in the emerging post-Cold War era, the very definition of what constitutes true security needs reassessing. Arguably, social, economic, and environmental issues are at least as important to the security—that is, the well-being—of nations and their citizens as safety from foreign attack, on which traditional national security concerns are focused.

This chapter begins by illustrating the ways in which environmental perils threaten national and global security. It then argues that military power is not only inadequate in this broader security perspective, but in addition the military economy preempts monetary and scientific resources needed to deal with the environmental crisis. Moreover, as the third and fourth sections document, the military sector—that is, the armed forces and the military industry—contributes significantly to environmental problems both during war and in peacetime. The environmental legacy of the war system joins a long list of solid reasons for moving toward serious disarmament. Unless humanity can find less violent ways of settling disputes, the fundamental incompatibility between the military and the environment will continue to confront us. But environmental considerations also play a role once the disarmament process gets under way. The final section discusses three major dimensions: first, the disposal of weapons and military equipment; second, the cleanup of military bases and rehabilitation of land holdings before they can be turned over to civilian use; and third, the conversion of arms-production facilities.

Redefining National Security

Over the course of history, and particularly during the half century of the Cold War, national security has come to be defined almost exclusively in military terms: the ability to deter or repel outside aggression. This growing reliance on force is counterproductive in at least three ways, however. First, with the spreading availability of weapons of mass destruction, the capability to truly defend a country's territory and population has been lost—and instead replaced by the capacity to destroy massively. Competitive national security policies have yielded international insecurity. Second, the unbridled pursuit of military power has meant a resource drain undermining economic vitality by retarding civilian R&D, slowing productivity growth, and contributing to indebtedness. And third, of central importance here, governments preoccupied with security threats of military origin have ignored the perils of environmental degradation.[2]

Environmental factors are often dismissed as irrelevant or unrelated to security issues. Yet military and environmental security share a fundamental objective: to permit people to go about their lives without undue harm. Although governments have appropriated the term, the dictionary definition of security contains not a hint of an exclusive military connotation: *Webster's Ninth New Collegiate Dictionary* defines security as freedom from danger, from fear or anxiety, from want or deprivation. The potential for economic upheaval and dislocation inherent in the environmental crisis poses threats to the well-being and safety of nations and individuals on a par with many wars.

National security is a meaningless concept if it does not encompass the preservation of livable conditions on earth. A reasonable definition of security needs to encompass breathable air and potable water, safety from toxic and radioactive hazards, an intact atmospheric ozone layer, a stable climatic system, and protective against the loss of the topsoil that assures us of our daily bread. The well-being of nations and their individual citizens depends as much on economic vitality, social justice, and ecological stability as it does on safety from foreign attack. Pursuing military security at the cost of these other factors is akin to dismantling a house to salvage materials to erect a fence around it.

Because environmental pollution and degradation respect no human-drawn borders, they jeopardize not only the security of the country in which they originate, but also that of others, near and far. Border-transcending environmental degradation most immediately affects neighboring countries. Disputes over water use and quality, for example, simmer in virtually all parts of the world. These involve water diversion, industrial and agrochemical pollution, salinization of streams through heavy irrigation, siltation of rivers, and floods aggravated by deforestation and soil erosion. An estimated 40 percent of the world's population depends for drinking water, irrigation, or hydropower on the 214 major river systems shared by two or more countries. In the Middle East, a water-scarce region, water has been a factor in previous wars and could play a prominent role in future conflicts.[3]

Deforestation seems an unlikely source of tension between nations. Yet by aggravating soil erosion and silt accumulation in riverbeds, it can lead to devastating floods. Denuded watersheds in the Ethiopian highlands have exacerbated floods in neighboring Sudan, devastating its capital, Khartoum, in 1988. The frequency and magnitude of flooding in Bangladesh has markedly increased, partly due to deforestation in the Himalayas since mid-century.[4]

The impact of pollution and ecological degradation originating in one country is not only felt in adjacent countries, as transboundary air pollution strikingly illustrates. Insecticides from Asia and southern Europe, for instance, are found in Arctic and Antarctic waters. All European countries are involved in an intensive exchange of air pollutants such as sulfur dioxide, a major component of acid rain. Norway and Sweden are large net importers of sulfur dioxide, originating primarily in Britain. Norway's foreign minister has said he considers the British reluctance to address the issue a problem as serious for mutual relations as trade and defense.[5]

Spurred by a continuous stream of new scientific evidence, attention is shifting to those aspects of environmental degradation that have an all-encompassing, global effect: the depletion of the ozone layer and global warming pose problems from which no nation can insulate itself. As monitoring and scientific understanding grows, it is becoming clear that the thinning of the stratospheric ozone layer, which protects life on earth from harmful ultraviolet radiation, is accelerating. Initially, it was believed that the depletion was taking place only over the poles and only in winter, but it is now significant in both the northern and southern hemispheres, and has now also been detected in summer, when ultraviolet rays pose the most serious hazard. Failure to rapidly phase out chlorofluorocarbons (CFCs) and other ozone-devouring chemicals—at a faster pace than current international agreements stipulate—presents a grave danger to human health, to agricultural productivity, and to marine fisheries. Already, significant crop damage and large numbers of skin cancers are inevitable, given the amounts of CFCs previously released into the atmosphere.[6]

The security of nations is similarly compromised by the greenhouse effect—the specter of global climate change brought on by the accumulation of carbon dioxide, methane, nitrous oxide, and other heat-trapping gases in the atmosphere. The prospect of an accelerated warming of the earth in coming decades puts the conditions essential to the stability of the biosphere in jeopardy. Shifting precipitation patterns and vegetation zones and rising sea levels caused by global warming threaten to disrupt crop harvests, inundate heavily populated low-lying coastal areas like the Bengal and Nile deltas, upset human settlement patterns, and undermine biological diversity.[7]

Third World nations face a particular predicament. Except for China (which burns large amounts of coal) and Brazil (where the decimation of the Amazon rain forest causes large-scale carbon release), global warming and ozone depletion are caused primarily by industrial countries: they account for 69 percent of CO_2 emissions and 84 percent of CFC production. Thus, while only a handful of countries enjoy most of the benefits associated with the use of fossil fuels and CFCs, all of humanity will suffer from the ecological repercussions.[8]

The Inadequacy of Military Power

If the above observations are accepted, it follows that the means of dealing with security threats and solving conflicts need to undergo scrutiny. The key traditional instrument for maintaining national security—military power—is wholly inadequate to provide security as understood in this broader perspective. (This does not mean that military security and armed conflict are no longer of importance; the recent Gulf War and the civil war in Yugoslavia serve as unpleasant reminders that the world community urgently needs to develop effective methods of peaceful conflict resolution and prevention.)

With regard to military security threats, the source of the peril is an easily identifiable foreign power. With regard to environmental hazards—the existence of transboundary pollution notwithstanding—the problem frequently is of domestic origin: the enemy is us. Although some countries generate a much greater volume of wastes and pollution than others, the unsustainable system of producing, consuming, and disposing of goods that characterizes virtually all economies today means that environmental degradation is a ubiquitous problem.

Obviously, military means cannot reverse resource depletion or restore lost ecological balance. Tanks, planes, and warships might be able to fend off a military attack, but no remedy exists to repel air- or water-borne pollutants. Former Soviet Foreign Minister Eduard Shevardnaze recognized this when he said that "the biosphere recognizes no division into blocs, alliances, or systems. All share the same climatic system and no one is in a position to build his own isolated and independent line of environmental defense."[9]

Environmental degradation is a problem very distinct from traditional conflicts. In the case of disputes over access, control, and allocation of natural resources among competing countries, it is possible to have a zero-sum game—that is, a winner and a loser. Environmental quality, however, is an indivisible goal. A zero-sum game is transformed into a no-win situation. Environmental security offers a more fruitful basis for cooperation and security among nations than military security because it is both a positive and inclusive concept. Whereas military security rests on the threat of annihilation, environmental security seeks to protect or to restore. While military security rests firmly on the competitive strength of individual countries (or coalitions of countries) at the direct expense of others, environmental security cannot be achieved unilaterally, but requires cooperative relationships among nations.

Security can no longer be achieved by exclusively national means; national security needs to be transformed into global security. Environmental reasons underscore the fact that nations are no longer the sole masters of their destinies. We have become accustomed to interdependence in economic affairs such as trade and investment, and we reluctantly acknowledge an uneasy mutual dependence for survival in the nuclear age. Interdependence in economic, military, and environmental affairs has already begun to erode traditional notions of security and even national sovereignty, but the structures of the nation-state system—especially the war-making capacities remain firmly in place. Because interdependence has come about by default rather than by design, it does not automatically generate the political will needed to adapt human institutions and thinking to new circumstances and requirements.

Military means not only are impotent in the face of environmental devastation, they also detract from environmental security in a variety of ways. The military consumes large quantities of resources and restricts society's ability to address environmental (as well as social and economic) problems, and it directly contributes to environmental problems both in times of peace and war.

To begin, the military sector preempts a sizable portion of the financial resources and scientific and technological capacities needed to stem environmental degradation and to assist in creating a sustainable economy. According to an estimate by Lester Brown and Edward Wolf of the Worldwatch Institute, the global community would need to expend a cumulative sum of about $774 billion during the final decade of this century to reverse adverse trends in four priority areas: protecting topsoil on croplands from further erosion, reforesting the earth, raising energy efficiency, and developing renewable sources of energy. While likely to be a conservative estimate and excluding other important areas, this sum is less than what the world currently spends for military purposes in one year.[10]

The resources poured into the military economy could go a long way toward meeting the environmental challenge (see the examples listed in table 1). For example, the United States spends roughly $300 billion for military purposes, compared with about $115 billion (by government and industry) on pollution control. Similarly, in Western Europe military spending stands at roughly $150 billion, while pollution control outlays are estimated at anywhere from $50 billion to $100 billion.[11]

Perhaps an even more telling indicator of current priorities is the money devoted to research and development. At an estimated $100 billion annually, world military R&D exceeds the combined governmental research outlays on developing new energy technologies, improving human health, raising agricultural productivity, and controlling pollution. Worldwide, some 25 percent of all R&D funds and of all scientists and engineers are devoted to military ends and thus unavailable to explore and develop ways to advance more environmentally benign production technologies. The share of governmental R&D outlays allocated to the military was as high as 70–75 percent in the United States and the Soviet Union in the late 1980s, but lower in other countries (50 percent in Britain and 30 percent in France, but 12 percent in the former West Germany and 3 percent in Japan).[12]

Warfare and the Environment: The Gulf War

From the Punic Wars in the third century B.C. on, armies have poisoned wells, salted soils, and destroyed crops to foil the enemy. However, over time the environmental impact of warfare has grown as sophisticated technology has boosted the firepower, range, and speed of weapons.[13] In addition, modern industries present many high-profile targets whose destruction can wreak environmental devastation on a vast scale. Modern warfare entails large-scale environmental devastation, as conflicts in Vietnam, Afghanistan, Central America, and the Persian Gulf amply demonstrate. Often, this is simply an inevitable consequence of the fighting, but

Table 1. Trade-offs between Military and Environmental Priorities

Military Priority	Cost	Environmental Priority
Trident II submarine F-16 jet fighter programs	$100,000,000,000	Estimated cleanup cost for the 3,000 worst hazardous waste dumps in the United States
Stealth bomber program	$ 65,000,000,000	Two-thirds of est. costs to meet U.S. clean water goals by year 2000
4 days of global military spending	$ 8,000,000,000	Action Plan over 5 years to save the world's tropical forests
Development cost for Midgetman ICBM	$ 6,000,000,000	Annual cost to cut sulfur dioxide emissions by 8–12 million tons/year in the U.S. to combat acid rain
2 days of global military spending	$ 4,800,000,000	Annual cost of proposed 20-year U.N. Action Plan to halt Third World desertification
6 months of U.S. outlays for nuclear warheads, FY 1986	$ 4,000,000,000	U.S. government outlays for energy efficiency, FY 1980–87
10 days of European Community military spending	$ 2,000,000,000	Annual cost to clean up hazardous waste sites in 10 European Community countries by the year 2000
3 B-1B bombers	$ 680,000,000	U.S. government spending on renewable energy, FY 1983–85
2 months of Ethiopian military spending	$ 50,000,000	Annual cost of proposed U.N. Anti-Desertification Plan for Ethiopia

Source: Michael Renner, *National Security: The Economic and Environmental Dimensions,* Worldwatch Paper 89 (Washington, D.C.: Worldwatch Institute, May 1989), table 8.

at least in some cases environmental modification techniques have consciously been employed as a weapon.[14]

The recent Gulf War provides an unfortunate illustration that warfare and environmental integrity are incompatible. It ranks among the most ecologically destructive conflicts ever. While the fighting was brought to a swift conclusion, the ferocious onslaught against the environment continues. Before retreating from Kuwait, Iraqi troops set fire to hundreds of oil wells that severely polluted the atmosphere and imperiled human health and harvests in the region; wellheads that failed to ignite spilled huge amounts of oil onto the ground, which threatens to taint underground aquifers; oil deliberately released into the Gulf waters is poisoning marine life; attacks on refineries, petrochemical plants, and chemical and nuclear facilities have likely released substantial quantities of toxic materials; and the massive movement of troops and their heavy equipment has imperiled an already fragile desert ecology.

Towering Inferno

It appears that 650 oil wells were set on fire (with an additional 100 damaged but unignited), and that as many as 6 million barrels of oil may have initially gone up in flames every day—almost four times Kuwait's production prior to the Iraqi invasion, or 9 percent of the world's petroleum consumption. After an agonizingly slow start, the firefighting effort gathered momentum, as the number of teams battling the inferno rose from five to twenty-seven and the ranks of those involved in the effort swelled to almost 10,000 workers. The last fire was extinguished on November 6, 1991.[15]

Richard Golob, editor of *Oil Pollution Bulletin* in Cambridge, Massachusetts, estimates that at least 1 billion barrels of oil have been released. Kuwait's oil minister, Hamoud al-Ruqba, mentioned a figure of 600 million barrels in November 1991, yet also estimated that Kuwait had lost 3 percent of its total oil reserves from fires and gushing oil wells—which would put the total loss at roughly 2.7 billion barrels (not including possible losses from structural damage to oil wells). Large amounts of oil gushed from damaged but unignited wellheads—at least 30 million and perhaps as much as 70 million barrels of oil are still covering the surface of the Kuwaiti desert. Forming an estimated 200 lakes (some of them more than a mile wide and several feet deep), the oil is gradually seeping into the ground, threatening to poison underground water supplies.[16]

The clouds of oil smoke lingering over the Gulf region for eight months likely contained large amounts of soot, sulfur dioxide, and nitrogen oxides (the major components of acid rain), and a large variety of toxic and potentially carcinogenic chemicals and heavy metals. We may never know exactly what substances were present because governmental assessment efforts were woefully inadequate. The National Toxics Campaign (NTC), a U.S. grass-roots group, found a number of toxic hydrocarbon compounds in the smoke in concentrations that exceeded U.S. health standards. For example, the NTC found high levels of 1,4-dichlorobenzene, which can harm the liver, kidneys, and respiratory system; and diethyl phthalate and dimethyl phthalate, both of which attack the respiratory system. The U.S. Environmental Protection Agency estimated that in March 1991 roughly ten times as much air pollution was being emitted in Kuwait as by all U.S. industrial and power-generating plants combined. Flying through the smoke clouds over Kuwait, scientists with the British Meteorological Office found that the concentration of soot, sulfur dioxide, and nitrogen oxides at an altitude of 6,000 feet was about 30, 20, and 10 times, respectively, the levels in a typical city plagued by air pollution.[17]

While the fires were burning the number of Kuwaitis suffering from respiratory problems was reported to be up sharply. Although considerable uncertainty persists concerning the long-term toll on human health, many air pollutants are thought to cause or aggravate a wide range of conditions, including blood disorders, respiratory problems such as asthma and bronchitis, coronary ailments, cancer, and possibly genetic damage. In independent assessments, George Thurston of New York University and Haluk Ozkaynak of Harvard University's Risk Assessment Group both predicted as many as 1,000 additional deaths in Kuwait—a 10 percent increase—over the course of one year.[18]

In parts of the the Gulf region, the smoke plume significantly diminished solar radiation, thereby lowering daytime temperatures and reducing the amount of rainfall. In April, daytime temperatures in part of Kuwait were as much as 27 degrees Fahrenheit below normal. Bahrain experienced its coolest May temperatures in thirty-five years. Reduced photosynthesis combined with the deposition of soot and other toxic materials imperils crops. In fact, reports from parts of Iran and Pakistan indicate that considerable crop damage has occurred. Saudi crop production has fallen by an average of 40 percent, according to the *Washington Post*.[19]

The Geography of Pollution

A huge area—from the waters of the Nile to the snows of the Himalayas, from the Black Sea to the Indian Ocean—was susceptible to acid rain and soot fallout ("black rain") from the Kuwaiti oil fires, according to the Max Planck Institute for Meteorology in Hamburg, Germany. Acid deposition is known to destroy forests and reduce crop yields. It can also activate several dangerous metals normally found in soil—including aluminum, cadmium, and mercury—making them more soluble and therefore more of a threat to water supplies and edible fish. The World Meterological Organization reported in July 1991 that the environmental effects of the Kuwaiti oil fires have been felt as far away as Chad and the South Pacific. Kuwaiti soot has also been detected in Japan, Hawaii, and parts of the continental United States.[20]

Whether the atmospheric effects could be of a global nature was a hotly contested issue among scientists even before the war started. While soot from Kuwait has evidently traveled around much of the globe, it appears that the quantity that was lofted into the upper atmosphere (at 35,000 feet or more, where it can remain for months or even years) is too small to set off any significant changes in global climate patterns. It turned out that, contrary to expectation, the soot particles easily bonded with water and most of them were therefore washed out of the sky. Still, this unhappy episode had all the trappings of a huge, uncontrollable game of roulette.[21]

Oil on the Water

The oil spilled into the Gulf waters is posing a severe test for marine ecosystems. Now estimated at some 6–8 million barrels by the Saudi government, the spill is by far the largest in history—twenty-five to thirty times the size of the 1989 Exxon Valdez accident in Alaska.[22]

Following "routine" spills (an average of 2 million barrels is lost every year during peacetime) and additional ones during the eight-year Iran-Iraq war, the Persian Gulf was already a highly stressed environment, in poor condition to withstand additional ecological assaults. A relatively shallow sea, it is essentially a closed ecosystem with only a narrow outlet to the Arabian Sea through the Strait of Hormuz. Because Kuwaiti oil is of a light weight grade, up to 40 percent of it may have evaporated. The warm waters of the Gulf allow the remaining oil to decompose fairly rapidly, but significant amounts foul shorelines or poison the sea bottom. The Gulf waters are calm, with little wave action to break down the oil slick.[23]

From the beginning, the focus of the Saudi government's containment and cleanup effort was on protecting the country's desalination plants. Natural habitats were left to fend for themselves, and roughly 350 miles of Saudi coastline—from the Kuwaiti border to Abu Ali island—are now blanketed with oil. By September 1991, about 1.5 million barrels of oil had been recovered from the sea. Yet the oil has simply been dumped in pits dug in the desert; if it is left there—one option being discussed—it will gradually seep into the soil and may contaminate the groundwater.[24]

Considerable harm to Gulf fish and other wildlife—including porpoises, turtles, and seabirds—is inevitable since many nesting and spawning grounds—mud flats, sea grasses, salt marshes, and coral reefs—have been soaked in oil. Up to 80 percent of Saudi Arabia's coastal mangrove swamps are dead or dying, according to a recent *Wall Street Journal* report. An estimated 20,000 to 30,000 birds were killed. Some areas are so contaminated that they had to be declared off-limits to fishing, threatening the livelihoods of commercial and subsistence fishers. The Saudi shrimp industry, for example, has been severely affected and is considered unlikely to recover before the end of the decade. If large quantities of plankton have been killed or poisoned, the entire food chain in the Gulf may be threatened. "It will take at least two decades for the marine life in the Gulf to recover from this war," according to Khalil Thaqfi, a Saudi health official.[25]

Desert Wasteland

The presence, during the Kuwait-Iraq crisis, of more than 1 million soldiers with their immense arsenals has placed severe strains on the already fragile desert ecology of Kuwait, Saudi Arabia, and Iraq. Normally inhabited only by Bedouins, the desert of the Arabian peninsula cannot bear such a massive burden. Desert vegetation is sparse, but it helps to stabilize and protect the soil. Tanks and other vehicles disrupted and compacted the soil and destroyed plants whose root systems are often close to the surface. As a result, the ground in many areas has been rendered susceptible to accelerated erosion. Seeds that lie dormant for large parts of the year, but which spark to life during spring rains, were likely affected. The incidence of sandstorms may well be increased. If a significant portion of the desert vegetation is destroyed, dry spells might be lengthened and the region's ecological balance could be tipped into long-term decline. It may take decades or even centuries for the desert to recover from the massive prewar maneuvers and the tank battles, according to John Cloudsley-Thompson of the University of London.[26]

Another immediate and long-term peril stems from unexploded bombs and mines littering large parts of Iraq and Kuwait. Gar Smith reports that as much as 20 percent of the 1 million land mines laid by Iraq may remain undetected after cleanup efforts. Of roughly 140,000 tons of explosives dropped by the allies on Iraq and Kuwait, perhaps 10 percent failed to explode and must be cleared. (British demolition specialists estimate that at least one quarter of the unexploded ordnance they have been disarming came from U.S. warplanes.) Again, many bombs will likely remain undetected, and disarming those found—particularly the "smart bombs"—is extremely difficult. Since the end of the war, 200 people in Kuwait alone have been killed by land mines and more than 1,000 wounded.[27]

Kuwait is no longer an occupied country, but it has been transformed into a disaster zone. With such results, it is difficult to distinguish between victor and vanquished. Indeed, the war's ecological impact extends far beyond the battlefield, blurring the distinction between the combatants and noncombatants, and affecting countries that were not party to the conflict and had no say over its course.

The Military's Peacetime Assault on the Environment

Whether advertently or inadvertently, warfare entails environmental devastation. yet the military's war against nature begins before the first shot is fired and continues after a cease-fire. Even in peacetime—preparing for war—the military contributes to resource depletion and environmental degradation, in some instances heavily. The production, testing, and maintenance of conventional, chemical, biological, and nuclear arms consumes substantial amounts of energy, generates enormous quantities of toxic and radioactive substances, and contaminates the earth's soil, air, and water. Keeping troops in a state of readiness imposes a heavy toll on large tracts of often-fragile land.

Land Use

Modern armed forces require large expanses of land. A 1982 UN study noted that "military requirements for land have risen steadily over the course of this century owing to the increase in the size of standing armed forces and, more particularly, the rapid pace of technological advances in weaponry." The report predicted continued growth in the military demand for land.[28]

The best information on military land use exists for the United States. The Department of Defense directly holds 100,000 square kilometers, an area equivalent to the state of Virginia. In addition, the armed services lease a total of about 80,000 square kilometers from other federal agencies, and an unknown amount of land owned by the states is devoted to military purposes. The U.S. Department of Energy's nuclear weapons complex, meanwhile, spreads over 10,000 square kilometers. Altogether, at least 200,000 square kilometers—2 percent of total U.S. territory—is devoted to military purposes.[29]

In what used to be the Soviet Union, the Defense Ministry controlled about 420,000 square kilometers, roughly 2 percent of total Soviet territory. In the republic of Kazakhstan, more land is devoted to military purposes than is used to grow wheat.[30]

Direct military land use in Western Europe is estimated at 1–3 percent of the total land mass. Yet indirect or nonexclusive use tends to be much higher. In the Netherlands, for instance, direct use stands at 1.15 percent of the country's territory, but indirect uses of both land and water surface areas (and the airspace above) are believed to add another 10.5 percent. At least one-third of the ecologically unique but fragile Waddensea and half the Dutch sector of the North Sea are used militarily. In Britain, the total land area controlled, leased, or held on license by the armed forces came to about 4,500 square kilometers in 1989. In the former West Germany, the national armed forces had exclusive access to about 2 percent of the total territory, or almost three times the combined area of all nature preserves. Including indirect land use, the military's control came to 5.6 percent (U.S. Army forces stationed in West Germany occupied 1,000 square kilometers, or 0.4 percent of the territory). The Soviet armed forces stationed in what used to be East Germany controlled an estimated 2.5–4 percent of the land, while installations of the East German army covered another 1.7 percent. Soviet troops in Poland occupied some 1,730 square kilometers, or 0.5 percent of all the land.[31]

Global estimates of direct military land use outside of wartime are sketchy at best. It is believed to be around 1 percent of the earth's total land area (approximately 1.5 million square kilometers). This may sound small, but it represents an area roughly the size of Indonesia. It is unclear whether the estimate includes the former Soviet Union (where an area the size of Sweden was under direct control of the Defense Ministry). To arrive at a truly comprehensive measure, however, the space occupied by arms-producing enterprises would need to be added to the land controlled by the armed forces themselves—information that is unavailable.[32]

In a world dramatically short of productive land, any unproductive and destructive use of territory seems a misplaced priority. The military appetite for land increasingly collides with other needs, such as agriculture, habitat protection, recreation, and housing. Beyond the land formally under the military's domain lie far larger areas that are used to varying degrees by the armed forces. While these may not be off-limits to civilians, they are often damaged or rendered dangerous or unusable even by occasional military use. Land used for war games is prone to suffer severe degradation. Maneuvers demolish the natural vegetation, disturb

Table 2. The Military's Use of Petroleum Products: United States and the Soviet Union, 1987

	UNITED STATES		SOVIET UNION	
Petroleum Product	Military Use	Share of Total Domestic Use	Military Use	Share of Total Domestic Use
	(million tons)	(percent)	(million tons)	(percent)
Jet Fuel	18.6	26.9	11.8	33.9
Diesel Distillate	4.4	3.0	3.8	4.9
Residual Fuel Oil	0.5	0.9	n.a.	n.a.
Gasoline	0.3	0.1	1.4	1.7
Other[1]	0.7	0.4	0.3	0.4
Total, Military	28.1[2]	3.4	17.4[3]	3.9

Source: Author's calculations, based on Tom Cutler, "Myths of Military Oil Supply Vulnerability," *Armed Forces Journal International,* July 1989.

1. Includes lubricants, greases, refined products, and refinery fuel.
2. Includes 3.6 million tons purchased for stockpiling. At least one-third of the total is used on U.S. bases abroad.
3. Total does not add up due to rounding.

wildlife habitat, erode and compact soil, silt up streams, and cause flooding. In the former West Germany, maneuvers were held on as much as a quarter of the country's territory. Bombing ranges transform the land into a moonlike wasteland, pockmarked with craters. Shooting ranges for tanks and artillery contaminate soil and groundwater with lead and other toxic residues.[33]

Energy Consumption, Global Warming, and Ozone Depletion

Whether it is jets roaring through the skies, tanks rumbling across the land, or warships navigating the high seas, the armed forces use large amounts of energy, and thus contribute to air pollution and global warming. Unfortunately, however, few statistics are available. Petroleum products account for roughly three-quarters of all energy used by the armed forces worldwide, but by far the most important is jet fuel. Worldwide, nearly one-quarter of all jet fuel—some 42 million tons per year—is used for military purposes. The share rises to 27 percent in the United States, to 34 percent in the former Soviet Union, and to 50 percent in the former West Germany (see table 2).[34]

Again, data are most readily available for the United States. The U.S. Department of Defense consumes about 37 million tons of oil equivalent (mtoe) a year. This works out to 2–3 percent of total U.S. energy demand and 3–4 percent of oil demand, but would be somewhat higher if military-related activities of the Department of Energy and the National Aeronautics and Space Administration were included. The Pentagon, perhaps the single largest consumer worldwide, uses enough energy in twelve months to run the entire U.S. urban mass transit system for almost fourteen years.[35]

These figures would be considerably higher if energy used in manufacturing weapons were included. Up-to-date data in this regard, however, are virtually unavailable.[36] In 1971, producing arms in the United States used about 47 mtoe. An extrapolation for a more recent year—1989—can be made on the basis of 1971 and 1989 (inflation-adjusted) expenditures for U.S. domestic arms procurement and revenues from arms exports. Assuming that energy intensities have remained unchanged, this computation yields a figure of about 68 mtoe for 1989, almost twice the armed forces' direct use of energy. Assuming that energy efficiency in the arms industry improved on a par with civilian U.S. industry, the figure would be about 50 mtoe. Total U.S. military-related energy consumption would thus be at least as large as Australia's total consumption.[37]

Worldwide, energy use for weapons production may be assumed to be relatively lower because most countries do not have a significant arms industry. Still, the military sector's share of total oil and energy use may well be double the armed forces' direct share of 3–4 percent. If these assumptions are correct, the world uses about the same quantity of petroleum products for military purposes as Japan, the world's second largest economy, does for everything.[38]

There are virtually no data that would allow a detailed assessment of the military sector's contribution to air and water pollution. According to a 1983 estimate, emissions from the operations of the armed forces account for at least 6–10 percent of global air pollution. In the former West Germany, military jets emitted 58 percent of air pollutants generated by all air traffic over that country's territory.[39]

Little work has been done to date on the military's contribution to global warming. In 1988, the U.S. armed forces contributed some 46 million tons of carbon emissions, or roughly 3.5 percent of the U.S. total. If the U.S. share of global military spending—just under a third—is any indication, then the U.S. armed forces' carbon emissions would have to be tripled to arrive at a rough global estimate. The result of such a back-of-the-envelope calculation is about 150 million tons of carbon—nearly equal to the annual emissions of Britain. Again, if arms-producing industries were included, these numbers could well double.[40]

A similar dearth of information pervades the military use of ozone-depleting substances. The U.S. Department of Defense is a major user of Halon-1211 and CFC-113, accounting for 76 percent and just under 50 percent of total U.S. use of these two compounds, respectively—which together are responsible for 13 percent of all ozone-depleting gases. The military's share of other substances implicated in this global problem, however, is much smaller. In addition, the combustion of solid rocket fuel, used in strategic and tactical missiles and on the Space Shuttle (some missions of which are military), releases hydrogen chloride gas that, transformed into hydochloric acid, contributes to the depletion of the ozone layer—in a relatively limited way globally, but more significantly locally, in areas adjacent to launch sites.[41]

Military Toxics

In their incessant pursuit of prowess and preparedness, the armed forces are poisoning the land and people they are supposed to protect.[42] The production, maintenance, and storage of conventional, chemical, and nuclear weapons and other pieces of military equipment generate vast amounts of materials inimical to human health and environmental quality. These wastes include fuels, paints, solvents, heavy metals, pesticides, polychlorinated biphenyls (PCBs), cyanides, phenols, acids, alkalies, propellants, and explosives.[43]

Knowledge about the health effects of these substances remains limited, but it is suspected that human exposure through drinking, skin absorption, or inhalation may cause cancer, birth defects, and chromosome damage, or may seriously impair the function of a person's liver, kidneys, blood, and central nervous system. Having been dumping grounds for a lethal soup of hazardous materials for decades, military bases have become health time-bombs detonating in slow motion. Over time, the toxics migrate underground from their dump sites, tainting the soil and water of adjacent communities.[44]

The U.S. military is the largest generator of hazardous wastes in the country and quite likely the world. In recent years, the Pentagon generated between 400,000 and 500,000 tons of toxics annually, more than the top five U.S. chemical companies combined. Military purchases directly account for 13–16 percent of the final demand for chemicals in the United

States. And these figures do not even include the large amounts of toxics spewing from the Department of Energy's nuclear weapons complex.[45]

Assessing the extent of toxic contamination is akin to opening Pandora's box: the number of U.S. sites on which problems have been spotted mushroomed from 3,526 on 529 military bases in 1986 to 17,482 on 1,855 installations in 1990. In addition, more than 7,000 former military properties are being investigated. Some 97 bases are so badly polluted that they are already on the Superfund Priorities List, a number that could well double in coming years.[46]

Many sites owned or run by the Pentagon's contractors are similarly contaminated. According to a report by the National Toxics Campaign, the top ten U.S. weapons contractors are listed 133 times by the EPA as "potentially responsible parties" at the nation's 100 most serious Superfund sites. Boeing, maker of missiles and aircraft, has dumped some 24 million gallons of toxic waste in two landfills in the Seattle area over the past thirty years.[47]

The extent of pollution at the Department of Defense's 375 bases outside the United States remains shrouded in considerable secrecy, although some evidence has emerged that suggests there are substantial problems. Full and uncensored publication of 1986 and 1990 General Accounting Office (GAO) studies that identified significant contamination at U.S. bases in Italy, the United Kingdom, and West Germany was prevented by the Pentagon and the State Department. U.S. military installations abroad are exempt from the 1970 U.S. National Environmental Policy Act. Although U.S. forces on foreign soil should in theory comply with pertinent host-nation laws, in practice they have been exempt, because the host government and the local population have no effective means of enforcement. But host governments are beginning to demand compliance with their environmental rules. As the U.S. military prepares to withdraw from some of its European bases, the question of who will shoulder the cleanup costs looms large. The U.S. Army has spent some money on cleanup, but plans to turn over vacated facilities in western Germany without a major rehabilitation effort, even though there are at least 358 polluted sites.[48]

As Soviet forces withdraw from Eastern Europe, it is becoming clear that the bases they occupied are in desperate need of cleanup. In addition, fuel, wastes, and unexploded ammunition were dumped in many unmarked off-base locations. In Vysoke Myto in central Bohemia, for example, groundwater tests reveal toxics in concentrations 30–50 times the allowable levels. In Czechoslovakia, up to 8,000 square kilometers—

6 percent of the total territory—have been polluted or despoiled. In the former East Germany, some 700 locations are suspected to be contaminated, and at least 90 Soviet installations are severely polluted; up to 10 percent of the territory sustained some kind of damage due to military activities. At Lärz Air Base in Mecklenburg, for example, more than 50,000 tons of fuel leaked into the soil. An estimated 10 percent of East German territory has been despoiled by Soviet military operations. In Poland, the aquifer under Swinoujscie naval base near Szczecin has been polluted by fuel dumping; sewage from Chojno airfield flowed untreated into the Rurzyca river. The most severe cases of soil contamination in Hungary have been identified at air bases in Sarmellek, Tokol, and Kunmadaras, at a fuel depot at Petfurdo, and at the Huszar army post.[49]

Little is known about the toxics used in the arms industry and about workers' exposure to them. Military secrecy has hampered efforts to monitor and enforce safety at aerospace and other factories. Yet the manufacture of explosives, composite materials, and electronic components can endanger human health. The production of explosives and propulsion systems, for example, entails potential exposure to such hazardous emissions as chlorine gas, dibenzodioxins, and dibenzofurans. Phenol formaldehyde, methyl dianiline, and other chemicals used to bond composite materials (including carbon fiber and glass fiber) that make military aircraft lighter and stronger are thought to cause cancer when inhaled or absorbed through the skin; fiber fragments can damage the lungs and also cause cancer. In the manufacture of semiconductors, workers may be exposed to a multitude of substances that are suspected carcinogens, teratogens, or mutagens.[50]

Nuclear Wasteland

During the Cold War, staying ahead in the feverish nuclear arms race between the United States and the Soviet Union took precedence over the health and safety of those involved in producing the weapons. For decades, officials in the two countries knowingly subjected their unsuspecting citizens to the dangers of radioactivity in the name of national security. While the worst excesses belong to the past, the problems of nuclear waste will haunt future generations long after the last warhead is dismantled: plutonium, for example, has a half-life of 24,000 years.[51]

Since the forties, the United States alone produced some 60,000 atomic warheads. Either stored or assembled in warheads are 90–100 tons of weapons-grade plutonium and 500 tons of highly enriched uranium. Stockpiles in the former Soviet Union are believed to be roughly of the same magnitude. Every step in the bomb-making process involves severe environmental threats. At the now-closed Purex plant at the Hanford Reservation in Washington, the production of a single kilogram of plutonium generated about 1,300 liters of liquid high-level radioactive waste laced with hazardous chemicals, more than 200,000 kilograms of low- to intermediate-level waste, and almost 10 million liters of contaminated cooling water. Military nuclear reactors are responsible for an estimated 97 percent of all high-level nuclear waste and 78 percent of all low-level nuclear waste (both by volume) in the United States. Measured in curies, however, the military portion comes to 6 and 74 percent, respectively. The military-related high-level waste inventory in the United States has been estimated at about 1.4 billion curies. (A curie measures the intensity of radiation and is equal to 3.7×10^{10} disintegrations per second; by comparison, about 50 million curies were released during the accident at Chernobyl.)[52]

By 1989, more than 3,200 sites in about 100 locations owned by the U.S. Department of Energy (DoE) had been identified as having tainted soil, groundwater, or both (see table 3). More than fifty bombs the size of the one dropped on Nagasaki could be manufactured from the waste that has leaked just from Hanford's underground tanks. At Rocky Flats in Colorado, enough plutonium has accumulated in ventilation ducts to make seven nuclear bombs. After a large 1969 fire there, investigators found the highest concentrations of plutonium ever measured near an urban area, including around Nagasaki.[53]

Additional danger looms from wastes that have not escaped into the environment—at least not yet. Some storage tanks at Savannah River and Hanford holding plutonium by-products such as cesium, strontium, and iodine are apparently in danger of exploding, according to a government advisory panel. Should such a detonation occur at Savannah River, residents nearby could contract up to 20,000 additional cancers.[54]

Radiation is known to cause cancer, leukemia, multiple myeloma, brain tumors, thyroid disorders, sterility, miscarriages, and birth defects. Damage to the human body depends on the size and type of the radiation dose and on how fast it is absorbed. It is difficult to establish a causal link between a specific radiation exposure and adverse health effects. Recent studies conclude that the risks of ionizing radiation are three times higher than previously thought, and many scientists now believe there is no "safe" level of radiation exposure.[55]

Some 300,000 people, or half of those who ever worked in the U.S. nuclear weapons complex, are believed to have been affected by exposure to radiation. The question of health effects on workers remains conten-

Table 3. Radioactive and Toxic Contamination at Major U.S. Nuclear Weapons Production Facilities, 1990

Facility (Task)	Observation
Feed Materials Production Center, Fernald, Ohio (converts uranium into metal ingots)	Since plant's opening, at least 250 tons of uranium oxide (and perhaps up to 1,500 tons) released into the air. Off-site surface and groundwater contaminated with uranium, cesium, thorium. High levels of radon gas emitted.
Hanford Reservation, Wash. (recycles uranium and extracts plutonium)	Since 1944, 760 billion liters of contaminated water (enough to create a 12-meter-deep lake the size of Manhattan) have entered groundwater and Columbia River; 4.5 million liters of high-level radioactive waste leaked from underground tanks. Officials knowingly and sometimes deliberately exposed the public to large amounts of airborne radiation in 1943–1956.
Savannah River, S.C. (produces plutonium and tritium)	Radioactive substances and chemicals found in the Tuscaloosa aquifer at levels 400 times greater than government considers safe. Released millions of curies of tritium gas into atmosphere since 1954.
Rocky Flats, Colo. (assembles plutonium triggers)	Since 1952, 200 fires have contaminated the Denver region with unknown amounts of plutonium. Strontium, cesium, and cancer-causing chemicals leaked into underground water.
Oak Ridge Reservation, Tenn. (produces lithium-deuteride and highly enriched uranium)	Since 1943, thousands of pounds of uranium emitted into atmosphere. Radioactive and hazardous wastes have severely polluted local streams flowing into the Clinch River. Watts Bar Reservoir, a recreational lake, is contaminated with at least 175,000 tons of mercury and cesium.

Sources: "Status of Major Nuclear Weapons Production Facilities: 1990," *PSR Monitor* (Washington, D.C.: Physicians for Social Responsibility), September 1990; Robert Alvarez and Arjun Makhijani, "Hidden Legacy of the Arms Race: Radioactive Waste," *Technology Review*, August/September 1989.

tious, however, in part due to DoE's refusal to release sufficient data. A February 1991 report by the Office of Technology Assessment notes the lack of sufficient data about off-site human exposure and concludes that "published reports and available data can neither demonstrate nor rule out the possibility that adverse public health impacts have occured or will occur as a result of weapons site pollution."[56]

Mikhail Gorbachev's glasnost gave the world first insights into the consequences of the Soviet nuclear weapons program. At Kyshtym in the eastern Urals (the Soviet counterpart to Hanford), perhaps over 6,000 workers were exposed to radiation of more than 100 rem—a dose that can produce cancer many years later. Cesium, strontium, and other liquid radioactive wastes were dumped into the Techa River from the late 1940s to 1952. The river became so polluted that traces of radioactivity showed up in the Arctic Ocean, nearly 1,000 miles away. Those living along the Techa had to be evacuated. From 1952 on, nuclear waste was dumped into nearby Lake Karachay; the heat of the radionuclides began to dry out the 10-square-kilometer body of water. By 1988, it contained 120 million curies of strontium-90, cesium-137, residual plutonium, and other long-lived isotopes, two-and-a-half times more than was released at Chernobyl. The lake is now being covered by a thick layer of concrete to contain the radiation. In September 1957, a chemical explosion occurred at a high-level radioactive waste storage site at Kyshtym. The accident severely contaminated 15,000 square kilometers of land that was home to more than a quarter-million people. The explosion released about a third as much overall radiation as at Chernobyl and forced the evacuation of 10,000 people.[57]

Warhead testing is the final phase in the development of nuclear arms, but it was the activity that elicited the earliest health and environmental concerns. From 1945 to 1990, 1,908 bombs were exploded at more than thirty-five sites around the world. Roughly a quarter of all tests, most of them before 1963, were conducted in the atmosphere, injecting far more radioactive debris into the atmosphere than the Chernobyl accident did. The fallout may have caused as many as 86,000 birth defects worldwide and may eventually result in some 150,000 premature deaths. Although underground testing has cut down on radiation, some still escapes into the atmosphere (known as "venting") and some is also suspected of leaching into groundwater.[58]

In the United States, individuals exposed to nuclear fallout include 400,000 "atomic veterans" (soldiers ordered to observe atmospheric testing), 100,000 test site workers, and a similar number of "downwinders" living in parts of Nevada, Arizona, and Utah. Yet millions more Americans are thought to bear trace amounts of plutonium in their tissues and organs. Between 1946 and 1958, the U.S. government conducted sixty-six atmospheric tests in the Marshall Islands. High levels of radioactivity in the soil and food crops have rendered Bikini Atoll in the Pacific uninhabitable since 1954. Many inhabitants of Rongelap—downwind from

Bikini—have developed thyroid tumors. From the early 1980s on, increases in the number of leukemia cases, brain tumors, and thyroid cancers have been registered in French Polynesia, the site of more than 160 French tests since 1966. In Australia, where Britain conducted nuclear tests from 1953 to 1963, 400 square kilometers of Aboriginal land has been contaminated. The Soviet Academy of Medical Sciences determined in 1989 that residents of Semipalatinsk, near the main test site in Kazakhstan, had experienced excess cancers, genetic diseases, and child mortality because of radiation exposure from pre-1963 atmospheric tests. A total of nearly 500,000 people were exposed to radiation. In 1988, the incidence of cancer was 70 percent above the national average. Kazakh activists claim that life expectancy in the republic has declined by four years over the past two decades, and that the number of people suffering from blood diseases has doubled since 1970. The Radiology Research Institute in Semipalatinsk has found that the 500,000 people living near the test site show incidence of cancer 40 percent higher and leukemia 50 percent higher than in other regions of the Soviet Union.[59]

Ecological Conversion

As the East-West confrontation fades away and progress is made toward disarmament, a number of environmental challenges and opportunities present themselves in three key areas of conversion: (1) the disposal (and in some cases possible civilian reuse) of military equipment, (2) the cleanup of military bases and land before they can be turned over to civilian uses, and (3) the conversion of arms-production facilities.

Military Equipment

Since Mikhail Gorbachev came to power in Moscow in 1985, a number of arms-control and disarmament treaties have been concluded; the Soviet Union (and recently the United States, too) has also undertaken a number of unilateral disarmament initiatives. Treaties include the 1987 Intermediate-Range Nuclear Forces (INF) Treaty between the United States and the Soviet Union, the multilateral Conventional Forces in Europe (CFE) Treaty signed in November 1990, and the 1991 Strategic Arms Reduction Talks (START) Treaty between the United States and the Soviet Union. Together, these measures mean that huge stockpiles of weaponry need to be disposed of. This disposal could take one of two forms: either the dismantling and destruction of weapons or the conversion and civilian reuse of military equipment (or the salvaging of parts and components thereof).

Considering the enormous resources expended in producing these arms in the first place, even an effort to use some equipment for civilian purposes cannot recoup these investments. In any event, civilian reuse is likely to be technically difficult and economically marginal: most of the military hardware has no intrinsic civilian value. Nevertheless, such a reuse is being attempted to a degree by the former Soviet Union, which needs to decommission large numbers of tanks, personnel carriers, and other equipment under the CFE Treaty. Already, several hundred SS-20 missile launchers proscribed by the INF Treaty have been transformed into self-propelled hoisting cranes.[60]

From a confidence-building point of view, destroying weapons is a better option than allowing for a civilian reconfiguration because the latter option cannot exclude altogether the possibility that converted equipment might later be refashioned again for military purposes. Arms reduction accords are likely to mandate the verifiable destruction of military equipment. The CFE Treaty, for example, offers four options for dealing with arsenals in excess of agreed deployment levels: destruction, withdrawal from the geographical area covered by the treaty (an option available only to the Soviet Union, the United States, and Canada), conversion to civilian use, or foreign sales. The treaty permits both NATO and the former Warsaw Pact to each convert a relatively limited number of pieces of equipment: 750 tanks, 3,000 armored vehicles, many combat trainers, and most helicopters. (The Soviet Union needs to cut its arsenal by about 12,000 tanks and a similar number of armored vehicles.)[61]

Yet the destruction of military hardware needs to proceed in an environmentally acceptable manner—an undertaking that no country or organization has yet much experience with. Concern is particularly focused on missiles, chemical warheads, and stockpiles of ammunition.

Under the terms of the 1987 INF Treaty, the United States and the Soviet Union had to destroy close to 2,700 rockets; another 2,000 long-range missiles will have to be disposed of under the START agreement, and unilateral reductions announced by Presidents Bush and Gorbachev in September and October 1991 consign additional launch vehicles to the scrap-heap. Yet, a careless demolition entails considerable air pollution. Missiles are, as *New York Times* science reporter William J. Broad put it, in essence "big tubes filled with exotic alloys, toxic chemicals and explosive fuels." Solid rocket fuel, when burned, can create clouds of dangerous chemicals and noxious fumes.[62] The destruction of U.S. Pershing missiles released aluminium oxide, titanium oxide, hydrochloric acid, and asbestos, and unleashed public protests in Utah and Colorado. The U.S. Air Force is now experimenting with a variety of ostensibly less polluting ways of disposing of solid rocket fuel.[63]

Congress passed legislation requiring the destruction of the U.S. chemical stockpile by 1997. The U.S. Army is planning to dispose of its stockpiles of nerve and mustard gas by incinerating them in plants on the uninhabited Johnston Atoll in the South Pacific and at Tooele (Utah), and at smaller facilities to be built in seven other states. In 1984, the National Research Council concluded that this was the safest method available. Even under the best of circumstances, however, the incinerators would emit toxins, and according to Greenpeace, "in a 'worst-case-scenario' prepared in 1987, the Army projects 8,896 to 62,773 deaths, depending on the site." Greenpeace has called for placing the weapons in storage until a safer disposal method is found. Yet many of these weapons are aging and deteriorating: the longer they are stored, the more likely it is that leaks will occur, with grave environmental consequences.[64]

Both the production and the destruction of ammunition constitutes a hazardous undertaking. The production of explosives entails potential exposure to emissions of chlorine gas, dibenzofurans, and dibenzodioxins. The countries of the former Warsaw Pact are now faced with the need to dispose of vast stockpiles. For example, the now-dissolved East German army had stocks of 290,000 tons of ammunition, and the Soviet troops now withdrawing from the former East German territory are believed to have stored at least another 1 million tons (though some estimates speak of 2.5 million tons). Experience with destroying ammunition is very limited; there is a bewildering variety of types, each of which requires different procedures for destruction.

The costs arising out of the physical destruction of arms—including verification measures and environmental safeguards—are substantial. Destroying chemical weapons, for example, is reckoned to cost more than their production. Estimates for the U.S. stockpile range from $4–10 billion, while General Vladimir Pikalov, the former chief of the Soviet chemical forces, has put potential Soviet expenses at up to $20 billion. The cost to develop appropriate technology and to build plants to destroy stocks of ammunition in the former East Germany are estimated at anywhere from deutsche marks (DM) 500 million to DM 3 billion ($300–1,800 million at current exchange rates).[66]

Base Cleanup

As the previous section demonstrated, many military facilities and tracts of land are severely contaminated; before they can be seriously considered for civilian re-use, they will need to undergo a meticulous cleanup. The cost of repairing the damage wrought will be staggering. For the United States, nuclear decontamination costs may run to $200 billion, or $3.3 million for every nuclear warhead the nation has ever produced. Coping with toxic wastes at U.S. domestic military bases could reach between $100 and $200 billion, according to estimates from the Department of Defense Inspector General's office. Environmental damage caused by Soviet troops in Hungary and Czechoslovakia has been estimated at $810 million and $120 million, respectively. In Poland, the damage, including losses from the inability of using sites for commercial purposes, has been put at $4.8 billion. In the former East Germany, the rehabilitation of fuel-contaminated soils is estimated to cost DM 300 ($180) per cubic meter. Cleaning up the Maralinga nuclear test site in Australia may cost anywhere from $75 million to $450 million.[67] But the financial cost is only part of the story. The most severely poisoned areas may prove impossible to "clean up" or otherwise restore. Fenced-off and unsuitable for any use, they may become "national sacrifice zones," ghastly monuments to the Cold War.

Another enduring and perilous legacy of war preparation is found in the large tracts of land strewn with unexploded bombs and ammunition. In November 1989, for example, the Pentagon had to close off some 275 square kilometers of public land in Nevada after discovering 1,389 live bombs, 123,375 pounds of shrapnel, and 28,136 rounds of ammunition accidentally dropped outside an Air Force bombing range. It costs an estimated $250 million to rehabilitate a single square kilometer of strafed and bombed land. Robert Stone, Deputy Assistant Defense Secretary and the Pentagon's top land manager, acknowledged that land used for bombing practice often has to be closed to human use permanently because even an intensive effort will fail to locate all unexploded bombs.[68]

Plant Conversion and the Requirements of a Sustainable Economy

Arms production facilities, R&D labs, and design bureaus need to be switched to civilian use. This is the task that has received by far the most attention in the conversion literature. Plant-based conversion involves the following components: making an inventory of existing skills and equipment; identifying alternative civilian products; conducting engineering studies to determine the feasibility of producing these goods with present capabilities; retraining employees or upgrading their skills; refashioning machinery and production layouts where needed; preparing marketing studies to ascertain whether alternative products selected can generate sufficient demand; making new arrangements for raw material supplies and other inputs; and erecting civilian marketing networks.

A critical, if long neglected, point is that such a switch-over should involve not just a crossing of the military/civilian threshold, but putting much greater emphasis on ecologically sound ways of producing goods. Arguments for a conversion of the military economy to civilian use often focus on the adverse impact of military-led economic development on productivity. The corporate culture characteristic of the arms industry presents a great obstacle to functioning effectively in the commercial marketplace. However, if arms production yields to a typical civilian production system, then one problem will simply be traded for another. In a sense, not only the military industry needs converting and reorienting, but so does its civilian counterpart. An environmentally sustainable economy will have to give greater emphasis to conservation and efficiency, rely more on renewable energy, and extract nominally renewable resources only to the degree that they can regenerate themselves. It will need to minimize waste, maximize reuse and recycling, and avoid the use of hazardous materials. And finally, it will need to develop production technologies that are more environmentally benign and less hazardous to the health and safety of workers, and design products to be more durable and repairable.[69]

Could military contractors lead the way in moving the entire economy toward sustainability? They frequently pride themselves on being at the cutting edge of technological development, and in response to recent military budget cuts a number of them have come forward with claims of spectacular potential spinoffs from their military research, including lasers and sensors that could be used for environmental, medical, or other purposes.[70] Yet problems pervasive in the military economy—cost-maximizing and the kind of overdesign that Mary Kaldor at the University of Sussex has labeled "baroque"—should inject a measure of caution into overblown expectations.[71] There is also growing evidence that the military are no longer a technological avant-garde. A number of studies by the U.S. Defense Science Board, for example, concluded that the Pentagon purchases electronics products that are often five to ten years behind the state of the art and up to eight times more expensive than civilian models.[72] Finally, Michael Closson, executive director of the Center for Economic Conversion in California, sharply questions whether the "corporate culture" present in the arms industry can ever be amenable to environmentally-sensitive approaches:

> The General Dynamics and Lockheeds of the world are authoritarian, hierarchical, patriarchal, secretive and not particularly innovative. They are hardly the foundation upon which one could build a sustainable peace economy. . . . The sort of projects that they are best suited to are multi-billion-dollar manned space stations and voyages to Mars, exactly the type of activity we should not be pursuing at this point in time when we have so many Earth-bound problems to address.[73]

Still, there is no single, typical "arms producer." The companies making up the military industry belong to a wide variety of industrial sectors (aerospace, electronics, motor vehicles, shipbuilding, chemicals, machine tools, and others). They include huge conglomerates and small, specialized firms and ventures; some of them are highly innovative, while others are structurally or even technologically conservative. For some, military contracting is their mainstay, but for others it is a business of limited significance; some have a long history of building weapons, while others have only a fleeting involvement; some produce equipment that has only military applications, while others manufacture ordinary products that may be built to military specifications or are indistinguishable from civilian goods. In short, the ability of military contractors to convert—and to do so in an environmentally responsible manner—varies enormously. Thus, some companies may be well placed to respond in imaginative ways to the environmental challenge. Interestingly, among the conversion groups initiated by arms industry workers, some have specifically focused on environmental criteria in identifying possible alternative uses of their company's equipment and know-how (see table 4).

An ecological conversion process could be either supply-driven or demand-oriented. In the first case, the process would be focused on plant conversion, and the companies concerned would most likely seek to stay as close as possible to the production technologies and products that they are familiar with. The success of an environmentally inspired conversion process would, as discussed above, hinge primarily on the extent to which military contractors' know-how is useful and applicable to solving

Table 4. Environment-Related Conversion Proposals by Selected Workers' Alternative Product Working Groups, United States, Britain, and West Germany

Location, Year Started	Alternative Product Proposals/Management Response
United States:	
Unysis, St. Paul/Minneapolis, Minnesota, 1989	IBEW Local conducted skill audit and gathered over 40 alternative product ideas, focusing on pollution-control equipment, energy-efficiency technologies, and water-conserving irrigation systems. Management has refused to cooperate.
Britain:	
Vickers Shipyard, Barrow Alternative Employment (BAEC), 1984	1987 report, "Oceans of Work," assessed alternatives to Trident submarine production in marine technology and renewable energy.
West Germany:	
Blohm & Voss Shipyard, Hamburg, November 1980	Water & waste treatment, desalination, biogas, wind power for energy generation and shipping, and energy-saving technologies. The working group's activities put pressure on the company to engage in (relatively successful) diversification measures.
Krupp MaK (Machine Tools), Kiel, January 1981	Innovative rail systems, co-generation, wind power. Management mostly uncooperative, but pursued some ideas originally proposed by the working group, including a wind energy plant on the North Sea island of Helgoland.
MBB (Aerospace), Bremen, March 1982	Some 62 alternative product ideas, including solar collectors, biogas, wind energy, energy storage and transport systems, and high-tech zeppelins (for surveillance of North Sea environment). Management showed interest in pursuing wind-energy market.
MBB, Augsburg, 1988	Workers' group was catalyst in bringing about a partnership between MBB and city government to explore ways in which MBB's know-how can be applied to solving environmental problems. Initial focus on boosting energy efficiency and reducing water pollution in Augsburg's textile industry; later, technologies for a more environmentally benign urban transportation system will be explored.

Source: Michael Renner, *Swords Into Plowshares: Converting to a Peace Economy,* Worldwatch Paper 96 (Washington, D.C.: Worldwatch Institute, June 1990), tables 4 and 5.

environmental problems. The process would thus be shaped by the capabilities of military contractors and, in a sense, be captive to their interests. The probably preferable alternative is a demand-oriented approach. It would channel government spending from military budgets to R&D and procurement programs that help develop, and generate demand for, environmentally sound technologies and products. While such environmental markets would certainly be open to former military contractors, the conditions and parameters of success would not be (exclusively) defined by them.

Environment and disarmament are closely linked; considerations of environmental sustainability should receive greater attention with regard to disarmament and conversion. The environmental community could refine and strengthen the alternative-use concept by developing guidelines for an environmentally sound conversion process. But there is room for some cross-fertilization of ideas: equally important is the contribution that the conversion concept could make to the goal of creating a sustainable economy. Not only does the arms industry need to be switched to more peaceful uses, but the civilian industry needs to be converted to less environmentally destructive ways of manufacturing products. Achieving a greater degree of democratization in economic decision-making is central to conversion, which relies on the participation of workers in joint management/labor "alternative-use committees" to plan and implement a switch from military to civilian production. In effect, such committees would prepare a thorough audit of a company's capabilities applicable to civilian tasks. The same principle can be applied to cases in which a company needs to assess the environmental impact of its operations and examine the options available to it to survive in a more environmentally conscious world. "Eco-audits" could be prepared by joint committees of management, labor, community representatives, and environmental experts. The European Community is in the process of drafting a proposal for establishing such audits; after encountering industry opposition, however, the EC would make them voluntary instead of mandatory. As currently constituted, the proposal also does not provide for the work force to be consulted during an audit.[74]

Conclusion

This chapter has presented the argument that significant detrimental environmental impacts are a virtually inevitable consequence of both warfare and war preparation, and documented the environmental legacy of the war system. Environmental considerations present both challenges and opportunities in the disarmament and conversion process.

The environmental legacy of the war system is most discernible in the wake of armed conflicts. The recent Gulf War provides tragic evidence. Though it has been one of the most ecologically damaging conflicts ever, it is only one in a long series of highly destructive wars. With some prominent exceptions, the environmental effects of producing arms and keeping armies in a state of readiness—the permanent state of war preparation—are not as dramatic as the flaming inferno in Kuwait that could be seen on television screens around the world. But they are no less serious; cumulatively, they are more serious. Even less noticeable—to the general public, at least—are the indirect ways in which military research and spending priorities detract from solving environment (and manifold other) problems.

With the end of the Cold War, the environmental challenges of disarmament are becoming evident. Stocks of ammunition and weaponry need to be disarmed and disposed of in the environmentally least objectionable manner. Arms factories and military bases need to undergo a meticulous, lengthy, and costly cleanup. New technologies need to be developed and tried out, and large sums of money budgeted. The challenges are tremendous, but so are the opportunities. Rehabilitation efforts and an ecological conversion process—oriented toward the development of environmentally-sound products and production technologies—mean that immense alternative markets are emerging.

Coping with the environmental legacy of the Cold War is an unavoidable necessity. But if ecological considerations are taken seriously, there are implications not just for the past, but for the future as well. Not only has the radical political transformation in the former Warsaw Pact countries eclipsed military power as a prime determining factor in the East-West relationship, but there is also a nascent discussion about the need to conceptualize "national security" in much broader terms than traditional definitions suggest. Central to these new concepts is the recognition that security can increasingly be obtained only globally, not on an exclusively national basis. Such a redefinition of security implies that military power is less and less appropriate as a means of settling conflicts.

Notes

1. A milestone in the sustainable development discussion was reached with publication of what is widely referred to as the Brundtland

report: see The World Commission on Environment and Development (WCED), *Our Common Future* (New York and Oxford: Oxford University Press, 1987).

2. This section draws heavily on my earlier work. See Michael Renner, *National Security: The Economic and Environmental Dimensions,* Worldwatch Paper 89 (Washington, D.C.: Worldwatch Institute, May 1989).

3. "Environment and Conflict," Earthscan Briefing Document 40, International Institute for Environment and Development, London, November 1984.

4. Martin Wright, "Mixed Blessings of the Flooding in Sudan," *New Scientist,* 22 Sept. 1988; "Bangladesh Blames Neighbors for its Floods," *Panoscope,* December 1987.

5. Pesticides from Michael Weisskopf, " 'Toxic Clouds' Can Carry Pollutants Far and Wide," *Washington Post,* 16 March 1988. Sulfur dioxide from Hilary F. French, *Clearing the Air: A Global Agenda,* Worldwatch Paper 94 (Washington, D.C.: Worldwatch Institute, January 1990), and from Tomasz Zylicz, "European Airborne Pollution: Economic, Social, and Political Aspects of a Possible Reduction Program," Warsaw University, unpublished manuscript, 1986. Norwegian foreign minister quoted in Norman Myers, *Not Far Afield: U.S. Interests and the Global Environment* (Washington, D.C.: World Resources Institute, June 1987).

6. For some recent findings, see William K. Stevens, "Summertime Harm to Ozone Detected Over Broader Area," *New York Times,* 23 Oct. 1991.

7. For a review of the major issues with regard to climate change, see Christopher Flavin, *Slowing Global Warming: A Worldwide Strategy,* Worldwatch Paper 91 (Washington, D.C.: Worldwatch Institute, October 1989).

8. U.S. Environmental Protection Agency, *Regulatory Impact Analysis,* Vol. 1 (Washington, D.C.: 1987); also Matthew Wald, "Fighting the Greenhouse Effect," *New York Times,* 28 Aug. 1988.

9. Shevardnaze cited in Michael G. Renner, "Forging Environmental Alliances," *World Watch,* November/December 1989.

10. Lester R. Brown and Edward C. Wolf, "Reclaiming the Future," in Lester R. Brown et al., *State of the World 1988* (New York: W. W. Norton, 1988).

11. U.S. military spending from Executive Office of the President, Office of Management and Budget, *Historical Tables: Budget of the U.S. Government, Fiscal Year 1992* (Washington, D.C.: U.S. Government Printing Office, 1991); pollution control spending from Management Information Services Inc., "PABCO Expenditures," Washington, D.C., May 1990, and from Gary Rutledge and Nikolaos A. Stergioulas, "Plant and Equipment Expenditures by Business for Pollution Abatement, 1987 and Planned 1988," *Survey of Current Busisness,* November 1988. West European military spending from U.S. Arms Control and Disarmament Agency, *World Military Expenditures and Arms Transfers 1989* (Washington, D.C.: U.S. Government Printing Office, October 1990); pollution control expenditures from Mark Magnier, "Market Abroad for Pollution Control Beckons," *Journal of Commerce,* 8 Dec. 1989, and from Michael E. Porter, "America's Green Stretegy," *Scientific American,* April 1991.

12. Comparison of military and selected civilian R&D from WCED, *Our Common Future.* An estimated 27 percent of all U.S. scientists and more than 30 percent of British scientists are involved in military projects. See Michael Dee Oden, *A Military Dollar Really Is Different: The Economic Impacts of Military Spending Reconsidered* (Lansing, Mich.: Employment Research Associates, 1988), and Mary Kaldor et al., "Industrial Competitiveness and Britain's Defense," *Lloyds Bank Review,* October 1986. Share of governmental R&D in the United States and the Soviet Union devoted to military purposes from, respectively, Renner, *National Security,* and from Alexei Izyumov, "The Natural Experience of the USSR," paper presented at United Nations Conference on Conversion: Economic Adjustments in an Era of Arms Reduction," Moscow, August 13–17, 1990. Other countries from Organisation for Economic Cooperation and Development, *Main Science and Technology Indicators 1981–1987* (Paris, 1988), table 39.

13. This section draws heavily on my earlier work: see Michael G. Renner, "Military Victory, Ecological Defeat," *World Watch,* July/August 1991, 27–33.

14. The environmental impact of warfare has been treated in the following publications, among others: Arthur Westing, *Ecological Consequences of the Second Indochina War* (Stockholm: Almqvist & Wiksell, 1976); Arthur Westing, *Weapons of Mass Destruction and the Environment* (London: Taylor Francis, 1977); Arthur Westing, *Warfare in a Fragile World* (London: Taylor Francis, 1980); Ralph Ostermann, "Umwelt als Waffe—Das Zerstörungspotential ökologischer Kriegsführung," in Arnim Beckmann, ed., *Umwelt Braucht Frieden* (Fischer Verlag: Frankfurt, 1983); Arthur Westing, ed., *Herbicides in War: The Long-Term Ecological and Human Consequences* (London: Taylor and Francis, 1984); Arthur Westing, ed., *Environmental Warfare: A Technical, Legal and Policy Appraisal* (London: Taylor and Francis, 1984); The Environmental Project on Central America, *Militarization: The Environmental Impact,* EPOCA/Green Paper Nol 3, San Francisco, 1990; Arthur Westing, ed., *Environmental Hazards of War: Releasing Dangerous Forces in an Industrialized World* (London: Sage Publications, 1990).

15. "Desert Storm Still Rages," *Friends of the Earth,* September 1991: 3; Youssef M. Ibrahim, "Most Oil Fires Are Out in Kuwait, But Its Environment Is Devastated," *New York Times,* 19 Oct. 1991; Matthew L. Wald, "Amid Ceremony and Ingenuity, Kuwait's Oil-Well Fires Are Declared Out," *New York Times,* 7 Nov. 1991.

16. Andre Carothers, "Oceans of Oil," *Greenpeace Magazine,* October-December 1991: 17; Ibrahim, "Most Oil Fires Are Out"; Wald, "Amid Ceremony"; Jennifer Parmelee, "Environmentalists Survey the Blackened Wasteland That Was Kuwait," *Washington Post,* 20 Dec. 1991

17. Matthew L. Wald, "High Levels of Toxic Substances Found in Kuwait Oil Fire Smoke," *New York Times,* 16 July 1991; Michael Weisskopf, "Oil Fire Pollution Assessed," *Washington Post,* 4 April 1991; Marlise Simmons, "British Study Disputes Lengthy Climatic Role for Kuwait Oil Fires," *New York Times,* 16 April 1991.

18. Michelle Hoffman, "Taking Stock of Saddam's Fiery Legacy in Kuwait," *Research News,* 30 August 1991: 971.

19. Peter V. Hobbs, "Summary of the University of Washington's Preliminary Findings on the Effects of the Smoke from the Kuwait Oil Fires on the Atmosphere," (unpublished paper, Atmospheric Sciences De-

partment, University of Washington, Seattle, June 21, 1991): 6; Tom Wicker, "Kuwait Still Burns," *New York Times,* 28 July 1991; Parmelee, "Environmentalists Survey. . . ."

20. "U.N. Virtually Out of Money to Pay to Combat Pollution from Gulf Oil Fires," *International Environment Reporter,* 17 July 1991: 401; Peter Hadfield, "Soot from Burning Wells 'Will Not Upset Climate' . . . but Falls on Japan," *New Scientist,* 6 July 1991: 16; Marlise Simmons, "Beyond Kuwait, Black Rain and Acid-Filled Clouds," *New York Times,* 16 March 1991; John Horgan, "Burning Questions," *Scientific American,* July 1991: 17.

21. John Travis, "As the Gulf Region Chokes, the Global Climate Breathes Easier," *Science News* 140 (1991): 25; "Black Smoke from About 3 Million Barrels per Day of Burning Kuwait Oil Likely to Fall to Earth Quickly, Scientists Say," U.S. National Science Foundation, news release, 24 June 1991: "NCAR Scientists Release Preliminary Results from Kuwait Oil Fires Study," National Center for Atmospheric Research, Boulder, Colorado, news release, 24 June 1991; Stephen H. Schneider, "Smoke Alarm," *World Monitor,* March 1991: 50–51.

22. U.S. Environmental Protection Agency, Gulf Task Force, "Summary of the Gulf Task Force/Non-Governmental Organization Meeting to Discuss U.S. Activities to Address Oil Well Fires in Kuwait," Washington, D.C., October 1991.

23. Louise Kehoe and David Thomas, "Difficulties with Oil in Narrow Waters," *Financial Times,* 28 Jan. 1991; William Booth, "War's Oil Spill Still Sullies Gulf Shore," *Washington Post,* 6 April 1991.

24. Thomas Y. Canby, "After the Storm," *National Geographic,* August 1991: 28; Ken Wells, "The Battles Are Over, But Gulf Environment Still Fights for Its Life," *Wall Street Journal,* 15 Oct. 1991.

25. Charles Sheppard and Andrew Price, "Will Marine Life Survive the Gulf War?," *New Scientist,* 9 March 1991: 38–39; John Horgan, "The Muddled Cleanup in the Persian Gulf," *Scientific American,* October 1991: 107; Wells, "The Battles Are Over"; Robert D. McFadden, "Oil Threatens Fishing and Water Supply," *New York Times,* 26 Jan. 1991;

Matthew L. Wald, "Gulf Oil Spill Vexing Cleanup Efforts," *New York Times,* April 7, 1991. Thaqfi quoted in Parmelee, "Environmentalists Survey."

26. John L. Cloudsley-Thompson, "The Destructive Effects of Warfare on the Desert Environment," *Environmental Awareness* 13, No. 2 (1990): 43–48.

27. Gar Smith, "Nuremberg Trials for Eco-Terrorism?," *Earth Island Journal,* Spring 1991: 50; Parmelee, "Environmentalists Survey."

28. Center for Disarmament, *The Relationship Between Disarmament and Development,* Disarmament Study Series No. 5 (New York: United Nations, 1982).

29. Pentagon-controlled and -leased land from U.S. Department of Defense (DoD), *Our Nation's Defense and the Environment: A Department of Defense Initiative* (Washington, D.C.: 1990), and from Edward McGlinn, "The Military Land Grab," *The Riverwatch* (Grayling, Mich.: Anglers of the Au Sable River), Winter 1990. Department of Energy land from Thomas B. Cochran et al., *Nuclear Weapons Databook, Vol. II: U.S. Nuclear Warhead Production* (Cambridge, Mass.: Ballinger, 1987).

30. Alexei Izyumov, "Conversion in the Soviet Union—and Possibilities for Cooperation in the Baltic Region," *Bulletin of Peace Proposals,* 22, No. 3 (September 1991): 274. Kazakhstan from Paul Quinn-Judge, "Soviet Writers Blast Nuclear Testing," *Christian Science Monitor,* 14 March 1989.

31. Netherlands from Paul J. M. Vertegaal, "Environmental Impact of Dutch Military Activities," *Environmental Conservation,* Spring 1989. British figure includes about 1,000 square kilometers used for agricultural purposes. See Secretary of State for Defence, *Statement on the Defence Estimates 1990,* Volume 2 (London: HMSO, April 1990), table 5.12. West Germany from Olaf Achilles, "Der Preis der Freiheit," in Olaf Achilles, ed., *Natur Ohne Frieden* (Munich: Knaur, 1988), and from "Environmental Damage from Military Forces Detailed," Joint Publications Research Service (JPRS), Environmental Issues (JPRS-TEN-91-011), Rosslyn, VA, 17 June 1991: 107. East Germany from Frank Marczinek, "Conversion of the Armed Forces in the GDR," paper presented at

United Nations Conference on Economic Adjustments in an Era of Arms Reduction, Moscow, August 13–17, 1990, from "Alles Zerwühlt und Kaputt," *Der Spiegel,* 1 Oct. 1990, and from "Die US-amerikanischen und sowjetischen Streitkräfte hinterlassen in Deutschland ein groβes Altlastenproblem," *Ökologische Briefe,* No. 11, 13 March 1991: 13. Poland from Bogdan Turek, "Soviet Troops are Devastating Polish Environment," UPI wire story, 27 Feb. 1991. A Polish newspaper report puts the land occupied by Soviet troops at 700 square kilometers, or .2 percent of Polish territory; see "Environmental Damage Caused by Soviet Forces Assessed," JPRS-TEN-91-014, 9 July 1991: 45.

32. Wolfgang Schwegler-Rohmeis, "Rüstungskonversion als Sicherheit spolitik," in Marcus Breitschwerdt, ed., *Rüstungskonversion. Facetten einer Strukturfrage* (Stuttgart: Wissenschaftsedition SPD Baden-Württemberg, 1988); Samuel S. Kim, *The Quest for a Just World Order* (Boulder, Colo.: Westview Press, 1984); Nicolai N. Smirnov, "The Impact of Conventional War on Natural Areas of the USSR," *Environmental Conservation,* Winter 1989.

33. Bruno Jerlitschka, "Umweltzerstörung durch Truppenstandorte und Manöver," in Arnim Bechmann, ed., *Umwelt Braucht Frieden* (Frankfurt: Fischer Verlag, 1983); Olaf Achilles, "Bodenbelastung und Flächenverbrauch durch Militär," *Forum Wissenschaft,* No. 1, 1989; Peter Grier, "Defense Contractors Go for 'Green' Look," *Christian Science Monitor,* 22 May 1990. West German maneuver space from Schwegler-Rohmeis, "Rüstungskonversion als Sicherheitspolitik."

34. Share of petroleum products from Gunar Seitz, "Ressourcenvergeudung durch Rüstung," in Bechmann, *Umwelt Braucht Frieden;* global share of military jet fuel use from Olaf Achilles, "Militär, Rüstung und Klima," MÖP Studie VII, Arbeitsund Forschungsstelle Militär, Ökologie und Planung, Bonn, West Germany, June 1990; U.S. and Soviet shares from Tom Cutler, "Myths of Military Oil Supply Vulnerability," *Armed Forces Journal International,* July 1989; West German figure from Schwegler-Rohmeis, "Rüstungskonversion als Sicherheitspolitik."

35. DoD share of total U.S. oil and energy consumption calculated from Energy Information Administration, Department of Energy (EIA/DoE), *Annual Energy Review 1988* (Washington, D.C.: U.S. Government Printing Office, 1989); comparison with urban mass transit is author's

calculation based on American Public Transit Association, *1989 Transit Fact Book* (Washington, D.C.: 1989).

36. The tri-annual *Manufacturing Energy Consumption Survey* compiled by the U.S. Energy Information Administration (EIA/DoE) provides data on the two-digit SIC code level, with more disaggregated information (on the four-digit level) only for four industry sub-groups that are not of prime importance for the military industry. The two-digit level is too aggregated for a meaningful comparison with published data of defense-related output by industry group—a comparison that would allow the preparation of an estimate of total energy consumption in arms production. The EIA is planning, however, to conduct a more detailed consumption survey for the next edition, to be published in 1994.

37. 1971 figure from Helge Hveem, "Militarization of Nature: Conflict and Control over Strategic Resources and Some Implications for Peace Policies," *Journal of Peace Research,* 16, No. 1, 1979; 1989 figure is author's estimate, based on data in Stockholm International Peace Research Institute (SIPRI), *SIPRI Yearbook 1990: World Armament and Disarmament* (Oxford: Oxford University Press, 1990), tables 5.4. and 7.1., and in Paul Quigley, "Arms Exports: The Stop-Gap Alternative to Pentagon Contracts?," *Bulletin of Peace Proposals,* 19, No. 1, 1988. Australian energy consumption—90.8 mtoe in 1988—from British Petroleum Co. (BP), *BP Statistical Review of World Energy* (London, July 1990).

38. Estimates for armed forces' energy use from Center for Disarmament, *The Relationship Between Disarmament and Development;* Achilles, "Militär, Rüstung und Klima"; comparison with Japanese oil consumption from BP, *BP Statistical Review.*

39. Global air pollution estimate from Seitz, "Ressourcenvergeudung durch Rüstung." West German jets' pollution is author's estimate based on data provided in Achilles, "Militär, Rüstung and Klima."

40. U.S. military carbon emission is author's estimate, based on EIA/DoE, *Annual Energy Review 1988;* on Gregg Marland et al., *Estimates of* Co_2 *Emissions from Fossil Fuel Burning and Cement Manufacturing, Based on the United Nations Energy Statistics and the U.S. Bureau of Mines Cement Manufacturing Data* (Oak Ridge, Tenn.: Oak Ridge National Laboratory, 1989); and on BP, *BP Statistical Review.*

41. Casey Bukro, "Military Faces Difficult Task in Ending 'War' on Environment," *Journal of Commerce,* 22 March 1989. Depletion potential of CFC-113 and Halon-1211 from Cynthia Pollock Shea, *Protecting Life on Earth: Steps to Save the Ozone Layer,* Worldwatch Paper 87 (Washington, D.C.: Worldwatch Institute, December 1988). Rocket and shuttle contribution to ozone depletion from Lenny Siegel, "No Free Launch," *Mother Jones,* September/October 1990; from Steven Aftergood, "Environmental Impacts of Solid Rocket Propellants," *FAS Public Interest Report,* September/October 1991, p. 6; from Steven Aftergood, "Poisoned Plumes," *New Scientist,* 7 Sept. 1991, 34–38; and from Warren E. Leary, "Study Calls for Effort to Limit Rockets' Pollution," *New York Times,* 18 Oct. 1991.

42. This section and the next section draw on my earlier work: Michael Renner, "Assessing the Military's War on the Environment," in Lester R. Brown et al., *State of the World 1991* (New York: W. W. Norton and Co., 1991), 141–145, and Michael G. Renner, "War on Nature," *World Watch,* May/June 1991: 18–21.

43. Heavy metals include beryllium, cadmium, chromium, mercury, lead, copper, zinc, iron, and others. They attack and weaken the cellular tissues of most organisms. Solvents include tri- and di-chloro ethylenes, ethanes and ethenes, carbon tetrachloride, methyl chloride, and trichlorofluoromethane (Freon). From *Uncle Sam's Hidden Poisons,* reprint from a *Sacramento Bee* series of articles published September 30–October 5, 1984 (Sacramento: Sacramento Bee, 1984).

44. Ibid.

45. Lenny Siegel, "The Growing Nightmare of Military Toxics," *Nuclear Times,* Spring 1990; "Turning the Wastes of War into a War on Waste," *Toxic Times,* Summer 1990; Will Collette, *Dealing with Military Toxics* (Arlington, Va.: Citizen's Clearinghouse for Hazardous Wastes, Inc., 1987). Emissions of top five chemical firms in 1988 from John Holusha, "Ed Woolard Walks Du Pont's Tightrope," *New York Times,* 14 Oct. 1990. Military share of final demand for chemicals from Lenny Siegel et al., *The U.S. Military's Toxic Legacy: America's Worst Environmental Enemy* (Boston: The National Toxic Campaign Fund, January 1991), 10.

46. DoD, *Defense Environmental Restoration Program;* Michael Weisskopf, "3,000 Military Base Sites Added to Toxic Cleanup List," *Washington Post,* 29 March 1991; Seth Shulman, "Toxic Travels: Inside the Military's Environmental Nightmare," *Nuclear Times,* Autumn 1990.

47. Siegel et al., *The U.S. Military's Toxic Legacy,* 8–9.

48. John M. Broder, "U.S. Military Leaves Toxic Trail Overseas," *Los Angeles Times,* 18 June 1990. For reports of contamination at U.S. bases overseas, see "Japanese Group Plans to Sue U.S. Navy for Violating NEPA," *Multinational Environmental Outlook,* 31 Oct. 1989; Jorge Emmanuel, "Environmental Destruction Caused by U.S. Military Bases and the Serious Implications for the Philippines," paper presented at "Crossroad 1991: Towards a Nuclear Free, Bases Free Philippines," Manila, May 14–16, 1990; and "U.S. Defense Department Lax in Environmental Protection at Overseas Bases, Official Charges," *World Environment Report,* 23 July 1987. U.S. Army plan from John G. Roos, "U.S. Army Plans to Turn Over Facilities in Germany in 'As Is' Condition," *Armed Forces Journal International,* September 1990. "U.S. Army Faulted for Environmental Damage," *JPRS-TEN-91-002,* West Europe, 29 Jan. 1991: 79.

49. Henry Kamm, "Americans Help Czechs Clean Up After the Soviets," *New York Times,* 24 July 1990; Peter S. Green, "Cleaning up After the Soviet Army," *U.S. News and World Report,* 28 May 1990; Vera Rich, "Departing Red Army Leaves its Rubbish Behind," *New Scientist,* 2 June 1990; "Alles Zerwühlt und Kaputt," "Das wird eine Gratwanderung," and "Die Fliegen als Erste Raus," all in *Der Spiegel,* 16 July 1990; "Environmental Inspectors to Visit Soviet Bases," Foreign Broadcast Information Service (FBIS) Daily Report/Soviet Union, Rosslyn, Va., 30 Aug. 1990; "Pollution Problems in Soviet Army Units Viewed," FBIS Daily Report/Soviet Union, 5 Sept. 1990; "Survey on Environmental Damage Left by Soviet Army," JPRS-TEN-91-017, 13 Sept. 1991: 32.

50. "Secrecy Hides the Hazards of Working in the Aerospace Industry," *New Scientist,* 8 April 1989; Kenneth B. Noble, "Health Troubles at Military Plant Add Mystery to Top-Secret Project," *New York Times,* 18 Sept. 1988; K. Geiser, "Health Hazards in the Micro-Electronics Industry," *International Journal of Health Services,* 16, No. 1, 1986.

51. "Defending the Environment? The Record of the U.S. Military," *The Defense Monitor,* 18, No. 6, 1989; Howard Ball, "Downwind from the Bomb," *New York Times Magazine,* 9 Feb. 1986; Keith Schneider, "Atom Tests' Legacy of Grief: Workers See Betrayal on Peril," *New York Times,* 14 Dec. 1989; Keith Schneider, "U.S. Admits Peril of 40's Emissions at A-Bomb Plant," *New York Times,* 12 July 1990; Francis X. Clines, "Soviets Now Admit '57 Nuclear Blast," *New York Times,* 18 June 1989.

52. U.S. warhead production and plutonium and enriched uranium stockpiles from Cochran et al., *Nuclear Weapons Databook, Vol. II;* Cochran et al., *Nuclear Weapons Databook, Vol. IV: Soviet Nuclear Weapons* (New York: Ballinger, 1989); and from "Status of Major Nuclear Weapons Production Facilities: 1990," *PSR Monitor* (Washington, D.C.: Physicians for Social Responsibility), September 1990. Waste products per kilogram of plutonium from Karen Dorn Steele, "Hanford: America's Nuclear Graveyard," *Bulletin of the Atomic Scientists,* October 1989. Military portion by volume from "Defending the Environment? The Record of the U.S. Military"; military portion by curies from Scott Saleska et al., *Nuclear Legacy: An Overview of the Places, Problems and Politics of Radioactive Waste in the United States* (Washington, D.C.: Public Citizen Critical Mass Energy Project, 1989). U.S. high-level inventory from Radioactive Waste Campaign, *Deadly Defense* (New York: Radioactive Waste Campaign) 1988.

53. Number of contaminated sites from Committee to Provide Interim Oversight of the DoE Nuclear Weapons Complex, Commission on Physical Sciences, Mathematics, and Resources, National Research Council, *The Nuclear Weapons Complex: Management for Health, Safety, and the Environment* (Washington, D.C.: National Academy Press, 1989); number of locations from Keith Schneider, "In the Trail of the Nuclear Arms Industry," *New York Times,* 26 Aug. 1990; Nagasaki bomb comparison from Michael Satchell, "Uncle Sam's Toxic Folly," *U.S. News and World Report,* 27 March 1989; plutonium in Rocky Flats ventilation ducts from Matthew L. Wald, "Doubt on Safety at Weapon Plant," *New York Times,* 21 June 1990; 1969 fire from Fox Butterfield, "Dispute on Wastes Poses Threat to Weapons Plant," *New York Times,* 21 Oct. 1988.

54. Matthew L. Wald, "Hanford's Atom Waste Tanks Could Explode, Panel Warns," *New York Times,* 31 July 1990; Robert Alvarez and

Arjun Makhijani, "Hidden Legacy of the Arms Race: Radioactive Waste," *Technology Review*, August/September 1989.

55. Larry Thompson, "Scientists Reassess the Long-Term Impact of Radiation," *Washington Post*, 15 Aug. 1990; "ICRP to Recommend More Stringent Human Radiation Exposure Limits," *Multinational Environment Outlook*, 16 Oct. 1990.

56. Martin Tolchin, "U.S. to Release Health Data on Nuclear Plant Workers," *New York Times*, 24 May 1989. "New Agreement Could Continue Department of Energy's Monopoly Over Radiation Health Research," *News Alert*, Physicians for Social Responsibility (PSR), Washington, D.C., 26 Oct. 1990; Daryl Kimball, Associate Director for Policy, PSR, Washington, D.C., private communication, 2 November 1990. Office of Technology Assessment, *Complex Cleanup: The Environmental Legacy of Nuclear Weapons Production* (Washington, D.C., February 1991).

57. Matthew L. Wald, "High Radiation Doses Seen for Soviet Arms Workers," *New York Times*, 16 Aug. 1990; Bill Keller, "Soviet City, Home of the A-Bomb, is Haunted by its Past and Future," *New York Times*, 10 July 1989; Zhores A. Medvedev, "The Environmental Destruction of the Soviet Union," *The Ecologist*, January/February 1990; Clines, "Soviets Now Admit '57 Nuclear Blast"; Vera Rich, "Thirty-Year Secret Revealed," *Nature*, 22 June 1989; David Dickson, "Kyshtym 'Almost as Bad as Chernobyl,'" *New Scientist*, December 23/30, 1989; Arjun Makhijani, Institute for Energy and Environmental Research, Takoma Park, Md., private communication, 23 October 1990.

58. The United States, the Soviet Union, and the United Kingdom stopped atmospheric tests in 1963 but France and China continued until 1974 and 1980, respectively. Number of tests from Stockholm International Peace Research Institute (SIPRI), *SIPRI Yearbook 1991: World Armaments and Disarmament*, tables 2A.2 and 2A.3. Birth defects from Barry Commoner, "Do Nuclear Plants Make Deadly Neighbors?" *Congressional Record*, 23 March 1972. Estimate of premature deaths from Bernd W. Kubbig, "Atomtests: Gefährdung für Mensch und Umwelt," in Bechmann, *Umwelt Braucht Frieden*. "Venting" from John Hanrahan, "Testing Ground," *Common Cause Magazine*, January/February 1989, and from "A Nuclear Unthreat," *Economist*, 29 March 1986.

59. Soldiers from Kubbig, "Atomtests"; Kim, *The Quest,* reports a number of 250,000 soldiers; workers from Schneider, "U.S. Fund Set Up to Pay Civilians Injured by Atomic Arms Program," *New York Times,* October 16, 1990; downwinders and their health effects from Ball, "Downwind from the Bomb"; Richard L. Miller, "Let's Not Forget Radiation in the U.S." *New York Times,* 27 June 1986, op-ed; Americans' exposure from Keith Schneider, "Senate Panel Describes Data on Nuclear Risks," *New York Times,* 3 Aug. 1989. Results of U.S. tests in Pacific from Ian Anderson, "Potassium Could Cover Up Bikini's Radioactivity," *New Scientist,* 10 Dec. 1988; Eliot Marshall, "Fallout from Pacific Tests Reaches Congress," *Science,* 14 July 1989. French tests from Bengt Danielsson, "Poisoned Pacific: The Legacy of French Nuclear Testing," *Bulletin of the Atomic Scientists,* March 1990. Australia from Ian Anderson, "Britain Asked to Foot its Nuclear Cleaning Bill," *New Scientist,* 31 Aug. 1991: 9. Semipalatinsk from Quinn-Judge, "Soviet Writers Blast Nuclear Testing"; from Olzhas Suleymenov, "We Cannot Be Silent," *Earth Island Journal,* Summer 1989; from Judith Perera, "Soviet Environmentalists Cite Health Problems Around Nuclear Testing Ground," *Multinational Environmental Outlook,* 5 Sept. 1989; from "Soviet Official Reveals Increased Radiation Hazard Near Semipalatinsk," JPRS-TEN-90-017 Soviet Union, 6 Dec. 1990: 79; and from Susan E. Reed, "Atomic Lake," *The New Republic,* 28 Oct. 1991: 12.

60. From Alexandri Remisov, "Disarmament Treaties and Conversion of Military Production in USSR," *IDOC Internazionale,* September/October 1988.

61. Institute for Defense and Disarmament Studies, *The Arms Control Reporter 1990* (Cambridge, Mass.: IDDS, 1990), section 407.B.

62. William Broad, "New Methods Sought to Dispose of Rockets With No Harm to Earth," *New York Times,* 17 Sept. 1991. Broad briefly discusses some of the alternatives examined.

63. Stephen Iwan Griffiths, "The Implementation of the INF Treaty," SIPRI, *SIPRI Yearbook 1990: World Armaments and Disarmament* (Oxford: Oxford University Press, 1990), 457.

64. Keith Schneider, "U.S. Plan to Burn Chemical Weapons Stirs Public Fear," *New York Times,* 29 April 1991; "Chemical Weapons Burn,"

Greenpeace Magazine, January/February 1991: 7; "Arms Controllers v. Greenpeace," *The Bulletin of the Atomic Scientists,* November 1990: 4–6.

65. Hazards of ammunition production from Vertegaal, "Environmental Impact of Dutch Military Activities." Ammunition stockpiles from Burckhardt J. Huck, "Abrüstung und Konversion in Deutschland," and from Werner Hänsel and Heinz Michael, "Rüstungskonversion in den Neuen Bundesländern," both in *Informationsdienst Wissenschaft und Frieden,* December 1990: 62; and from "Ecological Damage Caused by Withdrawing Soviet Soldiers," JPRS-UPA-91-010, West Europe, 11 June 1991: 91.

66. "U.S. Chemical Weapons Production: Poisoning the Atmosphere," *The Defense Monitor,* 18, No. 3 (1989): 5; Schneider, "U.S. Plan to Burn Chemical Weapons Stirs Public Fear," from Keith Schneider, "Military Has New Strategic Goal in Cleanup of Vast Toxic Waste," *New York Times,* 5 Aug. 1991; and Walter Goodman, "The Special Horror of Chemical War," *New York Times,* 23 Oct. 1990. German ammunition destruction costs from Huck, "Abrüstung und Konversion in Deutschland," and from "Die US-amerikanischen und sowjetischen Streitkräfte hinterlassen," 13.

67. Nuclear decontamination costs from "Problems Persist at Weapons Plants," *PSR Monitor,* September 1990. Toxic cleanup estimate from Siegel, "The Growing Nightmare of Military Toxics." Hungarian damage estimate from "Hungary, Soviet Union in Negotiations on Environmental Damage Caused by Troops," *International Environmental Reporter,* 14 Aug. 1991: 437. Czechoslovak estimate from "Cost of Ecological Damage by Soviet Troops," JPRS-TEN-91-015, 7 Aug. 1991: 32. Poland from "Environmental Damage Caused by Soviet Forces Assessed," JPRS-TEN-91-014, 9 July 1991. East German estimate from "Alles Zerwühlt und Kaputt," 121. Australia from Anderson, "Britian Asked to Foot its Nuclear Cleaning Bill."

68. Nevada example from Bert Lindler, "Foes Unite to Fight Military Proposal," *High Country News,* 12 Feb. 1990. Land rehabilitation cost from Edward McGlinn, Anglers of the Au Sable River, Grayling, Mich., private communication, 18 Feb. 1990. Robert Stone from Andrew Melnykovich, "Torn Between Cows and Jets," *High Country News,* 12 Feb. 1990.

69. For a more detailed discussion of the requirements of sustainability, see Michael Renner, *Jobs in a Sustainable Economy,* Worldwatch Paper 104 (Washington, D.C.: Worldwatch Institute, September 1991).

70. For spinoff claims, see for example William J. Broad, "Defense Industry Goes Hustling to Make a Buck Without the Bang," *New York Times,* 8 April 1990.

71. Mary Kaldor, *The Baroque Arsenal* (New York: Hill and Wang, 1981).

72. "A Healthy Military-Industrial Complex," *U.S. News and World Report,* 12 Feb. 1990: 43.

73. Michael Closson, "Expanded Horizons," *Plowshare Press* 15, No. 2 (Spring 1990): 4.

74. David Thomas, "Brussels Backs Down on 'Eco-Audit,'" *Financial Times,* 5 April 1991; "Öko-Audit: EG-Vorschlag für Betriebliche Umwelt-Kontrolle," *Ökologische Briefe,* No. 23, 5 June 1991.

4

The Obstacles to Real Security: Military Corporatism and the Cold War State

Gregory A. Bischak

Introduction

The national security state stands as the enduring legacy of the Cold War, representing the concentrated powers of the war-making institutions in the United States government, economy, and society. The continued influence of these institutions constitutes the most formidable obstacles to demobilizing from the Cold War and converting the military economy to civilian use. It has often been argued that the vested political and economic interests that have historically benefited from this system of power will resist any serious curtailment of the military's forces and with it the level of military spending.[1] Yet, the current situation offers some hope that this system of power might be dismantled as the ending of the Cold War has weakened the cohesive forces that have held together the national security state over the last forty-five years.

The ending of the Cold War seriously undermines the rationale for the continuance of a highly militarized national security policy. Yet, the institutionalization of the national security state makes a transition to a post-Cold War security policy extremely difficult. For these reasons it is necessary to understand the origins and dynamics of the national security state. Moreover, it is important to examine the vulnerabilities of the national security state after the Cold War, especially its emerging legitimation crises flowing from the collapse of the Soviet Union, and with it, the whole rationale of the arms race. These crises have further undermined the other legs of the national security state, namely, the practice of using military spending to stimulate the economy and the need for a high level of mobilization of the nation's science and technological resources.

The national security state secured its social support and legitimation by giving important sectors of society an economic stake in national security policy and by drawing together these social interests into consultative structures to advance this policy. This process of incorporating key sectors of society into a national security apparatus can be deemed a type of military corporatism. In this chapter, I will examine how military-serving science-based firms, organized labor, and elements of the scientific community became systemically incorporated into the decision-making process that shaped and supported the national security state. Of particular interest is how the junior partner, organized labor, was important in legitimating the policy and in controlling dissent. The respective roles of the major interest groups will be examined to show how they benefitted from the policies of military Keynesianism, the nuclear arms race, and perpetuation of anti-communism. Each of these policies has been antithetical to disarmament and conversion and even today exerts a powerful influence on the process of demobilizing from the Cold War.

Military Corporatism

It is the thesis of this chapter that through the national security state, science-based corporations together with state managers, organized labor, and branches of the physical sciences have been involved in a co-prosperity alliance founded on the military policies of the Cold War era.[2] The central material fact of the national security state's military corporatist policy was that the core participants all had an economic stake in the arrangement. Political leaders could counteract, to some degree, capitalism's business cycles by manipulating the levels of military spending; corporate leaders in military-related industries benefitted directly, while other business interests benefitted indirectly by ensuring the expansion of domestic markets. Meanwhile, international business interests were assured that the military apparatus guaranteed the international rules of the game. In exchange for labor peace, organized labor was guaranteed a lucrative field for union membership in high-paying jobs. The physical sciences enjoyed an unprecedented high level of governmental support for basic and applied research, while the engineering professions benefitted from expanded employment in developing new weapons systems in military-related industries. Meanwhile, state bureaucratic elites presided over an expanding bureaucracy of increasing military, economic, and political importance.

At its core, key representatives from the class interests comprising the central participants in the national security state's division of labor were incorporated into a hierarchical system. This included key corporations in high-tech and primary industries, the peak organizations of organized labor, the leading representatives of the sciences (especially the physical sciences), the bureaucratic state elites controlling the largest and most militarily important technological assets, and the political leadership of political parties and government. Each of these constituencies benefitted from an expansion of military spending.

These interests were incorporated into a neo-corporatist style of consultation on issues of national security policy making.[3] The central policy-making concerns of these military corporatist interests were the perpetuation of the strategic East-West confrontation and the specification of the size and composition of the military budget, especially the research and development and weapons-procurement budgets.

Both formal and informal governmental and non-governmental bodies have performed key functions in the national security state for representation and consultation, mobilization and legitimation, and decision making. These formal bodies include the obvious governmental agencies of the national security state such as the Department of Defense, Atomic Energy Commission and Department of Energy, NASA, the Central Intelligence Agency, and numerous other agencies of the federal government.[4] In addition, by design and accretion other bodies have grown up both within and outside the government to shape and direct policy. A large part of this has occurred through the extension of presidential powers and through informal or covert operations within government.[5] A more routine and direct form of interest representation by business, science, and labor occurred through deliberations during congressional hearings and the policy-making work of expert panels appointed to detail major legislative and organizational policy changes. Alongside this process there has grown the well-known activities of overt lobbying and influence outside government through industrial trade associations, science and technology groups, and other channels.

The intersection of these social interests within the military-related state structures established a close working relationship among representatives from all apsects of the technical division of labor in military industry. Together, state managers and scientists in the federal agencies, business leaders from science-based firms, and organized labor have participated in promoting public acceptance of Cold War military policy and in endorsing high levels of military spending.

I advance the thesis of neo-corporatist industrial policy making to account for the pattern and stability of national security policy making. Neo-corporatist industrial policy has been characterized by Leo Panitch as a form of state economic intervention that is promoted and planned by leading organizations of interest representation, such as trade associations, trade unions, professional associations, and regulatory bodies, that are functionally related to the policy-making issues in question by virtue of their respective positions within the industry's technical division of labor.[6] These leading organizations of interest representation are sometimes called "peak associations." Accordingly, I argue that national security policy making has historically exemplified the features of neo-corporatist policy, with leading science-based firms representing key military industries and the peak associations of organized labor representing the majority of employees within these industries through the AFL and CIO (American Federation of Labor and Congress of Industrial Organizations). Further, these unions were accorded a consultative status in national security policy making because of their pivotal role in developing military industry, and moreover, because labor support helped to ensure wider public acceptance for large-scale government subvention of defense industries. Furthermore, the potential hazards to public health of nuclear technology made it all the more necessary for the government to enlist labor's participation so as to legitimize the industry and to assure public acceptance of the policy.

I should note here that contrary to some neo-corporatist theorists who hold that all parties in such corporatist consultation should have equal standing and input in policy making, I subscribe to the view advanced by Panitch that corporatist arrangements are usually hierarchical, with representive standing being asymmetical and constrained.[7] As I will show, labor's role was constrained by national security and scientific-technical issues, which often marginalized its contributions to the policy-making process. Nevertheless, labor was never completely ostracized because to do so might threaten to delegitimize the whole policy-making process.

Finally, military corporatism grew up as a variant of the broader form of economic corporatism that developed during the late stages of the Great Depression and became widely accepted after World War II. Kees van der Pijl, a Dutch political scientist, has argued that the heritage of the New Deal was the formation of an alliance among big business, organized labor, and the government that salvaged American capitalism by striking a productivity deal among these class interests.[8] This type of corporate liberalism was supported by international finance interests together with those domestic industrial sectors that depended on growing mass-consumption markets, principally in automobiles, electronics, and chemicals. Social peace was based on a high-growth and high-wage economy, which was achieved through the continuous modernization of mass production and the stabilization of the economy by government intervention to maintain employment and the overall level of demand. In this context, military Keynesianism was but one expression of the broader phenomenon of this productivity deal, which in this instance secured domestic markets for the science-based industries that produced high-tech military equipment in electronics, aircraft, instrumentation, chemicals, and the automobile industries. This model of economic growth and social integration was further extended through the development and projection of American military power to Western Europe to cement the trans-Atlantic alliance.

This account will focus on four aspects of military corporatism. First, I will examine the role of these social interests in promoting the practice of military Keynesianism to stimulate the economy throughout the Cold War era, with a special focus on the role played by key science-based firms in developing military industry. In addition the often conflicting tendencies within organized labor will be examined to show how the unionization of military industry workers by AFL and CIO labor federations functioned to forge a unified labor position on national security policy. Second, I show how military interests profited from and advanced weapons development, as well as harnessed science and technology for the Cold War. This will be shown through examination of industrial, employment, and budgetary trends in military spending, as well as by the role of these interests in public policy hearings before Congress on substantive policy issues. Third, I will examine how the vested interests of corporations, scientific research enterprises and laboratories, and organized labor have undermined public support for economic conversion. Fourth, there are several latent legitimation crises that have historically plagued the national security state and today represent a real threat to its continued existence.

Military Keynesianism

Following the Second World War, fear of renewed depression led policymakers to tentatively adopt the economic policy prescriptions of John Maynard Keynes, which called for government intervention to maintain employment and the overall level of economic activity through a combination of fiscal and monetary policies.[9] At first, the widely accepted objective of this approach was to maintain full employment through income-maintenance policies, public-works investments, and the regulation of interest rates to stimulate private investment. However, opposition quickly grew in the business community to an overreliance on full-employment policies because it involved increased economic intervention by the government, increased public competition with private interests for investment resources, and because such policies undermined the "normal" discipline of the labor market by removing the threat of unemployment.[10]

Indeed, the reliance on full-employment policies to counteract the onset of recession was never fully accepted by policy-makers, although these policies forestalled an economic slump after the Second World War because massive wartime deficit spending created large savings that were spent after the war and because income-maintenance policies, like the GI Bill, were implemented. Significantly, the concept and the term "full" was dropped from the Employment Act of 1946, due to opposition by many conservative interests.[11] Many business leaders expressed dislike for expanded government spending and argued that it should be confined to investments that would not compete with the private sector, such as roads, bridges, hospitals, and armaments. Of course, there are limits to the extent of such investments, which eventually reach saturation. Moreover, government spending that subsidizes consumption was seen as threatening to undermine the economic incentives of the labor market, and was therefore deemed unacceptable by many business interests.

The alternative to a permanent full-employment policy was a more restrained use of government intervention to stimulate the economy and an increased reliance on military spending as a means to regulate the level of economic activity; this approach has been characterized by some as "military Keynesianism."[12] Military spending is virtuous from the vantage point of the private sector because arms production does not directly compete with private production, nor is there the prospect of technological obsolescence because competitive rearmament requires continual modernization.

Before the onset of the Korean War, some prominent policy-makers began to embrace increased military spending as necessary to ensure permanent mobilization and as a means to stimulate key sectors of the economy. Perhaps the most notable statement of this policy came in the National Security Council report known as NSC-68, which called for permanent mobilization of the economy and society for war making against the Soviet Union.[13] A lesser-known but nonetheless influential report came from the Air Policy commission, which was appointed by President Truman in 1947. It argued that "(t)his country, if it is to have even relative security, must be ready for war. Moreover, it must be ready for modern war. It must be ready not for World War II, but for a possible World War III."[14]

This policy principally benefitted the science-based defense sectors, particularly in aircraft, electronics, radio and communications, and instrumentation, as well as the older established sectors in shipbuilding, primary metals, and the automobile industry. But higher military spending also had the collateral benefit of providing stimulus to the rest of the economy. Throughout the 1950s and 1960s, this doctrine proved somewhat successful as a means to regulate the level of economic activity through changes in military spending. Indeed, it was the observable effect of changes in military spending that led many to embrace it as an effective government tool to counter business cycles. This is not to suggest that the government exclusively relied on military spending to counter the business cycle, but rather, that it played an increasingly prominent role in the fiscal policies of the federal government.

Nowhere was this view more strongly embraced than by the presidency of Ronald Reagan, who called for a sustained military buildup. Economic pressures on the domestic economy compounded the appeal of renewed military spending, as the sagging domestic manufacturing sectors were reeling from increased international competition and an erosion of domestic market shares in civilian markets. Thus, the planned expansion of military spending readily filled the needs of the durable-goods sectors for alternative domestic markets.[15] As a result, the main military-serving industries became the central beneficiaries of the debt-financed fiscal policy that fueled economic growth in the period. During the Reagan buildup, military spending increased in real terms by fifty percent. Together with the short-term economic stimulus provided by the massive deficits engendered by Reagan's fiscal policy, military spending provided a burst of economic growth, which strengthened the conventional wisdom that military spending was good for the economy.

But military Keynesian policies have established a dubious historical record for their contribution to the performance of the U.S. economy. From 1950 through the mid 1960s (see figure 1), military spending probably stimulated the overall level of economic activity. But after the mid 1960s, it became an increasingly narrow basis to regulate the economy, with the stimulative effects becoming confined to certain military industries. Moreover, as a large body of evidence indicates, military spending has clearly exerted a negative effect on the level and rate of private fixed investment in the United States, thus contributing to lower economic performance.[16] Meanwhile, the absorption of between one-quarter and nearly one-half of total research and development funding by the military (see figure 2) has had a cumulative, deleterious effect on the pattern of research and innovation in the U.S. economy, leading to fewer productivity-enhancing innovations. Thus, by the late 1960s, in the midst of the Vietnam War, the demand stimulus from military spending began to be offset, if not swamped, by the long-run depletionary effects of devoting critical industrial and technological resources to the military.

Yet, despite the protracted winding down of military spending after Vietnam, this critical view of military Keynesianism did not become generally accepted. Indeed, the conventional wisdom about the economic merits of military spending persisted and was gradually reasserted during the Reagan military buildup. The persistence of the military Keynesian view is largely a product of the vested interests of those who have historically benefitted from militarism. These vested interests stand at the center of the corporatist arrangement that has successfully reasserted military concerns and continues to defend the high plateau of military spending after the Cold War. For these reasons it is important to examine nature and role of the prinicipal interests comprising military corporatism: the military-serving corporations, state managers, the scientific community, and organized labor.

Business Interests and the National Security State

At the heart of most critical accounts of the rise of the national security state stand powerful economic interests, especially the military-serving

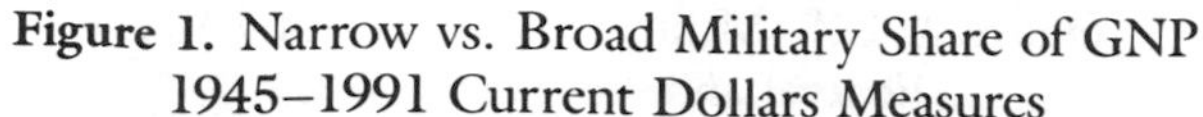

Figure 1. Narrow vs. Broad Military Share of GNP 1945–1991 Current Dollars Measures

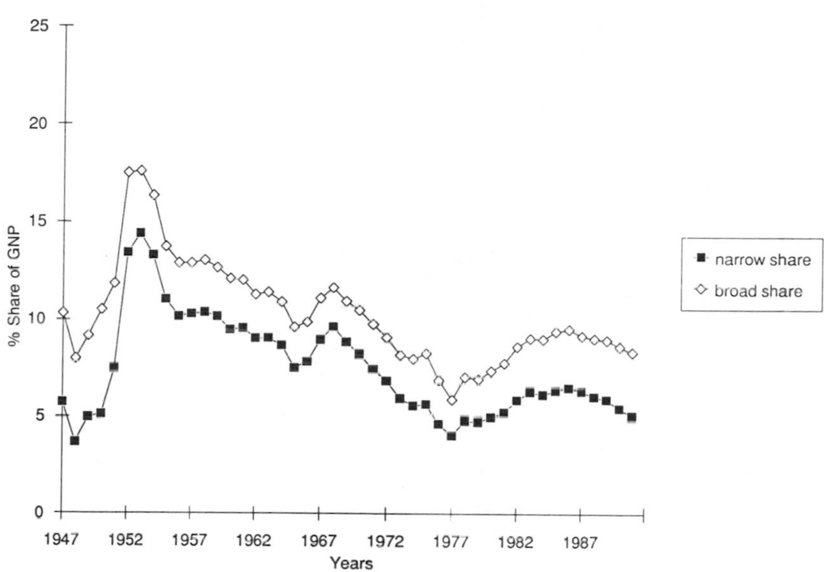

Source: Calculated from the Office of Management and Budget, *Historical Tables of the Budget of the United States Government Fiscal Years 1990 and 1991* (Washington, D.C.: Government Printing Office, January 1989 and January 1990), tables 3.3 and 15.1.

corporations. Contrary to the mainstream view within economics and political science, which holds that the extent of national security spending depends on public choice, alternative theories have argued that influential economic interests have determined the size and composition of military spending. In particular, some have argued that the military-serving corporations have been the dominant factor accounting for the persistence of high levels of military spending, protecting their interests by lobbying and influencing Congress.[17] Others have argued more generally that the capitalist system requires a permanent war economy, which acts as an economic support to counteract its tendencies towards economic stagnation.[18] A different economic motivation for military spending is advanced by those who argue that the threatened use of military force enhances domestic profitability by improving the terms of trade for U.S. firms relative to their competitors.[19] Still another perspective argues that

Figure 2. U.S. Military Share of Total R&D
Federal and Industrial R&D

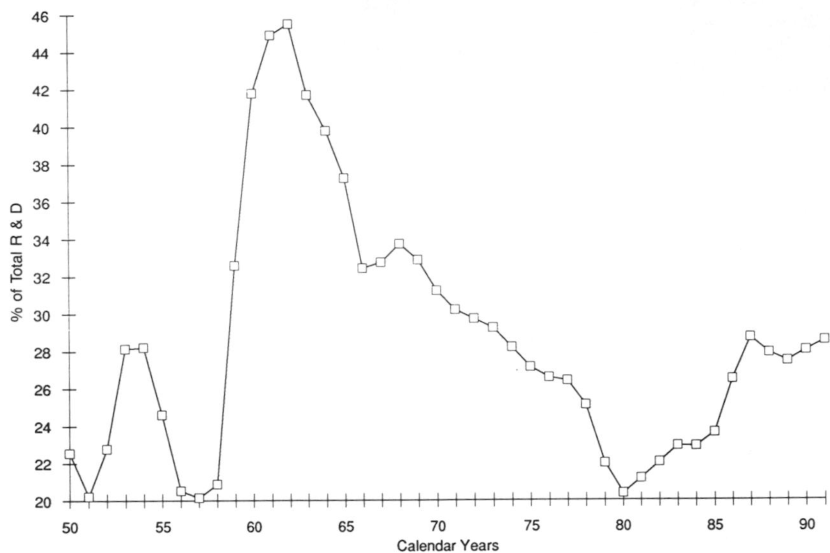

Source: National Science Foundation Review of Data on Research and Development, no. 33, (Washington, D.C.: National Science Foundation, April 1962), table 1; and National Science Board, *Science and Engineering Indicators –1991,* (Washington D.C., National Science Board, December, 1991) table 4.3.

U.S. militarism has essentially guaranteed the conditions of political stability necessary to promote the internationalization of capital. Thus, these last two perspectives hold that nonmilitary corporations also benefit from a permanent and sizable U.S. military establishment.[20]

We have already argued that military corporatism succeeded in welding together a diverse domestic constituency precisely because military spending was able to stimulate key domestic sectors of the economy, while providing a more general stimulus to the economy. This, however, was more generally the case during the first half of the Cold War period when defense constituted a relatively larger share of economic activity, and when the technological innovations of the defense industry were more readily transferred to the civilian economy. But as military spending became less of a general economic stimulus and more of a drag on economic performance, particularly private investment, the broader benefits of military spending have dwindled.[21] And while the maintenance and use of military force has helped to secure advantageous international terms of trade for U.S. producers vis-à-vis our trading partners, these more general economic benefits have been partially offset by the drain on the balance of payments of maintaining a large overseas military establishment.[22] Finally, U.S. militarism has fostered the internationalization of capital by guaranteeing the international conditions for trade, thereby enhancing the United States' bargaining position with other leading capitalist countries on a whole range of international political, financial, and economic issues.[23] But these advantages have eroded as the domestic economic power of the U.S. economy has declined relative to our chief competitor.

Accordingly, both domestic and international factors have contributed to the rise and stability of the national security state. However, the depleting effects of military spending on the domestic economy coupled with the growing internationalization of U.S. investment have narrowed the domestic basis of support for military spending.

The chief beneficiaries of domestic military spending have been the science-based firms that performed most of the research and development for new weaponry and that have been the prime contractors for much of the major procurement of these weapons. These firms possessed the unique capabilities necessary to conduct the research and to produce the high-tech equipment that the arms race demanded. In this regard, it is important to assess the nature and stability of military industry's structure in order to ascertain the extent to which the industry as a whole might act as a concerted and cohesive force in shaping policy.

The Structure of Military Industry

Two types of military-serving firms have dominated military industry throughout the Cold War: the highly militarily dependent science-based firm almost exclusively dedicated to military business; and the multidivisional firm, which operates large military divisions that supply significant, albeit usually minority shares, of the corporate revenues. These two types of large, high-tech firms have characterized the top 100 firms that together have accounted for over two-thirds of all prime military contracts during the 1964–1990 period. Indeed, representation among the top twenty-five military-serving firms has been remarkably stable, as table 5 indicates, with fifteen of these firms maintaining their positions in the top rungs of the industry throughout the 1964–90 period.

Table 5. Top Twenty-five Military Contractors and Subsidaries by Rank Based on Prime Contract Awards for Selected Years

Rank	1964	1970	1986	1990
1.	Lockheed	Lockheed	General Dynamics	McDonnell Douglas
2.	Boeing Co.	General Dynamics	General Electric	General Dynamics
3.	McDonnell Aircraft	General Electric	McDonnell Douglas	General Electric
4.	North American Aviation	AT & T	Rockwell Intern'l	General Motors
5.	General Dynamics	McDonnell Douglas	General Motors	Raytheon
6.	General Electric	United Aircraft	Lockheed	Lockheed
7.	AT & T	N. American Rockwell	Raytheon	Martin Marietta
8.	United Aircraft	Grumman	Boeing	United Tech.
9.	Martin Marietta	Litton Ind.	United Tech.	Grumman
10.	Newport News	Hughes Air.	Grumman	Tenneco
11.	Grumman Corp.	LTV Corp.	Martin Marietta	Boeing
12.	Sperry Rand	Boeing Co.	Honeywell	Westinghouse
13.	General Tire & Rubber	Textron	Westinghouse	Rockwell Intern'l
14.	IBM	Westinghouse	Textron	Litton Ind.
15.	Hughes Aircraft	Sperry Rand	Litton Ind.	Honeywell
16.	Avco Corp.	Honeywell	Sperry Co.	Unisys Corp.
17.	Bendix Corp.	General Motors	LTV Corp.	GTE Corp.
18.	IT & T	Raytheon	Texas Instru.	IBM
19.	General Motors	Ford Motor	IBM	Textron
20.	Thickol Chemicals	Avco Corp.	Eaton Corp.	LTV Corp.
21.	Raytheon Co.	American Motors	TRW	GENCORP
22.	LTV Inc.	RCA	Allied-Signal	TRW
23.	Westinghouse Electric	General Tire & Rubber	GTE Corp.	AT & T

Table 5. *(continued)*

Rank	1964	1970	1986	1990
24.	RCA	IBM	Royal Dutch Petroleum	IT & T
25.	GT & E	R. Morrison Knudsen	AT & T	Ford Motor
Top 100 Companies Cumulative Percentage	73.4%	69.74%	72.5%	66.28%

Source: U.S. Department of Defense, *Prime Contract Awards for the Top 100 Firms, 1964, 1970, 1986 and 1990,* (Washington D.C.: Government Printing Office, 1965, 1971, 1987, 1991).

Throughout the peaks and troughs of military procurement, there has been a striking continuity among the science-based firms representing the military-industrial suppliers from the aerospace, defense electronics, and transportation industries. And while some firms may have fallen out of the top twenty-five, virtually all have remained among the top hundred prime contracting firms, unless they have been absorbed by mergers or takeovers. Meanwhile, new entrants into the top ranks of military-serving firms resemble in strategies and structure the firms that have traditionally dominated the industry. Thus, there has been a remarkably stable structure to the industry that has, some have argued, promoted a political cohesiveness among these business interests in advancing military spending priorities.

The Politics of the Military-Industrial Complex

One popularly held view sees the military-industrial complex as an interlocking set of interests involving military-serving businesses, the Pentagon, and congress, which together have perpetuated military spending to the mutual benefit of each participant.[24] Military firms collaborate through a number of trade associations such as American Defense Preparedness Association, the National Security Industrial Association, the Aerospace Industries Association, and the Electronic Industries Associations.

Sometimes dubbed an "iron triangle," this relationship is comprised of ostensibly co-equal partners representing military-serving corporations, the top decision-makers in the Pentagon, and the Armed Services Committees from both houses of Congress (as well as the budget committees and representatives from military districts).[25] A number of contacts are established among these three interests through advisory committees, hearings, trade associations, direct lobbying, and campaign contributions. Yet, such elite theories implicitly assume that the military-serving corporations are the dominant actors in the process, with the Pentagon subsidizing the lobbying process. Furthermore, the links between the military-serving corporations and the Pentagon are reinforced by the frequent interchange of personnel, with many former military personnel moving into corporate positions to deal with military contracts and other matters.

The corporations exercise greater control over the whole process by shaping the arms race itself through the research and development programs that they manage, thereby ensuring them with lucrative follow-on procurement contracts.[26] National security requirements impose a high level of secrecy on such research, thereby removing many of these programs from public scrutiny. Review of these research programs is usually limited to closed committee hearings by select members of Congress. Thus, in this view Congress is more of a passive actor in the process, albeit the actor that controls the pursue strings.[27] However, the chairmen of the armed services committees benefit from the expansion of the military budget and therefore have an interest in playing along.

On the surface, this political account seems appealing since it focuses on the most visible and influential actors in the military decision-making process. Indeed, many of the elements of this account clearly reflect the way military decision making is conducted.[28] Yet, this account fails to show how such a process can maintain its legitimacy and stability over time. Moreover, such elite theories of the military decision-making process omit several key interests, including the scientific community, organized labor, and the media, all of whom have played important roles in the development and maintenance of the military system. By contrast, the military corporatist approach attempts to account for how these other social interests have contributed to the development and legitimation of the national security state.

Central to the success of military corporatism in maintaining the legitimacy of the system is the way in which the policy-making process has appeared to be open because the scientific community, organized labor, and other interests have been consulted on major decisions that may affect them. Clearly, the endorsement of the key players in the division of labor has enhanced public acceptance of major policies, particularly those that involve the procurement of expensive new weapons systems promising the creation of jobs. Furthermore, bipartisan agreement on major policy issues has added to the appearance of openness, despite the fact that many of the basic assumptions about United States foreign and military policy have been largely closed to debate and discussion within each political party since the onset of the Cold War.[29]

This closing off to public accountability has been questioned on several occasions during the Cold War as popular pressure and mobilization by citizens and grass-roots organizations have taken exception to the assumptions underlying the nation's foreign and military policies. On these occasions, Congress has often been motivated to initiate investigations, reforms, and sometimes an outright change in certain policies. These instances, where the ranks of military corporatism have splintered and the politics of national security decision making have been opened, have posed major legitimation crises for the national security state—a subject to which we will return in the concluding section of this chapter. The point to be made here is that corporatist political arrangements have made the decision-making process more complex and less rigid than the elite theorists have often suggested, which has made fundamental change more difficult, although not impossible.

Another layer is added to the political fabric of the national security state, and to the debate over its character, by a consideration of the role of the national security managers who have promoted the military doctrines that have helped to justify the arms race during the course of the Cold War.

National Security State Managers

The unprecedented growth of the state's security apparatus during the Cold War was fueled by three factors: the confrontation of state socialism and capitalism; the mobilization of science to continuously innovate new weaponry, especially strategic weaponry; and the practice of military Keynesianism, which provided an economic stimulus in the short run. As a result, the power of the national security state managers grew, permitting the extension of the military's command of resources. Some have argued that these managers have become so powerful that they have become the pivotal agents in determining national security policy.

So influential are these national security state managers that some theorists have postulated that they have gained control of key sectors of the economy to install a type of state capitalism.[30] Under this state capitalist formation, the nation's economic resources have been mobilized to expand the basis of power for the state managers through the ongoing militarization of the economy. Meanwhile, advocates of this state capitalism theory hold that the leading science-based military-serving private firms have fallen under the de facto control of the Pentagon as they have become dependent on military contracts for their economic livelihood.

There can be little doubt that the military and civilian professionals within the Pentagon, and their supporters in Congress and the executive branch, have sought to promote the expansion of military spending and their own bureaucratic control over resources. Indeed, the size and scope of the national security state has grown immensely during the Cold War, extending beyond the Department of Defense proper into the branches of the Departments of Energy, State, and Commerce, directly controlling other agencies such as Veterans Affairs, and influencing the policies of still other agencies such as NASA.[31] In addition, there are the various layers of the intelligence apparatus including the CIA, the National Security Agency, the Defense Intelligence Agency, the National Reconnaissance Office, and each of the individual services' intelligence operations.[32] Beyond these institutions lie the covert elements of the security apparatus, which have been sometimes termed the secret government.

In the economic realm there is little doubt that the military and its various institutional arms command formidable resources, including the majority of aerospace and shipbuilding production, and considerable shares of electronics, machinery, fabricated metal industries, and instrumentation production. The military-related aspects of manufacturing accounts for about 14 percent of total output. In addition, about one-third of all research and development funding in the United States is controlled by the military. By more comprehensive measures, the military controls at least 8.5 percent of the Gross National Product (GNP).[33]

Command of these resources has undoubtedly shaped the course of industry and technological change in the United States over the last forty-five years. Yet, it may be difficult to sustain the argument that the military state managers have actually installed a type of state capitalism in the economy. While the case can be made that militarily dependent corporations such as General Dynamics, McDonnell Douglas, and others are de facto controlled by the Pentagon, many of the other military-serving firms are multidivisional corporations that earn the majority of their revenues from their commercial divisions. These firms cultivate military business because it is profitable and provides another source of revenue besides their commercial divisions. It is more difficult to assert that these companies are under the de facto control of the Pentagon, even though their military divisions serve the Pentagon.

From the point view of the theory of military corporatism, the development of the military sectors of the economy was sustained by a set of mutually dependent historical, political, and economic factors that fostered the growth of these sectors and the state managers. Indeed, without the broader economic and political interest supporting the growth of the national security state, there is little reason to believe that it could have sustained its power. With these reservations, it is nevertheless clear that the state managers have exercised considerable influence over national economic policy, and are still seeking to maintain their control over these resources. Indeed, the critical basis of this control seems to lie in the technical resources that it commands.

The power of the state managers has been extended by the increasing reliance of the national security policy-making process on the technical expertise of a scientific strata within the bureaucracy to identify policy options and to determine in an allegedly technically neutral fashion the optimal policy.[34] The rise of the scientific technocracy within the national security apparatus has served to legitimate both the military doctrines and decisions themselves. Furthermore, technocratic decision making has served to justify the imposition of secrecy to protect any technological strategic advantage against our adversaries. Perhaps most importantly, the reliance on continuous scientific research to develop new and more powerful weapons has meant that the military has absorbed a very significant share of the nation's science and technology resources.

Labor's Role in Military Corporatism

From the inception of the national security state, labor has played a key role in national security policy making because of its position in the technical division of labor. Over the course of the forty-five years of industrial relations in military industries, the AFL and CIO have been the main organizations of interest representation for labor on national security policy issues. The AFL and CIO unions have represented the majority of workers in military-related industry throughout the Cold War,[35] and the union federation has marshalled union views on national security policy. Organized labor has generally supported increases in military spending because it has guaranteed a lucrative field of employment for industrial workers.

Public acceptance of national security policy and high levels of military spending rested in part upon the legitimacy bestowed by labor's participation. Indeed, the stability of military corporatism has been greatest when labor's views were generally consonant with other corporatist interests. Conversely, military corporatism has been most fragile when labor challenged key decisions of national security policy, particularly on such issues as disarmament policy and postwar reconversion planning.

Organized labor's views on the objectives and merits of military spending have been divided by political and economic issues within the various member unions. An early and decisive difference erupted over disarmament issues between pro-communist union leaders and the anti-communist forces within the industrial unions. Several other divisions emerged during the Cold War over issues of collective bargaining rights, job security, and health and safety, particularly relating to nuclear technologies. In the later stages of the Cold War differences began to emerge between the industrial unions and the service workers unions, as the expansion of military spending came at the expense of public-service-sector jobs. While at times these issues have opened fissures in labor's stand on military spending, by and large, the leading trade unions have supported the expansion of military production under the standard corporatist formula of job creation and economic growth.

A few years after World War II over 80 percent of the eligible workers in basic industries were organized by the two labor federations. Both AFL and CIO unions undertook organizing efforts throughout military industry. CIO unions were the most aggressive, led by the United Auto Workers (UAW) and the Oil, Gas, Coke, and Chemical Workers (later to become the Oil, Chemical and Atomic Energy Workers, OCAW). Of the former CIO unions that were expelled, the United Electrical Workers (UE) was the most active in military-related industries. The principal AFL unions were the International Brotherhood of Electrical Workers (IBEW), the International Association of Machinists (IAM), the Building and Construction Trades, and the Plumbers and Pipefitters Union.[36]

After the end of the Korean War, the growth of unionization in industry slowed, but the expansion of military spending to a higher postwar level made military industry one of the few growth sectors for unionization in the manufacturing economy. As figure 3 illustrates, after the Korean wartime peak, defense industry manufacturing employment settled to a plateau of around 12–14 percent. Employment growth came in the aircraft industry, radio and communications, ordnance, fabricated metal products, and the emerging atomic-weapons industry.

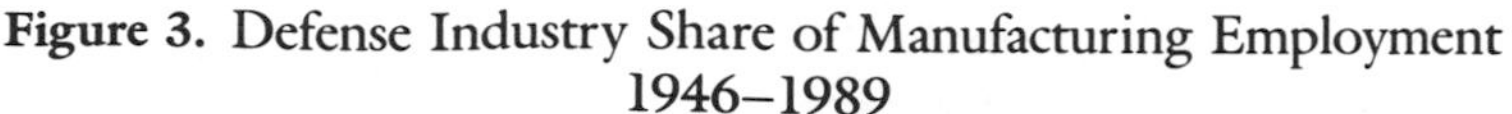

Figure 3. Defense Industry Share of Manufacturing Employment 1946–1989

Source: Calculated from Comptroller of the Department of Defense *National Defense Budget Estimates for Fiscal Years 1990 and 1991,* (Washington D.C.: Department of Defense, 1989 and 1990), table 7.7.

Following the merger of the AFL and CIO federations in 1955, the dominant trend was towards a thoroughgoing adherence to military Keyesianism, but some former CIO unions continued to call for general disarmament negotiations to diffuse the arms race. Meanwhile, the organizing gains from the expansion of military industry were largely due to the buildup of strategic bombers and nuclear weapons production. The UAW and the IAM garnered most of the membership gains from aircraft employment. Elsewhere in the nuclear fuel cycle the Metal Trades Council and OCAW managed to expand their unionization drives.

By the early 1960s, however, military-related industrial employment began to fall until the strategic missile buildup of the mid 1960s reversed the decline. This marked the beginning of a sustained increase in military-related industrial employment attending the Vietnam War. One countertendency was marked by the signing of the Partial Test Ban Treaty in 1963, which led to the termination of several plutonium production contacts and a severe reduction in nuclear weapons manufacturing employment. This event prompted some labor interest in the civil nuclear power program as a conversion opportunity, which in fact did provide some employment growth for nuclear-related unions in the 1960s.[37] Indeed, this conversion discussion resonated with the optimistic rhetoric that followed immediately after the Second World War, but it was not to be found more generally in the other unions that were benefitting from the Vietnam War buildup.

Post-Vietnam Conversion Initiatives by Labor

After the Vietnam War began to encounter widespread political opposition and the level of military spending began to be cut in 1969, organized labor revisited the idea of economic conversion. Indeed, Walter Reuther, then president of the UAW, issued his "Swords into Ploughshares" proposal for converting military industry to civilian production.[38] This initiative helped define the national debate over the downturn after the war, and began an effort to get some conversion legislation passed. While this effort succeeded in prompting study of the problem, little was done to implement a federal conversion program beyond some modest economic adjustment measures. Indeed, the failure of Congress to act, coupled with the opposition of the Nixon administration to a comprehensive plan, made the demobilization difficult for the nearly 1.5 million defense-industry workers that were laid off over the 1968–1976 period.

This experience had a profound effect on the trade-union movement, strengthening the resolve of some unions such as the Machinists and the UAW for putting in place a serious conversion program, while making other trade unionists wary of the promise of economic conversion. This legacy was carried into the debate over the proposed military buildup of the Reagan administration in the 1980s.

The Reagan Military Buildup

At the onset of the Reagan buildup an AFL-CIO sponsored survey found that over 60 percent of its membership surveyed did not support an increase in military spending.[39] This result partly reflected the changing composition of the union movement, as more members were represented in the public-sector work force. Since the military buildup was to come at the expense of social spending, the political arithmetic was all too easy for many trade unionists. Indeed, these unions, joined by the Machinist union, commissioned a study of the economic effects of the military buildup in order to evaluate the potential impacts.[40] The objective was to educate the union membership about the wider effects of military spending on the economy.

But as the buildup began in earnest, these unions turned their energies to oppose the strategic military buildup, particularly the MX missile.[41] Beyond opposing a senseless strategic arms race, the Machinists came to be in the vanguard of the conversion issue. Under the leadership of William Winpisinger, the Machinists advocated the development of a conversion program as a long-term job retention tool and supported the passage of comprehensive conversion legislation as sponsored by the late Congressman Ted Weiss (D-NY).

However, as the buildup picked up pace, the enthusiasm for conversion waned in the union movement as a whole, and in particular within the rank-and-file of the Machinist union as they became more interested in the jobs which it generated. Indeed, over 1.3 million military-related industrial jobs were added from 1980 to 1987. The unions within the nuclear-weapons sectors were especially benefitted by the strategic buildup, although many conventional weapons also generated jobs, especially in the moribund shipbuilding industry.[42] The predominance of promilitary unions in the these two industries helps to explain the Metal Trades Council pro-military position.

Throughout the buildup the leadership of the Machinists and the UAW continued to support conversion legislation, and once it became evident that military spending had crested, they renewed their efforts to solidify support within the trade-union movement. In 1990 and again in 1992, the AFL-CIO annual conference passed resolutions calling for national economic conversion legislation as a means to retain jobs in the manufacturing sector and to plan a smooth transition to civilian work. The specter of losing nearly one million jobs over the next five years has deepened the interests of trade unionists in a comprehensive conversion plan. Yet, to date only modest adjustment measures are in place and none are geared to job retention.

Barriers to Conversion

As the foregoing account makes clear, the institutions of the national security state and the practice of military corporatism constitute formidable barriers to demilitarizing this nation's domestic and foreign policies and converting the resources to civilian uses. It is, however, useful to consider how these institutions and interests relate specifically to the problem of conversion.

In the case of organized labor, military spending has become the last refuge of a national industrial policy that is explicitly tied to the domestic economy. Decades of erosion in manufacturing employment because of import penetration and the globalization of production have narrowed the basis of industrial unionism. Indeed, since military production represents one of the last sectors of high-wage unionized employment, it is understandable why the industrial unions have opposed deep cuts in military spending. Thus, in this context, organized labor has often seen conversion as a last resort, rather than as an attractive alternative strategy for generating self-sustaining jobs. This outlook is reinforced by the fact that the defense corporations employing these industrial workers most often resist conversion efforts because conversion does not fit into the corporate strategy and structure of these military-serving firms.

Military-serving corporations continue to pursue defense contracts even in an era of declining business because they are often highly profitable. In addition, the very strategy and structure of the military-serving firms tend to predispose them to military work. In the case of the multidivisional science-based firms that perform military work, such as General Electric and Boeing, they have historically operated both commercial and military divisions. In most cases, the commercial business accounts for the majority of the revenues, but the strategic plans of these multidivisional firms call for their defense divisions to secure business from the public sector so as to diversify the business of the firm. Thus, private-sector work is usually confined to their commercial divisions.

During the several downturns in military spending of the Cold War era, these firms have usually sought to shrink their defense divisions, rather than converting them to civilian work. This strategy is consistent with the strategic requirements of the corporation since conversion of the defense division would most likely compete with the existing product lines of their commercial divisions. In order to avoid intra-firm competition, the defense division must either hunker down to get a bigger piece of a shrinking pie, or identify conversion opportunities in nonmilitary public-procurement markets. Since the alternative public-procurement sectors are much smaller than military work, this strategy has led these firms to pursue marginal adjustment strategies such as diversification and downsizing.

Meanwhile, the highly dependent military firms with little or no commercial work in their civilian divisions face fewer options when military spending contracts. Their lack of commercial experience makes conversion a daunting task, especially since the management and engineering personnel are used to producing high-performance, high-cost, high-maintenance equipment, rather than the low-cost, low-maintenance, high-quality demanded in commercial markets. For these reasons, the top management often opts for diversification through selling off their defense operations and acquiring commercially oriented businesses. But since there is often little connection between the business practices and requirements of the defense business and the new commercial operations, these mergers and acquisitions have often been unprofitable for the defense firms.

In these circumstances, an expansion of civilian public procurement would seem to be an attractive solution to promote the conversion of the defense industry. Moreover, such public investment, especially in infrastructure, would meet the needs of organized labor for developing domestic-based production that would not migrate overseas. Indeed, when the federal government modestly increased its investments in the areas of alternative transportation and energy during the 1970s, many defense firms pursued these fields of public investment as conversion alternatives (a topic that is treated at greater length in chapter 5 of this book).

But such alternative public R&D and procurement for transportation, energy, and infrastructural investment has often been blocked by other vested interests in these sectors. In particular, in the transportation field, the auto-oil-industrial complex has long resisted the expansion of public transportation alternatives to the automobile. Indeed, the history of how the U.S. auto and tire companies bought up and closed down municipal transportation systems demonstrates their power and clout.[43] In the case of energy policy, the oil and gas industries and the nuclear-power interests have benefitted from this nation's de facto industrial policy, which has encouraged and subsidized the "hard" energy path.[44] Public investment in renewable energy technologies and energy conservation has been paltry by comparison, and has been effectively resisted by the vested interests. Thus, nonmilitary interests also impede the process of economic conversion.

Despite these obstacles, there is reason to believe that even these vested civilian industrial interests are reaching their limits as the environmental crisis begins to force a broad-based reconsideration of the nation's transportation and energy technologies.[45] Moreover, a nascent political coalition is beginning to form in the United States among environmentalists, trade unionists, and peace and human-needs groups that are together pressing for a peace dividend to fund a large-scale program to build an environmentally sustainable infrastructure. The prospects for advancing such a program are enhanced by the profound legitimation crisis that the national security state is experiencing with the end of the Cold War.

The Legitimation Crises of the National Security State

With the end of the Cold War and the breakup of the Soviet Union, a new legitimation crisis arises for the national security state, namely how to justify its continued existence. All the theories of balance of power and arms race deterrence collapse with the fall of the Soviet Union. And while the national security planners have labored to shift the focus of national security operations onto the instability in the Third World and Eastern Europe, the far-flung operations of the Cold War lack a sufficient rationale. Indeed, this aspect of the legitimation crisis might be properly termed a rationality crisis for the national security state.[46]

So profound is this crisis that it actually extends into several dimensions, involving economic, political, administrative, technological, and environmental factors. This manifold crisis threatens the continued existence of the national security state and the military corporatism that underpins it. But while this crisis has uniquely contemporary causes, the origins can be traced back to critical episodes earlier in the Cold War. Examining these other crises can help us to understand the dynamics of the current situation.

The Technocratic Legitimation Crisis

One of the first fundamental challenges to the national security state grew out of the scientific controversy in the mid 1950s about the biological effects of fallout from atmospheric nuclear testing. This controversy opened a fissure in the corporatist arrangement among scientists, the military, and the government. Indeed, the emergence of scientific dissent for the first time put to public scrutiny issues of national security. A legitimation crisis arose because the allegedly scientific and technically neutral basis for national security policy was questioned. This questionning, in turn, lent tremendous power to the nascent peace and environmental movements. Indeed, these two movements owe much of their social origins in contemporary American society to this watershed event, which ultimately culminated in the banning of atmospheric testing.[47]

The emergence of dissident union activity by environmentally progressive unions opened another fissure in corporatist relations, and threatened the stability of public support for military policies. This occurred in the late 1960s and early 1970s when questions were raised about the occupational health and safety for workers within the nuclear-weapons industry. While dissident factions of labor in the United Mine Workers and OCAW did manage to publicize questionable regulatory and policy issues, the leverage of these factions was undercut by the complicity of dominant unions with industry interests. Indeed, the pro-military unions within the AFL-CIO, together with the centralization of decision making on security policy, largely preempted the challenge of labor's minority view.[48]

But the dissident views were given further credibility when some of the Atomic Energy Commission's own scientists began to question the very data that many of the environmental and health and safety standards were based on.[49] This scientific dissent fundamentally challenged the technical basis of national security decision making for it was no longer possible for the experts to go unquestioned.

These technical challenges began to extend to strategic decisions about the deployment of the Anti-ballistic Missile (ABM) system. In 1969, this heated public debate prompted scientists to choose sides for and against deployment. The success of the peace movement and the scientific community in halting the ABM deployment and in fostering an ABM treaty represents one of the blows against military corporatism. No longer was it possible for the military to count on the unquestionning allegiance of the scientific establishment.

Indeed, the defections by elements of the scientific community from the national security technocracy became a more or less routine aspect of the subsequent debates over other strategic and scientific security issues in the years to follow. Today, one of the most important challenges to the military corporatist interests is the disposition of the scientific and technical resources being released after the Cold War. This issue will be the watershed event of the post-Cold War period and will be decided on both technical and political grounds. But at the heart of this contest lies the issue of the democratic nature of our society, an issue that poses yet another aspect of the legitimation crisis.

Democractic Crisis

The culture of secrecy engendered by the national security state has had a pervasive effect on civil society; it has eroded the capacity of the nominally representative civilian government and the judiciary to openly control their own security functions, thereby producing a legitimation crisis for our democratic system.

In the face of the alleged anti-monopoly and anti-bureaucratic attitudes of the American people, these bureaucracies have grown to enormous size and wield a technological power that is unmatched in the world. Perhaps more disturbing is the fact that many societal interests have not been included in policy making on defense, space, and nuclear-energy technologies because of the security barriers that have surrounded such decisions.

With the permanent emergency of the Cold War now gone, there is no longer a rationalization for the persistence of these institutions. What is called for is a revitalization of American democracy to end the reign of secrecy and the logic of technocratic decision making. At the very least, every institutional practice that places a limit on democractic accountability ought to be scrutinized in the full light of public opinion. This principle should guide the formation of critical legislative initiatives, ranging from efforts to terminate the covert state, to efforts to open its books by preserving its official records under an independent and public control, to the drafting of a new National Security Act based on the principles of economic, social, and environmental security.

The Economic Crisis

The erosion of U.S. economic performance signals that our de facto industrial policies are no longer delivering the goods. These trends have begun to produce a legitimation crisis for military Keynesianism, as the costs of military spending have begun to overshadow its alleged benefits. Today, as the nation seeks to address this profound crisis, the national security state is attempting to redefine its own mission in order to maintain its control over the resources necessary to deal with these problems. Thus, in the post-Cold War era, an immediate task for those groups working for change must be to challenge these efforts by the military corporatist interests.

Throughout the Cold War, the challenges to the national security state have been advanced by countervailing movements organized in civil society by labor, the peace movements, the civil rights movement, religious groups, and scientific and environmental organizations to oppose these policies. These movements, comprised of diverse elements of society, have at different times fractured the structures of control and decision making by exposing the undemocratic and destructive nature of these policies. The success of these movements has hinged on showing that these policies do not materially benefit the stakeholders both inside and outside the military corporatist structures.

Notes

1. The many different schools of thought in espousing this view will be reviewed in the course of this chapter.

2. This account draws on the work of Kees van der Pijl, *Making of an Atlantic Ruling Class* (London: Verso Books, 1984), especially xiv, 88–115.

3. For a discussion of the concept of neo-corporatism see two anthologies by Philippe Schmitter and Gerhard Lehmbruch's *Patterns of Corporatist Policy Making* Sage Publishers Beverly Hills 1979; *Trends Towards Corporatist Intermediation,* Sage Publishers, Beverly Hills, 1982, 1979. For another approach to corporatism see van der Pijl, *Ruling Class,* especially the introductory comments that contrast the various concepts of corporatism.

4. For a detailed legal and institutional overview of the organization of the various organs of the national security state see Alice Cole, Alfred Goldberg, Samuel Tucker, and Rudolph Winnacker, eds., *The Department of Defense, Documents on the Establishment and Organization, 1944–1978* (Washington, D.C.: Office of the Secretary of Defense, Historical Office, 1978).

5. For an analysis of the extension of presidential powers see Marcus Raskin, "Democracy versus the National Security State," *Law and Contemporary Problems* 40, no. 3: 189–220.

6. See Leo Panitch, "The Development of Corporatism in Liberal Democracies" in Schmitter, *Patterns,* 119–147.

7. Ibid., 124–5.

8. See van der Pijl, *Ruling Class,* chapters 4 and 5.

9. For an analysis of the propagation of the concepts of J. M. Keynes and its influence on public policy see Alvin Hansen, *Business Cycles and National Income* (New York: W. W. Norton & Co., 1951, 1964), 501–544, 609–662.

10. For an excellent treatment of the sources of opposition to full-employment policies see Mikael Kalecki, "Political Aspects of Full Employment," *Political Quarterly* 14 (1943): 322–31.

11. See Nelson Lichtenstein, *Labor's War at Home, The CIO in World War II* (New York: Cambridge University Press, 1982), 218. Also see Hansen, *Business Cycles,* 106–7, 529–30, and 631–32.

12. See for example, Richard Barnet, *The Roots of War* (Atheneum New York, 1972), 165–168.

13. See Executive Secretary on United States Objectives and Programs for National Security, *NSC-68, A Report to the National Security Council,* 14 April 1950, in *Naval War College Review,* May–June 1975: 51–108. Also see James Cypher, "The Basic Economics of 'Rearming America,'" *Monthly Review,* November 1981: 11–27.

14. See Wayne Biddle, *Barons of the Sky* (New York: Simon & Schuster, 1991), 296–298.

15. For a detailed analysis of the shift toward an increased military share of total manufacturing output by industry group, see David Henry and Richard Oliver, "The Defense Buildup, 1977–1985: Effects on Production Output," *Monthly Labor Review* (U.S. Department of Labor), August 1987: 6. Also see Cypher, *Monthly Review.*

16. This inverse relationship of military spending and private investment has been rather convincingly demonstrated by numerous economic studies. For the most definitive and recent research see Michael Dee Oden, "Military Spending, Military Power, and U.S. Postwar Economic Performance" (doctoral dissertation, New School for Social Research, February 1992), especially chapters 2–4. Also see Michael Dee Oden, *A Military Dollar Really is Different* (Lansing, Mich.: Employment Research Associates, 1987), 20–29. In addition, see J. Davidson Alexander, "Manufacturing Productivity and Military Depletion in the Post-

war Industrial Economy," in *Towards a Peace Economy in the United States,* ed. Gregory A. Bischak, (New York: St. Martin's Press, 1991), 78–117. This last essay is an example of the "depletionist" thesis, which argues that military spending has a negative effect on the civilian economy by diverting public and private spending into unproductive activities. See also Seymour Melman, *Profits Without Production* (New York: Alfred A. Knopf, 1983). Also see Lloyd J. Dumas, *The Overburdened Economy* (Berkeley: University of California Press, 1986).

17. See Gordon Adams, *The Iron Triangle* (New York: Council on Economic Priorities, 1981), 19–26.

18. The neo-Marxian perspective is best represented by Paul Sweezy and Paul Baran, *Monopoly Capital* (New York: Monthly Review Press, 1966); their theory argues that military spending helps absorb the surplus capacity generated by the inherent tendencies of monopolized sectors of the economy. An early and prescient view of the role of military spending was laid out by Mikael Kalecki, a contemporary of the economist John Maynard Keynes, who held that the institutional and economic factors predisposed the capitalist economies to prefer military spending over other forms of state intervention to prop up a stagnating economy. See Kalecki, "The Political Aspects of Full Employment."

19. See Tom Riddell, "Military Power, The Terms of Trade and the Profit Rate," *American Economic Review* 78, no. 2 (May 1988): 60–65. Also see Samuel Bowles, David Gordon, and Thomas Weisskopf, "Business Ascendancy and Economic Impasse: A Structural Perspective on Conservative Economics: 1979–1987," *Journal of Economic Perspectives* 3, no. 1 (1989): 107–134.

20. Richard Barnet argues in the *Roots of War* that there are many domestic sources that account for the militarist and expansionary U.S. foreign policy characterizing the post-World War II period. Rather than simply being a result of the confrontation of capitalism and socialism, Barnet argues that economic pressures from within the United States required the buildup of a permanent war economy to combat its stagnating tendencies. Moreover, the search for markets and investment overseas carried the system forward into ever greater intervention. Marcus Raskin argues that the social and economic institutions have created a set of interlocking interests that supported the development of a closely cohesive

national security apparatus, which required high levels of military spending to resolve both the internal crises of American capitalism but also the external challenges to it. See Raskin, "Democracy versus the National Security State." A corporatist theory of the internationalization of the national security state in America and the American economy is advanced by van der Pijl in *Ruling Class*. A different perspective, the state capitalist theory, is advanced by Seymour Melman who argues that the nation's economic resources have been mobilized to expand the power of state managers through the ongoing militarization of the economy in *Pentagon Capitalism* (New York: McGraw-Hill, 1970), 1–34; also see Seymour Melman, *The Permanent War Economy* (New York: Simon and Schuster, 1974), and his *Profits Without Production*.

21. See Alexander, "Manufacturing Productivity and Military Depletion." See Oden, "Military Spending, Military Power": chapters 6 and 7 test the effects of military spending on aggregate economic performance and find that military spending provided stimulus through the mid-sixties, which tapered off to become a drag on economic performance.

22. For a detailed and rigorous economic analysis of how military spending and power has influenced the terms of trade, as well as the domestic and foreign investment patterns of capital, see Oden, "Military Spending, Military Power," 275–320.

23. *Ibid.*

24. This view has been advanced by Adams in *The Iron Triangle*, 19–26.

25. Ibid.

26. Ibid, 95–102.

27. Ibid, 26, 43–52.

28. See Ernest Fitzgerald, *The Pentagonists* (New York: Pantheon Books, 1988).

29. For examination of how bipartisan foreign policy was shaped during the onset of the Cold War see Richard Walton, *Henry Wallace, Harry Truman, and the Cold War* (New York: Viking, 1976).

30. Melman's, *Pentagon Capitalism.*

31. For an institutional history of the development of the national security state see Alice Cole et al., *The Department of Defense.* Also see Select Committee on Intelligence of the House of Representatives, *Compilation of Intelligence Laws and Related Laws and Executive Orders of Interest to the National Intelligence Community,* prepared for the use of the Permanent 101st Congress, 2d Session, (Washington, D.C.: U.S. Government Printing Office, September 1990).

32. For a detailed treatment of the evolution of these agencies see James Bamford, *The Puzzle Palace* (New York: Penguin, 1983).

33. See *The Economy,* (Washington, D.C.: National Commission for Economic Conversion and Disarmament, Winter 1992), 16.

34. For a treatment of the nature and dynamics of technocracy in modern society see "Dogmatism, Reason and Decision: On Theory and Practice in Our Scientific Civilization" in Jurgen Habermas, *Theory and Practice* (Boston: Beacon Press, 1973), 253–282.

35. See Department of Commerce, *Statistical Abstract of the United States* (Washington, D.C.: Government Printing Office) tables 249–50, 1950 edition; table 299, 1960 edition; table 370, 1971 edition; tables 713, 714, and 716, 1980 edition; table 665, 1988 edition; and tables 696 and 697, 1990 edition. Also see, Nelson Lichtenstein, *Labor's War at Home: The CIO in World War II* (New York: Cambridge University Press, 1983), 233.

36. See Richard Hewlett and Francis Duncan, *Atomic Shield, 1947–52: Volume II, A History of the United States Atomic Energy Commissions* (University Park: Penn State University Press, 1969), 342–347.

37. See Aris Christodoulou, *Conversion of Nuclear Facilities from Military to Civilian Uses* in *Converting Industry from Military to Civilian Economy,* ed. Seymour Melman (New York: Praeger, 1970).

38. See Gene Carroll, "How to Get Labor Involved," in *Economic Conversion,* ed. Suzanne Gordon and Dave McFadden, (Cambridge, Mass.: Ballinger, 1984), 219–230.

39. Ibid., 1.

40. See Council on Economic Priorities, *The Costs and Consequences of Reagan's Military Buildup* (New York, Council on Economic Priorities: 1982).

41. *Ibid.*

42. The degree of unionization within the nuclear energy industry can be ascertained from data from the Department of Energy, Industrial Employment Division, Washington, D.C., and the Metals Trades Department of AFL-CIO. This data indicates that unionization of non-exempt employment in the principal weapons-related activities comprised about 75 percent of the workforce. See U.S. Department of Energy, *Industrial Employment in Nuclear Related Activities 1991,* (Washington, D.C.: Government Printing Office, Nov. 1991); *Metal Trades Council 62nd Annual Convention Report,* (Washington D.C.: Metals Trade Council) Sept., 1991.

43. For a short history of this episode see Barry Commoner, *The Poverty of Power* (New York: Bantam Books, 1977), 177–183.

44. Ibid, chapters 3 and 4.

45. See for instance, Lester Brown, et. al., *State of World 1992* by Worldwatch Institute, (New York, W. W. Norton, 1992) especially chapters 3, 4, 8, and 9.

46. See Jurgen Habermas, *The Legitimation Crisis* (Boston: Beacon Press, 1975) for a comprehensive treatment of these concepts.

47. For a discussion of the controversy over nuclear fallout from atmospheric testing see Barry Commoner, *The Closing Circle* (New York: Alfred A. Knopf, 1971), 45–62.

48. See Harvey Wasserman and Norman Soloman, *Killing Our Own* (New York: Delta Books, 1982).

49. Ibid.

Part Two

The Making of Conversion Policy

5

Economic Conversion: The Key to Building a Peace Economy

Gregory A. Bischak and Joel Yudken

Introduction

A comprehensive economic conversion process involves many dimensions, beginning with the most fundamental issues of realigning our national priorities, and moving to more specific measures necessary to reallocate resources at the industrial and local levels so as to prevent or minimize the economic disruption from major military reductions. In the broadest sense, economic conversion involves a realignment of national priorities to reflect the lowered defense needs of a new era in international relations and to address important domestic needs. Already, the process of realigning our national budget priorities is under way, prompted largely by the dramatic events in Eastern Europe and arms-reduction initiatives. In addition, there is widespread recognition that many domestic social needs are currently unmet because of the constraints imposed by the budget deficit and high military spending. However, even with a shift in budget priorities that would help to maintain and stimulate the overall level of economic activity, some military-dependent industries and regions will suffer dislocation.

From the point of view of military-dependent industries, economic conversion is a strategy to redevelop the manufacturing business and employment into relevant civilian alternatives. History has shown that this can be accomplished through cooperative efforts of business, government, and the affected communities. Economically, conversion planning requires advance planning for market research, economic incentives for firms to develop new products and retool equipment, and the retraining of management, engineers, and the workforce so that they become accustomed to the cost-conscious norms of commercial work.

Where direct conversion of the industry and work force is not possible, there is need for economic adjustment assistance to help communities to diversify their economies through developing new civilian business to reemploy the affected work force. Moreover, where defense firms choose to shut down their plants rather than convert them, there is often need for specialized labor retraining programs to assist workers in moving into new jobs. These types of adjustment assistance are complementary to the overall process of converting the military economy, although, as we shall see, it would be a mistake to assume that adjustment assistance alone is sufficient to effect a smooth and efficient transition to civilian work. Moreover, as we shall see, there are ample reasons to reject the claims that market forces can efficiently reallocate resources from military to civilian work.

In this chapter we will examine the structural economic conversion problems facing the United States as it demobilizes from the Cold War. First, we will scrutinize several prevalent myths about economic conversion that have been circulated by the Pentagon and its supporters to undermine the conversion approach. We will endeavor to expose the preconceptions that underlie these myths and to show that contrary to conventional wisdom, conversion has succeeded in the past and can work today. Second, we will critically examine past federal policies toward major military downturns following the wars of the last forty-seven years and draw several important lessons for the present situation. Third, we will consider the possible scale and consequences of the post-Cold War conversion and examine the macroeconomic, industrial, occupational, and regional dimensions of such a conversion process. Finally, we will discuss what conversion and adjustment policies are needed to ensure that the nation makes the most of this opportunity to revitalize its economy, rather than worsening its recessionary and structural problems.

Shattering the Four Myths about Conversion

For years the Pentagon and its supporters have perpetuated several prevalent myths about economic conversion. The leading myth is that normal economic growth can deal with the economic disruption of a major reduction in military spending.[1] It is further asserted that the normal workings of market forces will efficiently reallocate resources to other uses. Thus, it is claimed that there is no need for extraordinary government intervention, which will only distort the efficient operation of the market.[2]

Myth One: Normal Economic Growth Will Absorb the Shock of Cuts

Some economists often seek to minimize the relative impact of military spending and cutbacks, claiming that since it comprises only 5 percent of the gross national product (GNP), fluctuations in defense spending would not perceptibly affect the economy as a whole. However, looking at broader measures of the military's share of GNP that include other types of military-related spending not usually counted, the military share of GNP rises to 8.4 percent in 1991.[3] Expanding the measure to more accurately include international security assistance, military functions of NASA, veterans affairs, military-related Department of Commerce activities, and the military share of interest on the national debt, clearly gives one a better assessment of its potential impact on the fluctuation in economic activity. Under this more inclusive approach it becomes evident that the size and composition of military spending can affect the level and pace of activity in the manufacturing sectors, investment, credit markets, and the direction and rate of technological innovation.[4]

From an aggregate perspective, dramatic cuts in military spending will affect the economy, especially in its stagnant condition. Under these conditions, it should be remembered that a 1 or 2 percent decline in a major component of GNP will undoubtedly slow growth if no compensating stimulus is found elsewhere. Already the limited military cuts planned by Defense Secretary Richard Cheney are expected to cause the nominal GNP share of military spending to decline to 3.5 percent by 1996, and by broader measures it will decline even more drastically.

In addition, defense-related activity is highly concentrated among industries, firms, regions, localities, and occupational groups. Thus, the impacts of military cuts will not be as easily absorbed by the economy as if they were spread more evenly throughout the society.[5] The concentration of economic dislocation in particular industries and regions poses special adjustment problems. In such cases many unemployed workers and managers are suddenly thrown into the labor market at the same time. In addition, many smaller suppliers that were previously tied to a single large prime contractor suddenly find their subcontracts terminated without compensation. These smaller firms often lack the access to capital and credit to develop new business ties, and some are forced into bankruptcy. The combination of reduced business and lower consumer spending by laid-off workers ripples through the wholesale and retail business sectors, forcing in turn additional layoffs.

Military cuts are exacerbating an already bad situation for workers, businesses, and communities in several key economic regions of the country, most notably California and the Northeast. In California, once the economic showcase for the nation, the decline in defense business has been a major contributor to the state's current economic woes. As aerospace is its largest industry in terms of shipments and employment, the cuts in major military aerospace contracts are creating very serious economic problems, especially in those counties (Los Angeles, Orange, Santa Clara) with the largest concentration of military industry. Moreover, the huge size of California's economy, which ranks as the eighth largest in the world, makes its problems national problems. As noted in *The New York Times,* the lingering California recession is clearly putting a crimp in the national economy's sputtering attempts at revival.[6]

These problems are amplified in a recessionary period, or a stagnant period with anemic economic growth of about 1½–2 percent per year. In these circumstances, the economy has difficulty supplying new jobs for new entrants into the labor market, let alone absorbing the workers displaced from military cutbacks. Indeed, studies of displaced workers have shown that the duration of unemployment varies widely by region, and not surprisingly depends on the particular phase of the business cycle. Nonetheless, the average duration of unemployment for displaced workers was about four and one-half months in the first half of the 1980s.[7] This length of time imposes great hardship on many workers, especially since unemployment benefits fail to cover the cost of living during the job search, thereby forcing workers to exhaust their savings. More recently, the unemployment system has covered only four out of ten unemployed workers, down from the previous level of seven out of ten workers during the last recession.[8] Thus, behind the rhetoric of market adjustment and job creation through growth lies a darker reality, where adjustment is measured in job loss, protracted unemployment, bankruptcies, and regional recessions.

Myth Two: Job Training Will Deal with Displaced Workers

A second myth is that in those cases where there are special hardships imposed on particular workers and communities, there are existing job training and adjustment programs that can remedy these problems. Nevertheless, critics have argued that, except for a small number of special cases of extreme dislocation, no special adjustment of conversion policies for defense-dependent workers and communities are really warranted. The problem is not only that the problems are in fact greater than often recognized, it is also that current job training programs are ill-equipped to help displaced defense workers retool for new occupations. These programs are largely geared to low-wage, low-skill job positions, whereas most defense production workers and engineers are coming from high-wage, high-skill jobs.[9] Moreover, many of these same skills are in decreasing demand because of the decline of the defense industry and because of the lackluster growth in the nation's manufacturing sectors.[10]

The question is usually raised, why should defense workers, who after all represent a relatively privileged sector of the work force, be selected out for special treatment, especially when many other workers during the deindustrialization of the 1970s and 1980s did not have the benefit of such supports? The suffering of one group of workers is not a good reason for denying help to another, even if the latter is better off. Moreover, the problem of defense-industrial dislocation is being created by government policies, not the ordinary workings of the marketplace. The problem is how to help defense-dependent industries make the transition from government-created and -controlled markets to civilian, commercially competitive markets. The government has a responsibility to help ease the pain of this transition for workers, communities, and firms, that has been created by its own policies.

The complaint about singling out defense workers for government aid, moreover, diverts attention from a more fundamental problem: the lack of adequate, comprehensive economic adjustment policies in the United States that address the needs of all workers and communities suffering from economic dislocation, whatever the cause. Economic adjustment assistance covers a wide range of activities, including: early warning about layoffs and/or plant closures to allow time for workers and communities to make necessary adjustments; retraining, relocation, and job-search assistance; unemployment benefits; and planning assistance for communities to aid economic diversification.

Largely in response to hard-fought political battles by communities and labor unions, many such measures have been instituted by federal and state governments, and even by private sector firms, over the past two decades. The federal Economic Dislocation and Workers Adjustment Assistance (EDWAA) program, established in 1988, is considered an improvement over its predecessor, Title III of the Job Training Partnership Act (JTPA).[11] In the defense sector, perhaps to avoid the problems of the massive aerospace layoffs in the late 1960s, some large contractors have instituted adjustment programs to help their workers, especially technical professionals, make the transition to other jobs. Nevertheless, U.S. adjustment policies fall short of those of most other major industrial nations.[12] Generally, given the U.S. track record over the last decade,[13] these policies are still not adequate for the needs of U.S. workers and communities; they are too fragmented, inconsistent, inappropriately targeted, and inadequately funded.

The problems of defense industry adjustment are unique in a number of ways, and require specially tailored programs. Some of these problems, which afflict defense engineers most of all, include overspecialization, obsolete technical skills, and inappropriate skills and experience for commercial-sector employment. The large concentrations in defense industry of certain occupational groups makes it harder for them to find jobs in commercial industries that have very different mixes of jobs and skills. This is exacerbated by the concentration of defense industry within specific communities, where large numbers of defense workers with similar skills are forced to compete for limited numbers of jobs in nondefense sectors, a problem further compounded by the decline of civilian manufacturing in these same communities during the eighties.[14] By and large, current federal and state policies, even the improved EDWAA, do not adequately recognize the special needs of defense workers under conditions of dislocation. Modification of EDWAA provisions, in which defense workers are specifically targeted, along with other explicit defense adjustment programs with sufficient levels of funding, will therefore be necessary, especially to handle the substantial economic dislocations caused by the coming large-scale military cutbacks.

Myth Three: Little Community Economic Assistance is Needed

A third myth is that economic development assistance is not needed to help defense-dependent communities make the transition to civilian economy because private investment can do the job. According to this view there is no need for government intervention and policies to encourage advance planning. Indeed, the Bush administration is so enamored with this view that it is carrying forward with the plans made under the Reagan administration for eliminating the Economic Development Administration (EDA). This Department of Commerce agency is charged with delivering economic assistance for distressed communities in general, and defense-impacted communities in particular.

However, as we have seen, the termination of contracts without targeted assistance means large-scale job loss, the threat of bankruptcy for many smaller firms, and further repercussions within the surrounding communities. Well-targeted policy can overcome the failures of the market economy and minimize the local economic disruption.

Where plants are closed, history shows that well-targeted economic assistance grants can leverage more money from state and local governments, which in turn can leverage private investment to revitalize the local economy through diversification. Indeed, studies by the Department of Defense's Office of Economic Adjustment (OEA) of community economic adjustment experiences observed that economic dislocation was minimized when there was prenotification about possible contract termination or shutdown.[15] In addition, where an industrial facility has been vacated, its reuse and marketability should be assessed promptly to help reemploy dislocated workers and to stimulate new business activity as rapidly as possible. Furthermore, the study recommended that the OEA and other economic adjustment agencies should provide funding to communities to evaluate the feasibility of reusing vacant facilities, as well as to plan for longer-term economic redevelopment. Finally, the study noted that while states and localities have made great progress in expanding their capabilities to respond to economic dislocation, the cutback in federal programs to assist them has made economic redevelopment more difficult.

While necessary, however, economic adjustment assistance is itself not a sufficient response to economic dislocation. Economic adjustment is really only a short-term, transitional palliative, which, in order to be truly effective, needs to be tied to broader strategies for economic development. What's the point of retraining workers for jobs that don't exist? Thus, we need to turn our attention to the problem of economic conversion of military-dependent industries and firms to civilian production, as a central and concomitant feature of U.S. industrial restructuring in the coming decade.

Myth Four: Conversion Doesn't Work

The fourth and most pervasive myth is that conversion simply doesn't work. This is the favorite line of the DoD and its OEA, which has been most recently restated by Kenneth Adelman, the former director of the U.S. Arms Control and Disarmament Agency.[16] Contrary to the conventional wisdom of the military establishment, an evenhanded review of U.S. economic history reveals that conversion does work when the political leadership establishes the conditions for success. Since the Second World War, the United States has experienced several major cuts in defense spending, all of which have led to various degrees of conversion from military to civilian business and have had varying economic impacts on the level of economic activity.

Post-World War II Experience

The most notable conversion effort was following the Second World War when the defense economy was reduced from about 40 percent of the GNP to about 6 percent of the GNP two years after the war. While national output fell somewhat due to the rapid decline in military spending, the level of employment and consumption was maintained through public policies instituted to counter the onset of recessions. Moreover, the massive deficit spending by the federal government during the war boosted private savings for business and consumers, which was then spent after the war on investment and consumer goods. Furthermore, Congress and the Executive branch committed the nation to a full-employment policy and passed the GI Bill, which helped maintain consumer spending by providing returning GIs with money to go to college.

Contrary to conventional wisdom, *the successful rapid transition to a civilian economy occurred because there was extensive planning* and policies were in place to cushion the economy from the shocks of demobilizing from the war.[17] Indeed, several planning boards such as the National Resources Planning Board and the Office of War Mobilization and Reconversion, among others, began to plan for reconversion before the war was over, with detailed plans developed as early as 1943. Furthermore, in 1943 the War Department was encouraging firms to begin planning civilian products for after the war. At the state and local levels, the Committee for Economic Development, a business group, had representatives working on local reconversion projects in over 1,800 communities by 1944. Furthermore, several major legislative initiatives were put in place to permit defense firms to begin civilian product development for the post-war period and to set up procedures for the sale of government-owned plant and equipment to private firms.

As is well known, these sales of government-owned plant and equipment led to the creation of whole new businesses in such new sectors as the aluminum industry, and fostered new competition in transportation equipment and electronics.[18] In short, the cooperative efforts of government and business to undertake advance planning and legislative initiative led to a successful conversion process.

Post-Korean War Experience

The winding down from the Korean War was extremely modest, reducing the defense share of GNP from 13.4 percent in 1953 to 9.4 percent in 1956. Yet, this reduction still left the defense share at more than twice what it was in 1948.[19] Thus, the policy of military Keynesianism began to take hold, creating greater incentives for military-oriented firms to extend their defense contracting operations.

Despite this tendency toward a permanent military-industrial base, following the Korean War, several major aerospace companies undertook to develop commercial products that drew on their technological expertise in defense work. Boeing Aircraft, the most notable example, launched its conversion effort with the objective of developing a commercial passenger and cargo jet transport capability.[20] Boeing devoted a substantial percentage of its management, engineering, and production talent to developing this commercial venture, which was viewed as a long-term investment in an emerging market. As is well known, Boeing eventually became the worldwide leader in manufacturing jet passenger aircraft, and today the commercial division generates the lion's share of its revenues.

Post-Vietnam Examples

The decrease in military spending from the peak of the Vietnam War to the subsequent trough in the mid seventies brought the defense share of GNP down from 9.1 percent in 1968 to 5.1 percent by 1977. In inflation-adjusted terms, defense spending declined over this period by over 34 percent. These deep reductions in defense spending led many defense contractors to explore civilian market opportunities, particularly in the mass transportation market and in alternative energy research and development.

Boeing-Vertol, Rohr Industries, Ingalls, and Allied-Signal Corporation undertook to produce light rail cars and electronic control switches for the growing urban mass transit market in the 1970s.[21] These cases were only partial successes. They all produced new products and won contracts. But each contractor was plagued by technological and cost-control problems that arose because they adopted the dubious military production engineering practice of concurrency in their commercial work.

Concurrency is the simultaneous prototyping and full-scale production of a product that has not yet been fully tested. This method has often been used by the military to accelerate the development and deployment of a new technology in order to gain a strategic advantage.[22] However, it is fraught with problems, since undetected errors in product design and production engineering usually require expensive redesign and retrofitting efforts to correct the defects in the product and the production process.

Boeing-Vertol's concurrent testing and design practices resulted in major problems with its orders for the Massachusetts Bay Transit Authority. Eventually they worked out many of the problems, although they incurred rather large financial losses. Later, they learned from this experience, drawing on it to more efficiently produce and deliver orders for trolleys for the City of San Francisco and light rail cars for Chicago. While Boeing-Vertol used mostly workers from their military production lines, it did not manage to reemploy a majority of its work force in the trolley and rail car production.

Sudden changes in federal R&D and procurement policies during the 1970s and early 1980s were principal factors confounding the conversion efforts of Boeing-Vertol and other defense firms. Boeing-Vertol's failure to stay in the mass transportation market was to a significant degree a result of large reductions in federal urban mass transit discretionary spending during the Carter and Reagan administrations. In addition, the failure of the Urban Mass Transit Administration to establish uniform standards for such vehicles contributed to the instability of the public market. Thus, public procurement and regulatory standards played a key role in creating and then destroying a conversion opportunity for aerospace firms.

A parallel conversion situation prevailed in alternative energy R&D. The oil price shocks of the 1970s stimulated large-scale increases in federal spending on alternatives. Several defense-related firms were attracted by this spending into alternative energy research, but they quickly exited when the money dried up in the early 1980s. Significantly, while the OEA's own study[23] covers many of these very examples, the OEA has failed to draw the obvious conclusion that linking and targeting federal R&D and procurement policies can create conversion opportunities for defense industries.

Contemporary Examples

As the United States begins to disengage from the Cold War, many defense firms have started to exit the military market by developing civilian markets. Several examples have already occurred since military spending began to decline from its 1987 peak. Some of the most notable examples involve several small to medium-sized firms, including Textron Aerostructures of Nashville; A. M. General of Mishawauka, Indiana; Air Industries of Bay Shore, New York; Curtis Universal Joint of Springfield, Massachusetts; and Frisby Airborne Hydraulics, Freeport, New York.[24] Nonetheless, many of these cases of industrial conversion have occurred on a limited scale and have succeeded in reemploying only a fraction of the defense-industrial workers in the civilian operations. Indeed, some smaller defense firms, such as the Fail Safe Technology Corporation of Los Angeles, report that the transition is very difficult for small businesses because of the lack of access to credit and investment capital, and the lack of broader federal support to facilitate the transition to civilian work.[25]

The difficulty of these firms to make the transition, and the lack of initiative from the larger prime defense contractors highlights the shortcomings of current federal policy. The failure of the current administration to put in place a set of structural conversion policies to promote the transition to civilian work and to prevent or mitigate the economic repercussions has meant that the nation has lost the opportunity to retain jobs and develop new civilian business alternatives. While Congress acted in 1990 on a modest defense adjustment amendment to the Defense Authorization Act of FY 1991, this three-year $200 million program failed to deliver timely and well targeted assistance to many defense-dependent regions. In addition, the DoD has delayed transferring the funds to the Department of Labor and Congress. Finally, the program provides no incentives for firms to convert, and does not create conversion opportunities through relevant civilian research and development programs.

Today, there is a conversion potential for aerospace firms similar to that of the 1970s in the mass transportation market, especially in southern California where such a change is under active consideration.[26] Yet, because there is little commitment by the federal government to stimulate such a business development strategy, the market opportunity remains unexploited. It is noteworthy that today the United States imports most of its mass transit rail-car equipment from Japan, Italy, and Canada.

In this context, one can see that economic conversion can and does work, given the proper political and economic conditions. What is lacking today is the political leadership to guide the nation and the economy towards a peace economy. The outlines of a sensible conversion policy are suggested by the lessons from past post-war wind-downs. First, the nation needs to invest its peace dividend in critical civilian fields, including human resource programs, emerging new technologies, and the physical infrastructure. Second, there is an evident need for structural economic policies to facilitate the transition of businesses, workers, and communities into relevant civilian work. But to date, there has been little analysis of the scale and dimensions of the post-Cold War conversion problem that faces the nation. Thus, the political leadership has accepted the prevailing myths about the conversion problem, hoping that the transition will be as painless as often suggested in the economics textbooks.

The Scale and Consequences of Post-Cold War Conversion

The actual size of the post-Cold War downturn and its probable costs in terms of job loss and economic dislocation is a subject of speculation. Compared to the 12 percent cut from the Pentagon budget over the last half of the 1980s, the Bush administration estimated in early 1991 another 20 or 25 percent reduction in defense expenditures by 1996.[27] According to Department of Defense projections this would translate into 1,130,000 jobs lost over the 1991–1996 period.[28] John Steinbruner and Walter Kaufman, however, claim that a more realistic appraisal of the international environment by defense planners would yield a 40 percent cut in the military's budget over the next decade.[29] Indeed, in response partly to growing political pressures for more spending on domestic programs, the Bush administration proposed even deeper cuts, reducing defense spending levels from 1992 levels of $292 billion down to $240 billion by 1995.[30]

Presidential election year politics have raised the level of debate over the size of this peace dividend after the Cold War. Some have even called for a 50 percent cut in the Pentagon budget over the next five years. While the actual dimensions of peace dividend are still open to debate, there is little doubt that cuts on the order of 25 to 50 percent over five years will have serious economic repercussions.

In a study entitled *Converting the American Economy,* the economic effects of a such a large-scale shift in military spending to critical civilian needs was examined by use of a computer simulation to analyze the impact on the economy as a whole and particular industries and occupations.[31]

This hypothetical shift in spending resulted in an average of nearly 477,000 net new jobs created annually over the period studied.[32] Overall, new civilian employment more than offsets the job losses from the military-related cutbacks.

Industrial Effects

As table 6 shows, forty-one of the fifty-three major industry groups examined in this study showed net gains in employment from a shift away from defense spending. Job creation exceeded job losses in nondurable-goods industries, construction, transportation, utilities, mining, finance, real estate, insurance, wholesale and retail trades, services, and state and local government. In addition, a few durable-goods industries registered gains, including motor-vehicles producers, lumber, and furniture, as well as stone, glass, and clay industries.

Most hard hit were military-serving durable-goods industries such as aerospace and shipbuilding (represented here by "rest of transportation equipment"), electrical and electronic equipment, nonelectrical machinery, instruments, fabricated metal products, and primary metals, with losses averaging nearly 166,000 jobs per year. It should be emphasized that these projected job losses were over and above what "normal economic growth" would absorb. Thus, the results indicate that there is a clear need for some targeted policies to deal with this dislocation. However, the results also show that alternative civilian spending would substantially compensate for the military reductions in fabricated metal products, primary metals, and nonelectrical machinery. Nonetheless, the losses in these durable-goods industries, together with the layoffs averaging nearly 500,000 troops and 155,000 civilian Department of Defense employees, would pose the largest problem for economic conversion and adjustment.

The other affected industries suffer relatively minor losses. These could be mitigated through advance planning and targeted assistance to promote diversification for these less military-dependent industries and services.

Occupational Effects

At the occupational level, the compensated shift in spending stimulated job creation in some jobs, but other occupations suffered net losses. Overall, scientific and engineering occupations showed net gains averaging

Table 6. Impact of Alternative Priorities on Jobs (Average Annual 1991–1994)

	Jobs Lost From Military Spending Cuts	Jobs Gained From Civilian Spending Increases	Net Jobs Gained or Lost
NET GAIN INDUSTRIES			
Durable Goods			
Lumber	−4,850	+16,100	+11,250
Furniture	−4,700	+6,200	+1,500
Stone, Clay & Glass	−5,600	+14,950	+9,350
Motor Vehicles	−6,200	+7,700	+1,500
Non-Durable Goods			
Food	−6,500	+10,750	+4,250
Tobacco Manufacturers	−150	+200	+50
Textiles	−4,550	+5,500	+950
Apparel	−4,950	+6,850	+1,900
Paper	−4,950	+8,950	+4,000
Printing	−11,550	+29,050	+17,500
Petroleum Products	−1,100	+1,500	+400
Rubber	−9,550	+10,250	+700
Leather	−500	+800	+300
Construction	−40,850	+258,400	+217,550
Transportation, Utilities & Mining			
Mining	−7,800	+10,250	+2,450
Railroad Transportation	−2,550	+2,850	+300
Trucking	−23,300	+25,800	+2,500
Local/Interurban Transportation	−1,150	+7,300	+6,150
Communications	−13,950	+17,600	+3,650
Public Utilities	−7,250	+10,900	+3,650
Finance, Real Est. & Insurance			
Banking	−11,150	+15,350	+4,200
Insurance	−12,950	+24,350	+11,400
Credit & Finance	−9,250	+14,300	+5,050
Real Estate	−21,200	+39,500	+18,300
Wholesale & Retail Trade			
Eating & Drinking Establishments	−46,050	+52,100	+6,050
Rest of Retail	−72,400	+128,950	+56,550
Wholesale	−59,500	+74,400	+14,900
Services			
Hotels	−17,100	+17,750	+650
Personal & Repair Services	−20,450	+30,050	+9,600
Private Household	−5,900	+8,900	+3,000

Table 6. *(continued)*

	Jobs Lost From Military Spending Cuts	Jobs Gained From Civilian Spending Increases	Net Jobs Gained or Lost
Services *(continued)*			
Automobile Repair & Service	−8,500	+13,900	+5,400
Miscellaneous Business Services	−94,900	+111,400	+16,500
Amusement & Recreation Services	−7,300	+11,650	+4,350
Motion Pictures	−2,050	+3,500	+1,450
Medical	−34,900	+155,500	+120,600
Miscellaneous Professional Services	−33,700	+86,550	+52,850
Education—Public & Private	−35,250	+186,250	+151,000
Non-Profit Organizations	−36,300	+373,300	+337,000
Agriculture, Forest & Fisheries Ser.	−6,050	+18,050	+12,000
Federal Government—Civilian	0	+49,350	+49,350
State & Local Government	0	+180,850	+180,850
NET LOSS INDUSTRIES			
Durable Goods			
Primary Metals	−12,200	+9,700	−2,500
Fabricated Metal Products	−28,100	+24,100	−4,000
Non-electrical Machinery	−23,250	+20,600	−2,650
Electric & Electronic Equipment	−66,450	+20,100	−46,350
Rest of Transportation Equip. (missiles, aircraft, ships, tanks, etc.)	−101,200	+5,600	−95,600
Instruments	−20,050	+9,400	−10,650
Miscellaneous Manufacturing	−8,000	+3,700	−4,300
NonDurable Goods			
Chemicals	−12,650	+12,300	−350
Transportation, Utilities & Mining			
Air Transportation	−8,700	+7,250	−1,450
Other Transportation	−7,150	+4,600	−2,550
Federal Government—Military			
Uniformed Military Personnel	−498,500	0	−498,500
Non-Uniformed Military Personnel	−205,250	0	−205,250
Total Net Change	−1,688,000	+2,165,000	+477,000

(*Source:* M. Anderson, G. Bischak, and M. Oden, *Converting the American Economy: The Economic Effects of an Alternative Security Policy* (Lansing, Mich.: Employment Research Associates, 1991), 27.

over 19,400 jobs. This was due to increased spending on civilian-oriented R&D. However, there were considerable net losses in the military-oriented field of aero/astronautical engineering amounting to an annual average of nearly 3,000 jobs. In addition, there were net losses that averaged nearly 5,000 jobs among engineering technicians. A few other engineering fields registered relatively minor net losses.

Net gains were registered in most other major occupational groupings including managerial jobs, educators, nonprofit-sector workers, law, health care, technicians, marketing and sales, secretaries and administrative support, service occupations, agriculture, construction, mechanics and installers, and most transportation service workers.

Significant occupational dislocation occurred, however, among many skilled and semi-skilled production occupations. These are production jobs that are closely linked to the military durable-goods sectors. They include such skilled occupations as precision metal workers, inspectors, numerically controlled machine operators, and various machine tool operators. These net losses averaged nearly 23,000 jobs, with semi-skilled assemblers adding another 19,300 in net job losses. Other net losses in civilian occupations were relatively minor.

While alternative civilian spending stimulates net employment gains for the economy as a whole, the industrial and occupational results show the need for economic conversion planning and economic adjustment measures. New markets and job openings do not necessarily ensure that resources currently devoted to military ends will be readily and easily transferred to civilian markets and jobs. Indeed, there are distinct obstacles to converting highly specialized producers of military equipment to civilian production. In addition, troop cutbacks at military installations and layoffs by prime contractors will affect supplier firms and the surrounding communities. These issues show the need for a national and regional economic conversion and adjustment policy.

A Program for Economic Conversion

As we have seen, the post-Cold War decrease in military spending presents the nation with both a challenge and an opportunity. In order to meet this challenge and make the most of the opportunity, a comprehensive economic conversion program must be enacted that includes both a fiscal conversion of our national budget priorities and a structural conversion program to smooth transition for industries, communities, and workers.

A structural economic conversion policy would include economic incentives for advance planning by firms to develop new products, retool and reorganize production, and to develop marketing capabilities. In addition, an adequately funded retraining program is necessary to retrain managers, engineers, and the rest of the work force for commercial work and to provide relocation assistance. In defense-dependent communities there is need for well-targeted support for local diversification and development.[33] These provisions provide the framework and incentives for military contractors to seriously evaluate opportunities in public and private civilian markets and for communities and workers to adjust where conversion cannot be undertaken.

Conversion planning is necessary at the industry and firm level because market forces alone cannot ensure the efficient transfer of labor and capital to civilian production. Market forces tend to fail in many military-related sectors largely because the market structure in which military-serving firms operate is not competitive. Moreover, the lack of efficient cost- and quality-control techniques in military production make it very difficult for firms to adapt their management and production practices to civilian markets. Furthermore, most firms lack marketing experience in commercial markets. More often than not these factors lead the management of many military-serving firms to simply lay off workers and hunker down for more defense work. Where that fails, the corporate managers of multi-division firms often opt to write off facilities because the multi-division firms usually already have commercial divisions that cannot readily absorb the excess capacity.

These conversion planning proposals do not force management to convert facilities, but rather they merely provide incentives to draw on the knowledge of management, engineering, technical, and production workers to find out if conversion is feasible. Nor does conversion planning provide ongoing subsidies, price supports, or other market interventions that would distort basic market allocation mechanisms.

Clearly some defense facilities cannot be profitably converted, particularly those that manufacture nuclear weapons and are very contaminated. In these cases, conversion planning tools provide workers and communities with an orderly, participatory process to cope with layoffs, and support to diversify the local economy, provide income support, relocate, and retrain displaced workers.

Another conversion challenge is retraining and employing the large number of uniformed and nonuniformed personnel of the DoD displaced due to defense cuts. Most uniformed personnel have access to some benefits which will allow them to go to college or vocational training institutions, but the existing benefits of the Montgomery Program should be expanded in order to assure greater access to educational and job-training programs so necessary to reenter the civilian economy.

A fiscal conversion policy is needed to complement this structural conversion process. A new fiscal policy would redirect resources to renew the nation's economic base and address the difficult task of conserving and restoring the environment. Redirecting scientific and technical resources towards basic and applied research on critical economic and environmental needs would stimulate development of new products, production processes, and markets and provide conversion opportunities for many high-tech military industries. Infrastructural investments in transportation and environmental protection would likewise generate new demand and conversion opportunities. Not only would these investments compensate for reduced military spending, they would also improve the nation's competitiveness and enhance the quality of life of all of its citizens.

For forty-five years our nation has pursued an industrial policy designed to make a military power second to none. This policy has succeeded brilliantly, but at a high cost. Today, we need an industrial policy geared to restoring our nation's economy. Economic conversion should be at the forefront of efforts to rebuild the U.S. economy and to meet the pressing human needs so long neglected during the Cold War.

Notes

A brief discussion of the Clinton administration's program in response to unemployment in the defense sector is presented in an appendix at the end of this volume.—Eds.

1. See Council of Economic Advisors, *Economic Report of the President,* (Washington, D.C.: U.S. GOP, February 1991), chapter 7.

2. See Murray Weidenbaum, "The Problems with Economic Conversion," (paper presented at the American Economic Association meeting, New Orleans, December 1991).

3. These shares are for fiscal year 1990 and the data are from the *Historical Tables, Budget of the United States Government,* table 3.3. The methodology for this analysis is drawn from an article by Paul Murphy, *The Military Bite of the Budget,* Washington, Defense Budget Project.

4. See Michael Dee Oden, *A Military Dollar Really Is Different,* (Lansing, Mich.: Employment Research Associates, 1987) for an overview and detailed literature survey on these issues. Also see J. Davidson Alexander, "Manufacturing Productivity and Military Depletion in the Postwar Industrial Economy" in *Towards a Peace Economy in the United States,* ed. Gregory A. Bischak (New York: St. Martin's Press, 1991).

5. See Ann Markusen and Joel Yudken, *Dismantling the Cold War Economy,* (New York: Basic Books, 1992); and Ann Markusen, Peter Hall, Scott Campbell, and Sabina Dutrich, *The Rise of the Gunbelt* (New York: Oxford University Press, 1991).

6. Richard W. Stevenson, "The Sputtering California Miracle," *New York Times,* 17 Oct. 1991: D1, D117.

7. See Bureau of Labor Statistics, *Displaced Workers 1981–1985* Bulletin #2289, (Washington, D.C.: Government Printing Office, September 1987), table B-9, p. 23.

8. See Center on Budget and Policy Priorities, "Erosion of Unemployment Coverage" (Washington, D.C.: Center on Budget and Policy Priorities, September 1991).

9. See U.S. Congress, Office of Technology Assessment, *Worker Training, Competing in the New International Economy,* (Washington, D.C.: Government Printing Office, 1990), especially chapter 1. Also see John D. Donahue, *Shortchanging the Workforce, The Job Training and Partnership Act and the Overselling of Privatized Training* (Washington D.C.: Economic Policy Institute, 1989), 14–20.

10. See Bureau of Labor Statistics, "Industry Output and Employment: A Slower Trend for the Nineties," *Monthly Labor Review,* November 1989, 35, table 6.

11. A discussion of EDWAA and evaluation of adequacy of economic assistance programs appears in U.S. Congress Office of Technology Assessment, *After the Cold War: Living With Lower Defense Spending,* (Washington D.C.: Government Printing Office, 1992.) The authors, one of whom participated on the OTA panel for this report, do not agree with the report's assessment in all aspects.

12. See U.S. Congress, Office of Technology Assessment, *Technology and Structural Unemployment: Reemploying Displaced Adults* (Washington D.C.: Government Printing Office, 1986), 16, 23. OTA notes that "labor policies to avoid displacement, to assist workers who are displaced, and to offer retraining to adult workers have generally been less active in the United States than in some other industrial democracies. Most European countries and Canada have programs designed to deal with displacement. Even in Japan, where the active government role is small, social and business customs often provide a high degree of security for some of the work force (primarily male)" (p.23). It observes, for example, that the Canadian Industrial Adjustment Service (IAS) "reaches many more workers, in relation to the size of the size of the Canadian labor force than Title III does for the U.S. work force" (p.16).

13. Ibid., 3, 16. According to the OTA, "Title III [of JTPA] served 96,100 workers in its first 9 months, and another 132,200 workers were newly enrolled in the full program year July, 1984–1985. This is probably less than 5 percent of the eligible population." It further notes, "whether Title III is an effective and sufficient response to the problem of worker displacement is questionable" (p.16).

14. Markusen and Yudken, *Dismantling,* 143–145.

15. See National Council for Urban Development, "Previous Community Economic Adjustment Experiences," in *Economic Adjustment/Conversion* (Washington, D.C.: Office of Economic Adjustment, July 1985), 23–36.

16. See Kenneth Adelman and Norman Augstine, "Defense Conversion: Bulldozing the Management," *Foreign Affairs,* Spring 1992: 26–47.

17. See Jack Stokes Ballard, *The Shock of Peace: Military and Economic Demobilization after World War II* (Washington, D.C.: University Press of America, 1983).

18. Ibid. Also see J. Davidson Alexander, "Conversion Planning: 1945 and 1990," (paper presented at the American Economic Association meeting, Atlanta, Georgia, December 1989).

19. These computations come from the Office of the Comptroller, Department of Defense, *National Defense Budget Estimates for FY 1990/91* (Washington, D.C.: Government Printing Office, March 1989) 118, table 7.5.

20. See Murray Weidenbaum, "Obstacles to Conversion," *Bulletin of the Atomic Scientists,* April 1964, for his discussion of the post-Korean War conversion efforts in Boeing and the aerospace industry. Curiously, Weidenbaum, who was a Boeing economist, plays down the success of Boeing's efforts because they did not immediately lead to a rapid growth in the commercial division's sales revenues. However, the key point is that the commercial division developed out of the transfer of resources from the defense work force and production capacity, and eventually led to the commercial division generating more sales revenues by the end of the 1960s.

21. The study of the Office of Technology Assessment *After the Cold War* examines some of these cases studies. In addition, see Office of Economic Adjustment, *Economic Adjustment/Conversion*, chapter 7 for an analysis of these cases.

22. For an analysis of the practice of concurrency see Anthony DiFilippo, *How the Military-Serving Firm Differs from the Rest,* ECD Briefing Paper 10 (Washington D.C., National Commission for Economic Conversion and Disarmament, March 1991), 4–5.

23. See Office of Economic Adjustment, *Economic Adjustment/Conversion,* 40.

24. For more details on these and other cases see Gregory A. Bischak and James Raffel *Successful Conversion Examples* (Washington,

D.C.: Commission for Economic Conversion and Disarmament, December 1991).

25. See James Raffel, "Los Angeles Faces the End of The Cold War," *The New Economy* (Washington D.C.: National Commission for Economic Conversion and Disarmament), Summer 1991.

26. Ibid.

27. Eric Schmitt, "U.S. Weapons Makers Intensify Lobbying Efforts as Budgets Fall," *New York Times,* 6 Aug. 1991: 1, D6.

28. Reported in Richard W. Stevenson, "So Far, St. Louis Handles Arms Cut," *New York Times,* 8 Aug. 1991: D1, D11.

29. William W. Kaufman and John Steinbruner, *Decisions for Defense: Prospects for a New Order* (Washington, D.C.: The Brookings Institution, 1991): 54–55.

30. Eric Schmitt, "Pentagon Making a List of Choices for Spending Cuts," *New York Times,* 24 Nov. 1991: 1, 32.

31. See M. Anderson, G. Bischak, and M. Oden, *Converting the American Economy: The Economic Effects of an Alternative Security Policy,* (Lansing, Mich.: Employment Research Associates, 1991).

32. This section of the paper draws upon the authors' work, *Converting the American Economy.*

33. These are the key elements of House Resolution 441 (1992), a comprehensive conversion proposal advanced by the late Congressman Ted Weiss (D-NY).

6

Capitol Hill and Conversion: A Summary of Recent Congressional Action

Maggie Bierwirth

Introduction

The first substantial appropriation for economic conversion was approved by Congress in 1990, building on efforts to pass economic conversion legislation that began in 1964 with Senators George McGovern (D-SD) and Charles Mathias (R-MD). In the 1970s, Congressman Ted Weiss (D-NY) introduced a similar bill in the House of Representatives; his colleagues Nicholas Mavroules (D-MA), Sam Gejdenson (D-CT), and Mary Rose Oakar (D-OH) introduced their own legislation in the 1980s, when other members of Congress joined the effort, and by 1992 a virtual cottage industry in economic conversion bills had sprung up. This chapter will focus on the legislative process of developing an initial, $200-million consensus conversion amendment to the 1990 Defense Authorization bill, and will briefly describe a follow-on $1 billion package.

The View from Capitol Hill

The process of developing a consensus among legislative approaches to conversion began in December 1988, almost a year before the fall of the

Berlin Wall. Initially, then-Speaker Jim Wright asked the four House members who had introduced legislation—Weiss, Mavroules, Gejdenson, and Oakar—to form a working group to write a consensus bill for the purpose of assisting communities that would be impacted by the December 31 recommendations of the 1988 Base Closure Commission. That context was far more narrow than the sweeping reorganization of national priorities that would soon confront Americans as the Cold War ended, but for those who wished to see it, the handwriting was on the wall. Still, world events moved faster than legislative negotiations, and by the time the conversion package was considered by Congress, it seemed meager to many, especially to scholars and activists whose views, goals, and agenda were already well developed. The modest first attempt at conversion funding provided $200 million for job training and community economic development, and it addressed relatively simple goals:

1. to put new economic conversion provisions into law so that when more funding was needed, the program would already be on the books, on the assumption that it would be easier to increase funding for existing programs in the future than to start up a big one from scratch;
2. to begin to generate additional success stories of conversion and diversification, dispelling the myth that "conversion doesn't work," and removing that argument from the arsenal of conversion opponents when increased appropriations were needed;
3. to establish a precedent to underscore the principle that the federal government has a unique responsibility to provide assistance to communities that have dedicated their labor to defense contracts.

However, the congressional working group didn't begin and end with those simple goals. Along the way they struggled with larger objectives such as the need for extended unemployment compensation, specialized retraining for managers and engineers whose needs would differ from those of welders and sheet-metal workers, and the inadequacy of market forces to replace economic activity caused by defense cuts—particularly in hard-hit defense dependent areas.

Forging Consensus

The working group started with the four existing bills that they had written. Congressman Ted Weiss (D-NY) had introduced the most sweeping bill, a $1-billion-plus proposal to provide full health benefits and 80–90 percent of salaries to laid-off defense workers during their retraining period, to be financed by a 1¼ percent tax on defense contracts. Weiss's bill also required site-specific economic conversion plans from defense contractors, as a condition of doing business with the Department of Defense. The plans would be drawn up by alternative-use committees composed of labor and management representatives in a cooperative effort to develop mutually agreeable, technologically feasible, economically viable nondefense products.

Congressman Nicholas Mavroules (D-MA) sponsored a more modest bill that concentrated on providing job retraining, to be financed by setting aside a percentage of savings from defense reductions. Congresswoman Mary Rose Oakar (D-OH) wrote a bill incorporating community economic development assistance, job retraining, and unemployment benefits. Congressman Sam Gejdenson (D-CT) introduced legislation to provide $200 million for job training through the Job Training Partnership Act (JTPA) and community-based economic development through the Economic Development Administration (EDA).

The strength of the Weiss approach was its broad scope and emphasis on planning ahead so as to minimize the difficulties of economic transition. Ironically, the scope of the bill also made Weiss's approach vulnerable to criticism, from those opposed to government intervention in business, from conversion opponents of course, and even from some conversion proponents who believed that its "cookie-cutter" approach—exacting the same requirements from all defense facilities, be they dedicated to defense products or already familiar with commercial markets—set the program up for failure by lacking sufficient flexibility to give workers and communities the option to convert their local economies if the defense plant couldn't or wouldn't "play ball." Strangely, similar criticisms of the Department of Defense, which often requires its contractors *not* to develop other products, are rarely heard.

The Mavroules bill was more modest, and its sponsor's reputation as a defense moderate gave the issue of economic conversion increased credibility among certain cautious or more conservative members of Congress. However, the bill's lack of economic development provisions restricted its most useful applications to communities with diverse, growing economies, where retrained workers would have the least difficulty finding new jobs, and where defense layoffs would have the least disruptive effect. The Gejdenson and Oakar bills' strengths were that they coupled economic development in advance of defense layoffs, to sow the seeds of new jobs early, with retraining provisions to prepare the work force for new jobs. Like the proposal that eventually became law, the most frequent criticism of the Gejdenson, Oakar, and Mavroules bills was that while their modest scope increased their chances for passage, they did not include adequate funding to address the nation's needs comprehensively.

Planning a Legislative Strategy

The compromise enacted into law included parts of the four bills discussed briefly above. The discussions that led to the first sizable appropriation for defense economic adjustment—$200 million—were complex and strove to incorporate the views of all the participants. Labor unions, public interest groups, and affected federal agencies took part. It took eighteen months to hammer out a legislative strategy, a bill, and amendments to implement it.

Early discussions among the members of Congress focused on whether the Weiss bill's requirement for facility-based advance planning by alternative-use committees was feasible. The bill called for labor-management committees at each defense production facility to draw up plans for alternative use, including new products that could be manufactured at the facility. In theory, the plans would be "shelf-ready" and available to guide production when defense contracts were terminated. Proponents of the Weiss approach are quick to point out that for the alternative-use committees to succeed, retraining of managers and engineers is a prerequisite so that they shed their habit of producing highly specialized weapons at any cost for the Department of Defense, and begin to inculcate the values of the commercial world: mass production at low cost. Even if such retraining were successfully accomplished, some of the congressional working group members questioned whether companies would be willing or able to comply with the advance planning requirement, going to the trouble and expense of conducting production analyses and marketing studies for new products, unless the defense market had already dried up. In a highly developed competitive global economy, it seemed unrealistic to some to keep marketing plans on the shelf while commercial competitors around the globe marched forward with new and innovative products.

However, the members of Congress agreed that a mechanism for advance preparation was desirable; if not site-specific conversion plans, then community-based diversification to generate and sustain new industries constituted a realistic and desirable alternative approach. Economic development grants for diversification could be funded for a relatively modest investment—$200 or $300 million to start, from a defense budget of nearly $300 billion. Gejdenson emphasized the importance of getting the program written into law, generating successes, and increasing funding in the future when the program's value had been demonstrated in fact as well as in theory. Mavroules felt strongly that it was critical to go forward with a proposal of modest proportions, for which a majority in Congress could be mustered with relative ease, rather than risk losing everything by advancing an ambitious proposal with slim support. Weiss understood that the 1¼ percent tax on defense contracts would not be part of the consensus legislation, but he wanted to include extended unemployment benefits as well as job retraining.

All the members of the congressional working group agreed that extended unemployment benefits were needed for defense workers, because even if diversification plans could be implemented quickly in the communities that needed them, the transition period from defense to new industries could easily take longer than the six months in which workers would receive regular unemployment benefits. In some cases, thousands of skilled workers were at risk of being laid off in regions where the entire economy was defense-dominated. New businesses take time to grow and prosper, and while they may absorb gradual increases in unemployment from defense layoffs, they could not absorb precipitous job losses. The proposal to provide extended unemployment benefits (beyond twenty-six weeks) to defense workers became embroiled in the much larger political question of extended unemployment benefits for the entire American work force.

The members of the congressional working group were doubtful that the Ways and Means Committee would agree to single out defense workers for benefits without examining the broader question of extended unemployment benefits for all workers, a controversial and time-consuming process with enormous potential impact on the federal budget. However, the Banking Committee and the Education and Labor Committee could be counted on to approve a bill or bills to provide legislative authority for additional funding for JTPA and EDA as part of a defense economic adjustment package. Then Congressman Mavroules would shepherd the finished bill(s) through the Armed Services Committee, for inclusion in the annual defense authorization bill, with a commitment from Chairman Les Aspin (D-WI) to provide economic adjustment funding in the defense bill.

The congressional working group generally agreed that all the economic adjustment ideas were meritorious, and that an approach that combined them all was the most desirable. They were reasonably sure they could get $200 million for a modest program of job retraining and economic development assistance, but they also wanted to provide extended unemployment, with a much higher price tag. Two possibilities were suggested: a single bill including all the provisions discussed above, or several bills, each focused on one element of the overall economic adjustment program. Including everything in one bill was a much riskier choice, because such a bill would have to be approved by at least four committees with jurisdiction over its programs and emerge reasonably intact, without major alterations—an unlikely scenario. However, a package of several bills, each one tailored to a single committee's jurisdiction, could be worked through the committees one by one, with confidence that some of the committees would report favorably, and those provisions could be included in the defense bill to form a core economic adjustment program. An even simpler solution was to move the JTPA and EDA provisions through the Education and Labor Committee and the Banking Committee, and then include them in the defense bill. With such a core program safely on its way to passage into law, all the advocates of an economic adjustment program—members of Congress, unions, and other public interest groups—could focus their efforts on the more ambitious and riskier extended unemployment provision, which would be offered as an amendment, regardless of how it fared in the Ways and Means Committee.[1]

This approach was enthusiastically received because the more cautious members of the congressional working group liked the guarantee that at least a modest core proposal could be included in the defense bill, where its opponents would have a hard time making the case to remove it by amendment, and passage into law was virtually assured. In addition, economic conversion advocates could focus more of their efforts on the

1. Under House rules, the committee with jurisdiction is entitled to mark up any bill that includes subject matter under its jurisdiction. In this case, the Banking Committee, the Education and Labor Committee, and the Ways and Means Committee were entitled to amend and approve the subject matter under their jurisdiction: the EDA, JTPA, and extended unemployment provisions respectively, if those provisions were included in the defense bill before it reached the House floor.

However, amendments made on the House floor must be germane to the bill under consideration, and in most cases must be made in order by the Rules Committee, which structures House debate. The committee of jurisdiction need not have considered the amendments, although they may request that the Rules Committee not make such amendments in order.

more ambitious extended unemployment plan, thus improving its uncertain chances for passage.

However, Chairman Aspin was reluctant to authorize programs outside the jurisdiction of the Department of Defense—the core JTPA and EDA provisions—in the defense bill. The plan was altered significantly, so that both the core proposal and the extended unemployment provisions would be offered as floor amendments. In the end, efforts to offer both a core and an unemployment amendment failed when Ways and Means Committee Chairman Dan Rostenkowski (D-IL) objected to extended unemployment being debated on the defense bill instead of in his committee. Thus, the Rules Committee made only one of the group's amendments, the core amendment, in order.

On September 18, 1990, the House of Representatives approved the core proposal in the form of an amendment to H.R. 4739, the National Defense Authorization Act for Fiscal Year 1991, providing $150 million for defense workers' job retraining through JTPA and $50 million in EDA funding for economic adjustment in defense-dependent communities. The amendment was offered by Congressman Mavroules, and was adopted by a vote of 288 to 128. During debate on the amendment, the members of the congressional working group circulated flyers to their colleagues with the heading "Don't Leave Defense Workers Defenseless."

The Senate, virtually without debate, had included its own economic adjustment provisions in its version of the defense bill, in the dead of night on August 3, 1990. The Senate provisions were a noncontroversial place-holder, to ease their passage in the Senate, but were crafted to reflect the general outline of the House defense economic adjustment program. After both chambers had passed their respective versions of the defense bill, a conference committee meeting was held to resolve differences, and with minor changes, the House's economic adjustment provisions became law in November 1990.

The Real Battle: Implementation

Then the real struggle began. Despite the roadblocks overcome, getting the money to the communities where it is needed has proven more difficult than passing legislation. The Department of Defense (DoD) raised a host of objections to the plan, despite its enactment into law, and in May 1991, Congressman Mavroules held a hearing to ask DoD representatives why the funds had not yet been transferred. In the glare of public opinion, the DoD witnesses stated publicly that the transfer would be duly accomplished. An unusual amount of constituent activity had been generated to turn up the heat on the DoD to release the money, with activists and local elected officials frequently contacting the Office of Economic Adjustment (OEA) to find out when regulations to implement the law would be published, and when grant money would be available.

However, not until August 1991, did the Department of Labor receive the $150 million in JTPA funds. And after the DoD had dropped its objections to the plan, the Department of Commerce (which oversees EDA) raised new ones. To satisfy the Department of Commerce's objections, language was placed in a Fiscal Year 1992 appropriations bill to facilitate the funding transfer to EDA. More than a year had passed, and the modest $50 million that was meant for advance preparations for defense cuts was still hostage to bureaucratic objections.

1992: A Billion for Conversion

In the fall of 1990, just when the first conversion appropriation was being signed into law, a budget agreement was formed between congressional leaders and the Bush administration. Enacted into law as the Budget Enforcement Act of 1990, within the Omnibus Budget Reconciliation Act of 1990, the agreement placed spending caps on defense and nondefense discretionary spending, and further required that if spending reductions were made below the caps, the resulting "savings" would be devoted to deficit reduction (that is, those funds could not be transferred from defense to nondefense spending, or vice versa, without passing special legislation, potentially opening up issues which were even more controversial, such as taxes). While the budget agreement didn't affect the $200 million for conversion, which had already been signed into law, it put severe constraints on conversion legislation under consideration in 1992.

On March 31, 1992, the House of Representatives voted on a bill to take down the budget "walls" between spending categories, thus providing for the transfer of funds from defense to nondefense discretionary spending. By vote of 187 to 238, the House failed to pass the bill, and as a result, any funding available for conversion would have to be spent by the Department of Defense. This provision was so objectionable to many activist groups that they circulated letters on Capitol Hill asking Congress to reject such a conversion plan, even though the available funding was $1 billion.

Despite the groups' efforts, broad bipartisan support was achieved for the $1 billion conversion amendment authored by Armed Services

Committee Chairman Les Aspin (D-WI) and offered by Congressman Martin Frost (D-TX). Within the Department of Defense, the amendment called for:

- development of dual-use (military/civilian) technologies through consortia (joint efforts) of defense firms and the DoD;
- a defense technology extension program that will make information or manufacturing processes and technologies available for dual-use applications, especially for small businesses;
- technical support services for small business defense contractors to assist them in bringing new products to market;
- expansion of the Small Business Innovation Research (SBIR) program, which helps small businesses develop new technologies and products;
- education and training programs for former defense personnel, especially in teaching and environmental services;
- economic adjustment assistance planning for states and local governments;
- health benefits, job placement, and early retirement for certain terminated DoD civilian personnel.

Although this program is likely to be funded at a level that was beyond reach just two years earlier, and conversion proponents agree that the $200 million appropriated in 1990 is woefully inadequate to address the nation's needs, the program faced opposition from conversion advocates on the grounds that civilian agencies are the appropriate ones to administer the transition to nondefense activities, and the program's emphasis on dual-use technologies was misguided, as the potential for civilian use of defense technologies is limited and dual-use manufacturing would be favored at the expense of other industries.

The Limits of Congressional Policy-Making

Implementing large-scale policy changes such as the constructive industrial policy represented by economic conversion and diversification is extremely difficult to achieve without presidential leadership. No parliament in the world is expected to function without a prime minister, and likewise Congress constitutionally must rely on a chief executive, the president, to carry out its programs. When Congress makes appropriations and the administration is reluctant to spend them, the limits of congressional policy making become readily apparent, as they did in this case where the executive branch found ample opportunity to engage in stalling tactics and foot-dragging.

In sum, the $200 million economic adjustment package passed by Congress was limited by the constraints of legislative procedure, the fact that it was embedded in larger issues including extended unemployment compensation and industrial policy, and the lack of presidential leadership. These difficulties are not minor or coincidental; they reflect basic philosophical differences about the need for advance planning and the federal government's role in the economy.

All this suggests the need for a new approach, one that can garner a large and powerful political constituency to help break through the logjams of resistance to change. The time is ripe for a new debate on national priorities. It must be cast not in terms of "how do we convert excess defense capacity?" but "how can we reinvest defense savings to improve national economic security?" Every American has a stake in the latter question, not just defense-dependent communities fearing lost bases and contracts, or activists seeking reduced defense spending to finance domestic programs.

An economic adjustment agenda for the 1990s must include increased federal demand and funding for infrastructure, energy, transportation, and environmental projects, from research and development to large- and small-scale construction. There is substantial skills overlap in these areas for defense workers and companies because they involve technology, metal fabrication, and government contracting. Such projects can also serve as a bridge to commercial technology by providing start-up research grants that will enable defense companies to develop new technologies and products—in energy, for example—that can then be sold to both the public and private sectors. Low-cost loans and export assistance are also critical, inexpensive elements of a federal commitment to transitional assistance for defense companies. Such programs will provide added incentive for defense companies to make the substantial risks of private capital needed to diversify and convert their product lines.

The difficulties encountered in passing the first economic adjustment package illustrate the need for a broad cross section of the American people to make clear demands of their democratic system of government. The 1990s are a crucial time for creative leadership. If the American people demand that a debate on national priorities be part of presidential and Congressional elections, the democratic process will finally have to respond with a comprehensive economic policy. Only in that context can the needs of defense-dependent communities really be met.

7

Converting the Military Industrial Economy: The Experience of Six Communities

Catherine Hill, Sabina Deitrick, and Ann Markusen

Introduction

The fate of the military budget hangs in the balance, and will continue to do so for years to come. The end of the Cold War could mean the dismantling of a huge and very expensive arsenal of highly automated, high-tech weaponry that is regarded by many as having sapped the productive vigor of the economy and deflected resources from pressing social and infrastructural needs. In this chapter, we address the task of converting this segment of the economy to other uses, differentiating demand-side from supply-side approaches. We distinguish four alternative models of conversion, each organized around a different target: converting the company, converting the community economic base, converting the worker, and converting the facility.

After some discussion of each approach, we scrutinize the last of these, which is the most difficult and yet the most attractive in terms of retaining jobs and stabilizing communities. After stating both strict and broader criteria for judging success, we present six geographically dispersed and industrially diverse case studies that, while not successful in the narrow sense, have had an impact on public thinking about the formidable task of conversion. Partially as a result of these efforts, several states have passed legislation to assist conversion. In other cases, ongoing organizations continue to pursue conversion and/or other economic development endeavors. As a group, the cases demonstrate the ability and willingness of defense workers to plan for civilian work. In some, local conversion planning has led to an alliance between labor and peace organizations that has strengthened the political clout and institutional capabilities of both.

Finally, we address the conditions that have facilitated or impeded success across the case studies. The conversion efforts share several common obstacles: the unsuitability of current defense business practices for competing in commercial markets, the opposition of key management people to joint planning, and disarray or antagonism among potential members of alternative-use planning coalitions. We conclude that worker participation and unity enhance prospects for success, that success requires early warning and financial disclosure on the part of the company, that state or federal government intervention and funding will be necessary for the conversion of many facilities, and that workers and peace activists can overcome differences and work in coalition. We compare facility conversion to the more general case of plant closings and conclude that conversion, because it involves product and market shifts, will require technical assistance from outside parties, particularly in marketing, financial analysis, and social cost accounting. Conversion efforts in the 1980s have not reproduced the success of the World War II conversions, or even the efforts undertaken in the post-Vietnam era (see chapter five.) Nevertheless, we do not conclude that conversion doesn't work; rather, we observe that without government planning both on the demand and supply sides of the equation, community and labor efforts will face an uphill battle. In conclusion, we recommend that government undertake conversion planning linking the capacities of local companies with a national agenda to redirect military spending toward social and infrastructural needs.

The task of economic conversion attracted considerable interest and debate by the late 1980s.[1] Conferences on conversion were held all over the country—in Orange County in California, in Boston, in Columbus, in Seattle, in Harrisburg. Technical assistance groups who had been laboring on the issue for a decade, including the Washington-based National Commission on Economic Conversion and Disarmament and the California-based Center for Economic Conversion, found themselves overwhelmed with inquiries. At least two major constituencies, sometimes at odds, are involved in current conversion efforts: first, the peace movement, with its fears that economic stakes in the military budget will block disarmament, and second, workers and their unions, community groups, and politicians whose livelihoods are threatened by military cutbacks. Despite their vastly different perspectives, in the conversion efforts we investigated, aside from some instances of miscommunication, these groups were able to work together.

The Conversion Nexus: Supply and Demand When Governments Are the Market

In many ways, the problem of defense-plant or base conversion resembles that of any plant closing. Imminent closure threatens the loss of jobs and tax base to the community, while individual workers must face an uncertain labor market and the shock of a move, a premature retirement, or sinking to a lower rung of the labor market. Yet conversion of defense facilities is a unique problem, because the $300 billion market sector in which such economic units operate is distinctly different from that of sectors like steel, food processing, or insurance, where sales are made on an open commercial market. While defense manufacturers can sell abroad, marketing to foreign governments remains tied to the foreign-policy directives of politicians.[2]

The biggest difference lies in the demand side of this market. Instead of a host of individual consumers or a modest number of big business buyers, firms and plants in the military market sell to a government bureaucracy, the Pentagon and, through its foreign military sales program, to foreign governments. Generally, weapons systems for the United States military account for the bulk of military contractors' orders, with foreign sales accounting for a significant portion of some military equipment such as fighter aircraft.[3] The way the American military decides to buy a particular weapons system (or aircraft part, or uniform) is a complex process in which need is articulated by one or more military services (Army, Navy, Air Force), shaped into a budget request by the Department of Defense (DoD) and the president's Office of Management and Budget, and then reshaped by Congress in the appropriations process. To sell a product to this many-faceted customer requires a marketing system wholly unlike that familiar to companies operating in commercial markets, one requiring institutional knowledge of the customer and skill at lobbying Congress and military leaders. Furthermore, such sales are apt to be the culmination of a design, development, and planning process that can take as long as a decade, particularly for the high-tech portions of procurement. By the time money is appropriated for a program like the B-2 bomber, the relationship between buyer and supplier has been cemented, through prior contracts for research and development and construction of prototypes.

On the supply side, the military economy consists of a set of very large corporations, many of them born and bred on Cold War military budgets. Twenty corporations received 47 percent of the $145 billion in prime procurement contracts in 1988, more than $1 billion apiece. Some, such as General Dynamics, Grumman, and Martin Marietta, sell more than two-thirds of their output to DoD and NASA. Others, for whom prime contracts form a minority of sales—Ford, GM (Hughes), and Unisys, for example—have separate divisions devoted to military markets. Grouped around these prime contractors are thousands of subcontractors, many of whom are also heavily defense-dependent.

In contrast to commercially oriented production, these companies have relatively small runs or "batch" production systems, eschewing the economies of scale of mass production. They employ large numbers of specialized scientists and engineers and highly skilled blue-collar workers, compared to the preponderance of semiskilled assemblers found in commercial operations. Business planning is preoccupied with design and performance requirements, rather than with keeping costs down.[4]

The fact that a great deal of military equipment is produced by very large corporations often means that segments of management and labor within the industry have different stakes in periods of defense-spending decreases. Top corporate managers may prefer diversification—they may have milked profits from a recent buildup period to diversify into other nondefense fields through buyouts and mergers. Workers, including some engineers and managers, may see their futures tied up with the survival of the facility and support conversion planning. In small, one-plant businesses, this tension may be absent.[5] In the cases we studied, management was steadfastly opposed to conversion for defense facilities, while many workers supported conversion planning.

Much of the current debate in the peace movement on the appropriate target for activism centers on this demand/supply dichotomy.[6] Some would prefer to strike squarely at the demand side—through pressure on Congress to lower the defense budget. Others argue that the massiveness and interdependency of the military-industrial complex, and the vulnerability of the work force and communities dependent upon military spending, deter congressional action; on moral grounds, they argue for direct attention to the supply side. They stress the necessity to engage in direct plant-by-plant alternative-use planning along with worker adjustment programs.[7] The labor movement is increasingly interested in the latter approach, as are communities threatened with the destruction of a portion of their economic base. However, some peace activists are pessimistic about the prospects for conversion, preferring instead to align themselves with groups like educators, social workers, housing activists, and other constituencies who would presumably benefit from a change in national spending priorities.

Some question whether this kind of conceptual separation between the demand (state) and supply (private-sector) sides is meaningful at all. The relationship between the military-industrial sectors and the state is addressed by a considerable and lively literature.[8] Some scholars argue that the level and nature of military demand is predominantly shaped by foreign policy concerns to protect the national interest. Others stress the systemic needs of capitalism for a state that will police the world for the benefit of multinational corporations, while others argue that a recession-prone capitalist economy must dispose of its economic surplus in nonproductive activities like defense. Yet others argue that neither foreign policy nor systemic economic imperatives drive the defense budget. Instead, a segment of American industry in partnership with the Pentagon—the military-industrial complex—acts as a special interest group to bloat the defense budget at the expense of other public priorities and other segments of capital. In this latter view, supply drives demand.

These positions differ in their prognosis of the potential for defense reductions and the likely effects they will have on the economy. If foreign policy concerns really do drive the budget, then there is little need for a congressional initiative, because the present thaw will by itself drive down military spending. In this case, we need only worry about adjustment assistance. If the reductions are going to precipitate a serious recession, then linking conversion to a macroeconomic spending initiative is essential.[9] If the budget is determined by the power of the military industrial complex rather than by foreign policy or economic rationales, then an attack on Congress is essential. In this case, the economy could be expected to boom given the change to reordered priorities without much supply side intervention. Our analysis of the conversion efforts in the 1980s suggest that management opposition to conversion poses a formidable obstacle for a demand driven restructuring of the economy, and that failure to offer workers and communities a concrete alternative will result in their support of continued military spending at the federal level. We return to these more general issues about demand formation and its implications for conversion strategies in the final section of this chapter.

Four Adjustment Models

Several kinds of phenomenan have been described as conversion. We have identified four different approaches to conversion, each with a different target and each with different lead actors. They are the corporate-diversification model or "converting the company," the economic-development model or "converting the economic base of a community," the worker-adjustment model or "converting the individual employee," and the alternative-use model or "converting the facility." While our case studies involved only this last type of conversion, the first three models are important in that they represent alternative ways to conceptualize and remedy the impact of military plant or base closures.

Converting the Company

In the company-based model, conversion is a business adjustment process. When military dollars dry up, firms turn to commercial markets and attempt to diversify their facilities and/or investment funds. Firms play the lead role, and the goal is restored profitability for the company as a whole. As the Reagan buildup tapered off, many companies scrambled to diversify through acquisition, merger, or internal development. Some succeeded in bringing down their defense dependency ratios, although existing divisions remained even more military-oriented than before.[10] Raytheon is an example. Over two decades it purchased two appliance manufacturers, an oil exploration firm, an airplane manufacturer, and a publishing house, lowering its defense dependency by the mid 1980s to under 50 percent.[11] Relying heavily on acquisitions, the Raytheon strategy resulted in few crossovers of workers from military to commercial activities, and thousands of workers were laid off during periods of military cutbacks.[12]

A minority of firms have tried to market existing military products to commercial users or have embarked upon new product development. Only this last strategy promises to stabilize employment in existing plants under a scenario of extensive military spending cuts. The history of such efforts over the whole postwar period is far from encouraging. Murray

Weidenbaum surveyed a host of early conversion efforts and found that military-dependent firms had attempted to design and produce a variety of commercial items, ranging from canoes to computers to coffins. "With one major exception [commercial aircraft]," notes Weidenbaum, "these diversification attempts have each been relatively small in comparison with military equipment."[13] Likewise in a study of conversion and diversification efforts by six companies in the 1960s and 1970s, Robert DeGrasse found that few were successful at actual conversion of facilities. Rohr and Boeing-Vertol failed at their entry into the mass transit market. Raytheon's adaptation of microwave technology for home use and Kaman's ventures into guitar and bearings production are company success stories, but did not result in reemployment of the defense-related work force.[14]

One recent success story is the conversion of Frisby Airborne Systems on Long Island, which reduced its reliance on military contracts from 95 percent in 1985 to 35 percent in 1990.[15] Good management-employee relations and a coincidental surge in commercial aircraft sales helped Frisby make the transition. Nevertheless, the number of successful conversion cases is limited. Conversion advocates find themselves citing the same handful of success stories over and over, and executives like Greg Frisby are run ragged with requests to serve on panels and give public speeches. Most analysts have concluded that the big military contractors are still heavily committed to struggling over shares in a dwindling defense market and are most apt to diversify into other military or space lines rather than make the awkward transition to commercial markets.[16] Regrettably, no good comparative research has been done at the aggregate level on firms' strategies, failures, and successes. While we suspect that company-led diversification could work to preserve jobs more often than pessimists or anecdotal accounts suggest, the evidence to date is thin and discouraging.

Converting the Local Economic Base

The economic-development model places the local economic base at the center of its agenda, and the lead agents in this process are economic development planners, sometimes with the aid of the Pentagon. In this approach, planners attempt to "convert the community" by replacing the economic stimulus of the lost military dollar with other activities, sometimes reusing the site or space of a closed military base or plant. The existing kit of economic development tools are employed, including tax incentives, training assistance, and marketing help. One important difference between this approach and that of normal economic development activity is that the government is often willing to give away infrastructure at little or no cost.

Community economic adjustment has been the preferred strategy of the Office of Economic Adjustment (OEA) of the Department of Defense, a small unit in DoD whose funding has been maintained by Congress in the face of continual opposition from Republicans in the White House and top DoD management. According to the OEA, some 100 military bases that closed over the past 25 years have been successfully converted into schools, businesses, housing, and other uses, with a net civilian job gain of more than 64,680.[17] The OEA is explicitly opposed to conversion strategies that target particular facilities for conversion, arguing that traditional economic development strategies will suffice to revitalize formerly defense dependent economies.

Converting communities in this manner from their defense-dependent status employs familiar techniques for planners, but may fall into familiar traps. It is strictly a "professional" development model, banking on improving the business climate and on government incentives to private business to revitalize the community. In some instances, the costs of the incentives to private business may outweigh the benefits these companies bring to the community. No systematic research has been done evaluating diversification of military-dependent local economies through economic development approaches. Such research is badly needed, particularly to inform planners about the special opportunities and problems associated with government ownership of facilities.

Converting the Workers

The worker-adjustment model of economic conversion approaches the problem in the same vein but from the point of view of individuals. It counsels scrapping plants and letting companies exit, but helping workers cope through interim support, retraining, and placement services. The notion is that federal income support and adjustment programs be set up for workers in industries affected by military cutbacks, similar to those provided for other special classes of workers.[18] For example, the federal Trade Adjustment Assistance Act provides income support, including extended unemployment insurance, money for training, and relocation expenses, to workers who become unemployed due to import competition. The Title III program of the Job Training Partnership Act, which replaced the Comprehensive Employment and Training Act in 1982, is the other major component of the federal worker readjustment program. The Title III program has been criticized for its focus on short-term retraining and job search rather than on education, and the Trade Adjustment Assistance Act has been criticized for long delays in processing claims and covering too few workers.[19] In a version put forward by Oil Chemical and Atomic Workers' Union official Tony Mazzochi, a superfund would be created for displaced defense workers modelled on the GI Bill and environmental cleanup laws, where company contributions would enable displaced workers to return to school with income support for enough time to learn new analytical skills. Advocates for a superfund for displaced workers note that in the debate over the original GI Bill, many argued that war-related workers should be included in the assistance program. In the end, however, only veterans were included in the GI Bill.[20]

Only small-scale programs have been recommended for displaced war-related workers, and these programs were geared toward technical and professional staff rather than blue-collar workers. Defense-related layoffs of engineers and scientists in the early 1970s generated enough concern that the government created a Technology Mobilization and Reemployment Program that involved career counseling, job search grants, on-the-job training, and relocation assistance. An innovative component of this effort by state and local governments to place former aerospace engineers in professional jobs was unsuccessful due to workers' reluctance to relocate, confusion about how skills could be transferred, and a lack of funding at the state and local level.[21] A current effort along these same lines is underway in Florida. There, military personnel with scientific or technical backgrounds facing "involuntary separation" from the military are being placed in teaching positions. State education officials hope that these military personnel will fill the shortage of qualified science and math teachers in Florida. They expect the program to be more successful than its predecessors because expected military personnel cutbacks are more substantial.[22]

Although proportionally more engineers and scientists may be displaced in military industrial activity than in industries like auto and steel, blue-collar workers are still apt to lose jobs in greater numbers. Furthermore, their reemployment prospects are relatively bleaker than they are for the college-educated professional. Studies forecasting military workers' displacement experience suggest that blue-collar workers will be unemployed for longer stints and will experience greater declines in their relative incomes once defense plants close.[23]

Worker adjustment strategies "convert" the individual from a defense worker to a civilian worker. There are both operational and normative difficulties in pursuing worker conversion. The worker adjustment strategy assumes that jobs for retrained workers will exist in the marketplace. But if military cutbacks are substantial and add to recessionary tendencies, this may not be the case. Some critics raise normative issues. Do defense workers warrant special treatment? Why shouldn't workers whose industries have been undercut by an industrial policy favoring aerospace also be covered? Should workers who on average earn more and have had more education invested in them at public expense deserve adjustment assistance not offered to other displaced workers?[24] Defenders of such assistance argue that the public sector has a special responsibility to this group of workers and that achievements for them are a step in the door for other workers.

Converting the Facility

Facility conversion is the final model, which envisions alternative-use planning as a joint effort of community, labor, and management representatives. It is at once both more narrowly construed—targeted at individual sites—and more ambitious—aimed at maintaining livelihoods for existing workers in existing plants. It calls for more explicit institutional changes than the previous models, both in the planning and implementation stages. The beneficiary of considerable academic design work and of a number of singular experiments, this strategy is based on a view that management either can't or won't tackle facility conversion on its own. Management requires a blend of "instruction and imposition," involving participation of workers, community groups, and government. In this model, the initiating impulse comes from outside plant management—from the workers, the community, the peace movement, and/or local government staff.

Inspiration for contemporary alternative-use planning came originally from the plan by the workers of Lucas Aerospace in Britain to convert their facility in the 1970s. Since then, a number of scholars have worked on designs for such planning, chief among them Seymour Melman, long-time scholar of the military-industrial complex and a staunch advocate of conversion.[25] These designs favor decentralized conversion, eschewing another Washington bureaucracy. They advocate mandatory alternative-use planning, paid for by companies (and presumably recoverable from government contracts) and conducted by joint local committees of management, labor, and community representatives. Committees researching alternative uses would have access to company data and to outside consultants and marketing help in drafting a new business plan. Government would pitch in with funds for retraining, transitional income support, and coordination via a National Economic Conversion Commission. A version of such alternative-use planning is contained in the bill H.R. 44 (102nd Congress), and it was a major bone of contention during the congressional debates on conversion in the summer of 1990. Alternative-use planning has not yet been adapted as law.

Despite the interest in this last approach, no evaluative research on cases of community/labor-initiated facility conversion has been conducted to date. Because alternative-use planning is more directly concerned with job retention than the other models described above, we decided to further investigate this model and "test" it against experience to date. In the course of our research, we chose to focus on a half dozen controversial and specific cases of facility-based conversion in the past decade, to see how well each matches up to the Melman model and what each reveals about the politics and implementation of such an approach. The results help to illuminate the other models as well, since facility conversion can be an element in a company diversification or community economic development strategy.

Facility Conversion: An Evaluation

The Research Design

Over the period of the first six months of 1990, we investigated six cases of community/union-initiated efforts at facility conversion, four at privately owned plants and two at government-owned, contractor-operated facilities. The six were chosen on the basis of the relatively well-developed campaigns that were conducted on each site, the fact that each involved large numbers of jobs, and the availability of primary and secondary sources.[26] To find them, we canvassed all the groups in the U.S.—from the peace and labor movements, and plant closings—who had been active in and/or interested in conversion. Those sites that we chose were by and large the best-known efforts and together constitute a set of "best practice" cases. The cases are geographically representative and cover a fair spectrum of types of military production: Quincy Shipyards, a division of General Dynamics, making military ships in Massachusetts; Blaw-Knox foundry, a subsidiary of White Consolidated Industries, making tanks in Indiana; the Long Beach plant of McDonnell Douglas, making military aircraft in California; Lockheed Shipyards, Marine Division, outside Seattle; Philadelphia Naval Yards, repairing and overhauling military ships; and a Unisys Corporation plant in Minneapolis producing military computer systems for the Navy. Some of the efforts had been completed as of our inquiries, while others were still in developmental stages.

In each case, we either interviewed the various parties to the effort, including management, labor, and representatives of the community, and/or we relied upon secondary sources where others had already done this investigative work. In each case, we asked the following questions. What did the facility make, who owned it, and what was its current predicament? Who initiated the conversion effort? Who were the leaders of the effort? Was there funding and staff for the effort, and who provided it? How broad was the participation in the effort, both on a group-by-group basis and by members within each group? What was the alternative-use strategy? Was there a social cost calculus applied? What were the attitudes of each of the major players as the process unfolded? What public policy and political issues were generated? How well did the effort "succeed" on the basis of the narrow and broad criteria? How generalizable are the lessons from each?

Criteria for "Success"

In order to evaluate these conversion initiatives, we must first specify the criteria for gauging "success." In this case, because the constituency for conversion is diverse, we developed both narrow and broad criteria. The narrow, and more demanding, goal is the preservation of jobs in the community in the existing plant. Does the alternative-use plan provide a similar number of jobs with similar salaries and wages? Is the plan "practical" (i.e. can stockholders make an acceptable return on investment)? This narrow criterion is the one of most immediate interest to workers, managers, and local governments directly involved in a military facility closing.

Because the peace movement is also a constituency for conversion planning, and given the magnitude of the changes necessary for successful conversion, a broader criterion is also appropriate. In it, conversion planning can be considered a success if it succeeds in educating management and workers, on the one hand, about their prospects, and educating voters, including peace activists themselves, on the other hand, about how difficult a contraction might prove and how badly conversion is needed.

In other words, a conversion effort, even if it fails as a jobs-preservation project, might have salutary effects overall. On the supply side, each effort moves us up the learning curve and helps to educate and empower the constituencies most affected, while on the demand side, it can feed into the sophisticated crafting of a political response to the spending-preserving efforts of the military-industrial complex. While this is more difficult to measure, it is important to recognize how these efforts contributed to the conversion debate overall.

Six Conversion Efforts: A Synopsis

Quincy Shipyards. Quincy Shipyards, a 180-acre yard located south of Boston, belonged to General Dynamics, the biggest purely military conglomerate in the nation. Quincy Yard employed more than 11,000 in the 1960s and 5,000 workers as recently as the mid 1980s, although the number of jobs fluctuated with the rise and fall of big projects. In 1982, its future looked grim as a large commercial effort failed and competition for military contracts heightened. Employment had fallen to 1,100, and the yard seemed destined to be smaller and more military-dependent than ever. At that point, a group of activist rank-and-file workers in the local shipbuilder's union initiated the South Shore Conversion Committee, creating a coalition with local peace activists. Without management, outside consultants, or local government involvement, they researched alternative uses themselves and proposed that the yard pioneer in making an ocean thermal energy conversion plant/ship to produce electricity at sea. Other new products not requiring major new investment included oil rigs, rail cars, and bridge spans. The South Shore Conversion Committee hoped to link up shipyard workers nationally with the peace effort, redirecting their industry toward civilian activities.

The Quincy effort ran into a number of organizational problems. On the whole, many rank-and-file members of the union were either indifferent or hostile, as was the "old guard" of the union leadership. At least one of the leaders interpreted this in retrospect as a strategic error in organizing. "The peace movement preached morality," he said, "and closed people's minds."[27] There were practical problems with organizing, too. Many of the workers were commuters eager to hit the road after work rather than attend lengthy planning meetings. The City of Quincy, reeling from a lawsuit that awarded General Dynamics $28 million for overassessment of property, was in no position financially to support alternative-use planning for the yard.

More importantly, General Dynamics adamantly opposed the alternative-use effort. The company claimed to have researched alternatives without finding a viable product. Moreover, the company had just completed a financially disastrous commercial venture building liquefied natural gas tankers. General Dynamics focused its energies on getting new Navy contracts, and in 1983 it was successful with a $409 million contract for cargo ships for the Navy's Rapid Deployment Force.

The new contract was a kiss of death for the conversion effort, distracting the attention of all but a few committed activists. However, the Navy contract won in 1983 proved to be the shipyard's last and in 1986 the facility was closed. In the final six months of the shipyard's operation interest in conversion renewed, and the State of Massachusetts commissioned a study on the shipyard's future, which concluded that shipbuilding was impractical until 1988 when the commercial shipbuilding market was forecasted to improve. The consultants noted that a new owner could make money on the yard but that the owner "will likely have an entirely different marketing philosophy, cost structure and pricing policy than the existing owner."[28]

General Dynamics sold the site to the Massachusetts Water Resources Department for $48 million, in essence, creating a cash bonus for the corporation for exiting. As of 1990, the government used the site for storing and shipping barge equipment. In 1991, the state hopes to have a secondary sludge treatment facility under construction. Other parts of the yard are used for the storage of vehicles. A 70-acre section of the yard was set aside for the shipbuilders' union for reuse as a shipyard. In 1990, 1,000 former shipyard workers created a plan to reopen the yard, of which they would be the new owners. Drexel-Burnham-Lambert has offered financing of $17 million contingent on a $10 million loan guarantee from the U.S. Economic Development Administration, who thus far have balked at the project. Advocates claim that the yard could take advantage of the strong global demand for shipbuilding and that the land and equipment costs of reopening would be minimal as the site is state owned and former General Dynamics equipment has been maintained.[29] Critics claim that increased foreign demand may be transitory as foreign governments may increase their shipbuilding capacities despite restrictive international agreements. Ironically, U.S. public and private capital investment may go to Poland's Gdansk yard rather than than to Quincy.

Overall, on the narrow criterion, the South Shore Conversion project was not successful. The yard was dismantled, and 5,000 jobs disappeared. The possibility of a smaller worker-owned shipyard has run into government opposition, although there may yet be a change of heart in the Economic Development Administration. Nor did the Quincy effort bear much fruit in terms of a larger effort at conversion planning, although one of the major participants did go on to work on the Philadelphia Naval Shipyards conversion effort. If anything, the Quincy case appears to have convinced Boston-area peace activists interested in conversion to concentrate on the demand side, working with groups such as teachers and housing activists to push for a change in federal spending priorities rather than targeting the point of production. On the other hand, the work done analyzing what could be made at shipyards and publicizing the social costs of closing was a valuable contribution to future conversion efforts.

Blaw-Knox Foundry. Blaw-Knox Foundry of East Chicago, Indiana, was a 70-year-old maker of heavy castings. Up through the late 1960s, it employed about 1,400 (mainly semiskilled workers) producing steel mill equipment, although about 15 percent of its output consisted of tanks, which it first made in World War II. But in the 1970s, a new conglomerate owner, White Consolidated Industries, began switching into production of the M-60 tank for both the Army and foreign governments. By the mid to late 1970s, the plant was making four to five tanks a day, working three shifts and employing approximately 2,500 workers. By then, Pentagon orders accounted for 85–95 percent of its output. Meanwhile, its steel business languished, chiefly because foreign competitors—especially the Japanese—made considerable inroads into the steel mill market on the basis of quality and aid in financing.[30]

In 1984, a researcher at the local Calumet Project on Industrial Jobs, a community-based anti-plant-closing group, spotted a note in the trade press suggesting that White might sell and/or close the plant. Its M-60 tank was being displaced by a fancier tank, the M-1, which did not require Blaw-Knox services. He notified the president of the Steelworker's Union local at the plant, who issued a call for a meeting, at which the Blaw-Knox Steering Committee was born. The committee consisted of representatives from the union, management, the community, and local and regional economic development agencies. They commissioned a study by A. D. Little, which recommended that the plant be retooled, at a cost of $20 to $24 million, to produce smaller-sized commercial castings. The investment was crucial, because despite twenty years of profitability and lucrative military contracts, White had not put in one cent of new equipment. While the government would have to put up between $4 and $7 million, the savings in social costs, which would be incurred if the plant with its 800 workers were to be shut down, would be substantial.

The alternative-use plan was never implemented, and the plant closed down in 1986. In the interim, White had sold out to another holding company, Nesco, which formed a new company called the Blaw-Knox Corporation, headquartered in Pittsburgh, who took control of the planning process and redirected it single-mindedly toward a lobbying effort to keep Pentagon orders coming. Cleavages within the conversion committee paralyzed opposition to Nesco's strategy. The union local refused to play a major leadership role, and the international union was preoccupied with collective bargaining issues. The community groups—the Calumet Project and the United Community Organization—had an alternative vision but little clout. They refused to lobby, trying instead to generate support for a public jobs authority with the powers of eminent domain, modeled on the successful Steel Valley Authority in Pittsburgh. The economic development people and the Indiana politicians, including the state's two senators and the local congressman, were co-opted into the company's losing strategy of begging for more tanks.

Although the Blaw-Knox effort did not succeed according to the narrow criterion of job preservation, it has borne fruit in a larger, ongoing effort on the part of the Calumet Project to avert plant closings and facilitate management turnover of endangered plants. In late 1989, the project published a much-quoted retrospective study of Blaw-Knox and more than a dozen other closings in the area, concluding that many of them (including Blaw-Knox) could have been averted had certain public policies and institutions been in place. Its ongoing efforts include a project to create and fund a public Jobs Authority that would operate an advanced warning system, provide "one-stop shopping" to plants in trouble, and give technical assistance and support to workers, unions, and business to stabilize jobs and prevent job loss. It would also assist in management turnover, using eminent domain if necessary.[31]

Philadelphia Naval Yards. The Philadelphia Navy Shipyard is part of a Navy base comprised of two dozen naval commands in Philadelphia. The Philadelphia Navy Base conducts engineering research and design and is a stable source of employment and income for many Philadelphians. The future of the shipyard and the adjacent Naval Hospital are much less certain. Like the Quincy shipyards, the Philadelphia yard has faced cuts in Naval spending with no commercial work to cushion the blow. The yard had several strikes against it in the competition for Navy work. As Jobs

With Peace activist George Lakey noted, "Philadelphia is a non-nuclear yard, which is reassuring for the health of Philadelphians but could be a disadvantage in the scramble for work."[32] Lakey also points out that Philadelphia's status as a government-owned yard was not necessarily an asset since privately-owned yards were increasingly undercutting the prices of the public yards. Because it was futile to demand that the Navy conduct commercial work on government property, conversion advocates suggested that "full use" for the yard be attained by portioning off a section of the yard for sale and then using that site for commercial work.

The League Island Development Corporation (LIDC) was a South Philadelphia neighborhood-based development organization with financial support from Jobs With Peace's Philadelphia office. It was a joint effort of neighborhood and peace activists. LIDC had an explicitly pro-labor conversion strategy:

> We believe that the skills of dislocated workers should not go to waste, but rather, should become a resource for economic development programs benefitting them and their communities. In response to long term decline, the Corporation has focused its initial programs on bringing underutilized sites in and around the Philadelphia Naval Base up to their most productive, job creating capacity.[33]

Despite its pro-labor position, the organization had little success with the Metal Trades Council that represented the approximately 10,000 workers of the yard. Jon Brandow, president of the LIDC, believes that there were tactical errors in the way peace activists approached workers in that they appeared to have an agenda.[34] Failure to gain union support became a major stumbling block for the conversion effort and the unions' persistent lack of interest that caused the LIDC to cease organizing.

A contributing factor to the effort's demise was the resolution of the immediate crisis. At the end of 1986 the Shipyard was informed that it would receive three major ship overhauls, which would keep nearly 10,000 skilled blue-collar workers busy through 1990. While the LIDC tried to raise the specter of 1991, workers were not interested. In the ensuing two years, the group refocused its work on two other major conversion projects: a shipyard in Chester, Penn., and the Naval Hospital that is adjacent to the shipyards.

The Philadelphia conversion organizing efforts have not been successful to date in terms of job retention or the reuse of the site. Continuing efforts in Philadelphia may yet bear fruit of that variety. However, like the Quincy shipyard effort, organizing in Philadelphia succeeded in publicizing alternative uses for the shipyard and illustrating the technical feasibility of conversion. Moreover, Jobs With Peace activists have gone on to craft and push state legislation to assist conversion efforts.[35]

McDonnell Douglas Aircraft. By the early 1980s, the former Douglas Aircraft Company in Long Beach, California, found itself in long-term financial difficulty. Once the leader in commercial aviation, the company never recovered from Boeing's entry into the jet airliner market in the late 1950s, nor had it recouped its development costs from the DC-8.[36] In 1967, McDonnell Aircraft of St. Louis had stepped in to attempt to "rescue" the larger Douglas. Unfortunately, the merger did not return Douglas to its former profitability or production levels. In the Long Beach plant that employed 33,000 workers at its peak in the late 1960s, employment plunged sharply over the intervening years. By the early 1980s, the Long Beach plant was operating at about 20 percent of capacity. Between 1980 and 1982, the number of United Auto Workers (UAW) at the plant fell from over 12,000 workers to under 5,000, while the engineering, scientific, and technical work force was cut in half from its previous level of 7,000. McDonnell chose to do nothing about continued attrition of the Douglas plant business. Instead, it was banking on a C-17 cargo carrier contract, even though it had yet to be approved by Congress.

After the rash of 1982 layoffs, UAW Local 148 President Robert Berghoff sought alternatives for reemploying his 10,000 members. The Los Angeles Coalition Against Plant Shutdowns (LACAPS), a broad-based coalition of labor, community, and religious activists, met with Berghoff to discuss the idea of conversion planning. The UAW's goals were to reemploy its workers and rebuild its strength in the plant. Working together with the state government and the Mid-Peninsula Conversion Project (MPCP, now known as the Center for Economic Conversion) and an unofficial representative of the engineers' union, the local identified several feasible alternatives for the plant, including light rail transit assembly, a co-generation project, and commuter aircraft production.

The transit project was particularly attractive, since two new light rail systems were underway in California, and Douglas management expressed interest in it. Plant managers and the union, working together with MPCP and the state, began to negotiate informally. While the labor-management committee was never formally established, management's willingness to consider workers' ideas seriously was a significant step.

Both labor and management felt they had stakes in the effort. The involvement of the state facilitated both labor and management's willingness to work together.

What then went wrong? McDonnell Douglas did not act fast enough on the transit project and lost the contract. Secondly, during the course of negotiations, Berghoff led a 113-day strike against a proposed two-tiered wage system and cuts in other benefits. It is unclear whether the strike affected the project, although Douglas representatives were willing to continue to negotiate with the union concerning new products. Perhaps most significantly, McDonnell management in St. Louis was ambivalent about the effort. It had earlier rejected attempts by Douglas to move into new product lines and continued to stress military work. The rail project was abandoned when Congress approved the C-17 for McDonnell Douglas.

The conversion effort was not a success in the narrow sense of preserving jobs. In 1990, the layoffs again numbered in the thousands, due to civilian-related layoffs and no new military prospects. The conversion effort did garner a fair amount of publicity in the Los Angeles area, however. It helped to put ideas about alternative high-tech production, and rail projects in particular, on the table; these ideas were picked up again with enthusiasm in 1990 when a number of local officials in Orange County began to search for projects to counter military cutbacks.

Lockheed Shipyards. On November 17, 1986, the Lockheed Shipbuilding Corporation locked out 685 union workers at its Seattle Shipyard with only 48 hours' notice after workers had received a 45 percent wage cut.[37] Lockheed demanded unilateral work-rule changes and refused to bargain in good faith. Many observers now believe that by the time of the lockout, Lockheed had already made the decision to close its Puget Sound operation, a shipbuilding subsidiary acquired in 1959 from Puget Sound Bridge and Drydock. After the lockout, the Seattle Worker Center stepped in to help. The Worker Center, organized in 1986 by representatives of labor, churches, government, industry, academia, and the community, served as an early-warning center for plant closures and intervened to help save jobs and to advocate for dislocated workers.

The Seattle Worker Center launched a campaign with two initiatives. First, it worked with people who were locked out and denied their unemployment benefits. Targeting bills to deal with employer-generated lockouts, the center helped the shipyard workers develop a legislative campaign to take to Olympia, the state capital. The campaign united locked-out workers across the state, and the effort succeeded in winning $5 million in unemployment benefits for those locked out. Second, the campaign aimed to convert the Lockheed Shipyards, targeting potential new operations in nonmilitary boat-building, such as fish processing boats.

The campaign ultimately failed in its effort to keep the yard open. The campaign did not receive the support of Lockheed management nor did it generate sufficient political clout to help keep Lockheed in Seattle. Lockheed permanently closed the Seattle yard in December 1987 and sold all its equipment at auction in May 1988. Only 45 percent of the ex-Lockheed workers found new jobs in the maritime industry. Many of the former Lockheed workers went to work for Boeing, just then enjoying an enormous boom.

However, the shipyard jobs campaign helped save other maritime jobs. The campaign was expanded to target the entire Port of Seattle. The Worker Center helped with a worker buy-out of a bankrupted tug and barge operation and a repair yard. The new worker-owners included many former Lockheed workers. The campaign also helped focus public attention on Puget Sound shipyards and shipyard job loss. It publicized the fact that between 1982 and 1987, shipyard jobs fell from 10,700 to 3,000. In response, the government embarked upon an eighteen-month research and development effort concerning the state of the industry and its prospects for future growth. The research effort culminated in a report for the governor and legislature, *Recapturing Markets for Puget Sound Shipyards*. Among other provisions, it recommended the creation of an industry-wide labor-management committee, and policy support for shipyard modernization and job retraining programs.

Unysis Defense Computer Systems. In 1986, Sperry and Burroughs corporations merged into the Unysis Corporation combining their military work into one Computer Defense Division heavily concentrated in the St. Paul, Minnesota, area with around 5,000 workers. Shortly thereafter, caught bribing consultants for bid-related information and suspended from bidding on Navy contracts for several months, Unisys lost ground to competitors. When the Navy, which accounted for more than 70 percent of Unisys's $2.4 million annual military sales, announced a shift to commercial grade from military specifications, Unisys's military sales slumped further. The company began a long series of layoffs with no apparent desire to convert military-oriented facilities to other uses.[38]

As early as 1985, concerned members of the International Brotherhood of Electrical Workers (IBEW) Local 2047 contacted the AFL-CIO

(American Federation of Labor and Congress of Industrial Organizations) and the State Task Force on Economic Conversion to ask for help in challenging these layoffs. A new working group, the Alternative-Use Project, was formed with members from the IBEW local, the state AFL-CIO, the Working Group on Economic Dislocation (an anti-plant-closing group), and Jobs with Peace. With technical and financial assistance from the state and city governments, the group hired an independent consultant to produce an alternative-use plan. The result was a careful analysis of over forty new product ideas, including pollution monitoring devices, automobile computers, home security systems, smart irrigation, low-power electronic lighting ballasts, adaptive technologies for the physically disabled, light rail transit controls, and monitoring systems. All could be manufactured, the study contended, with little or no change to equipment and with the existing work force.

However, the company remained adamantly opposed to alternative-use planning. It refused to meet with the project, rejected a request for a six-month moratorium on layoffs, and claimed that Unisys was already a "converted company" because it already had divisions producing for the commercial market. The company spokesman belittled the alternative-use study, suggesting that management had access to better engineering and new-product talent, which, however, it was unwilling to disclose or share. Ironically, the company has recently announced plans to build one of the products suggested in the task force's plan, a satellite-based remote sensing system, but plans to produce it in Salt Lake City rather than in St. Paul.[39] Because the company would not cooperate, additional funding for alternative-use planning provided by the state legislature could not kick in, since it required the participation of management.

To date, the Unisys project has not been a success in the sense of retaining jobs. However, compared with the preceding cases, it still has some chance of success in this narrowly construed sense, and the solid coalition continues to recruit advocates and amass technical assistance. More importantly, it has had a major demonstration effect on other efforts across the country. During a major layoff of 151 workers in January of 1990, the governor of Minnesota and the mayor of St. Paul were at the plant gates to welcome the fired workers and walk the picket line, the first ever where a union picketed for economic conversion.

Support for state legislation on conversion is growing. Two University of Minnesota professors researched the extent of Minnesota military dependence and conducted an analysis of job creation under an alternative social spending scenario, concluding that defense spending hurt the Minnesota economy.[40] State Representative Karen Clark continues to push legislation that would mandate alternative-use committees for defense companies in the state, reserving state development assistance for complying firms. This legislation could have an impact on Unisys if it expects to receive any assistance from the state.

The Cases Compared

From these cases, we can draw some tentative conclusions. We found that peace activists and labor unions were able to work together, and that the deeper the level of consensus among workers in particular, the more powerful the movement. In all cases, management opposed conversion planning, and this crippled the efforts. State intervention, then, is necessary if conversion is to take place. Early-warning legislation, particularly legislation that provides a long lead time, would prove useful so that organizers could speak with certainty about when layoffs or closure would occur and plan accordingly. Finally, organizers admitted to us that more technical assistance, particularly in marketing, would be useful. Workers may have good ideas about what products they can produce at a facility, but they don't know what products will sell.

These precursor cases mostly illustrate the obstacles facing conversion; however, they also indicate directions for overcoming these problems. By identifying the problems facing conversion in the 1980s, we can better consider prospects for conversion in the 1990s.

Leadership and Participation

The cases differ in the quality of leadership and the degree of broad-based participation in the conversion initiative. Where the initiative came from outside the union or the work force, as at the Philadelphia Naval Yards, developing clout to put pressure on the operator was almost impossible. Narrowly-based efforts, as in the Quincy Shipyards case, foundered because of lack of support from the majority of workers and the community, not to mention management. Without such political pressure, response by policy-makers in Massachusetts was too little and too late.

Labor participation and unity is particularly crucial to mounting a successful case. Unions bring with them an activist tradition. They know how to use strikes and pickets effectively for generating public support and media coverage. Larger trade union offices have resources for funding feasibility studies and research, and legal departments to help out. Where a rank-and-file dissident group lacked local union support, as at Quincy, management felt no need to take the effort seriously. Support at higher levels of the union hierarchy also helped, but was not crucial. Not having it at Blaw-Knox was a disadvantage, but at McDonnell Douglas, the local effort proceeded quite well without such support. At Unisys, where local union leadership was backed up by both the international and the state AFL-CIO, support from politicians and the public sector was easier to generate quickly.

On the other hand, an effort mounted strictly within the boundaries of collective bargaining is apt to degenerate into contractual demands for severance pay, job transfer rights, or control over subcontracting, issues that complicated the Blaw-Knox and Quincy cases. However, pioneering provisions about plant closings can be explicitly bargained into labor contracts. For instance, a machinists union local at Kohlmorgan Electro-optical Division in Northampton, Massachusetts, a 75 percent defense-dependent facility, bargained successfully for the establishment of a joint union-company committee to address issues of mutual concern, among them the prospects for work under future defense cuts.[41]

The cases illustrate that potential divisions between peace activists, communities, and trade unionists can and should be bridged.[42] Peace groups often bring with them financial resources, visibility, and staff support to supplement a workplace-based effort. Community groups, too, have helped out by bringing in politicians and local government support. The Unisys effort enjoyed community, peace-movement, and public-sector support and could enter terrain not generally accessible to workers and their organizations. Peace activists demonstrated their commitment to taking care of those most adversely affected by the demilitarization of the economy, while trade unionists came out strongly in favor of the peace dividend. As the president of IBEW Local 2047 Victor Globa put it, "We have taken the leadership to demonstrate that the cuts to the military budget do not have to cause job loss. . . . Our people are extremely talented and can make many useful and profitable products."[43] In the Blaw-Knox case, the union local refused the company's demands that they write patriotic letters pushing tank contracts to their congressional representatives.

Management Cooperation

To make conversion work, management must be willing to participate in the effort. In all six cases studied, key managers refused to cooperate in alternative-use planning, even when plant-level managers were favorably inclined. This coincides with other research findings and press accounts generally that most military contractors are neither interested in nor believe they are capable of refurbishing military-dedicated facilities to alternative production, but prefer strategies of acquisition and merger or, in the rarer cases of successful diversification, to undertake new plant construction elsewhere.[44] In one case where management initially joined the team, Blaw-Knox, it squelched the effort at its most creative junction and redirected it into political lobbying for more defense spending. At McDonnell Douglas, where the plant management participated actively, central-office corporate strategists undermined the commercial effort with their preoccupation with military work. The more or less predictable opposition of management to conversion initiatives forms a formidable barrier to the facility conversion strategy.

Management opposition was sometimes tied to evidence of incompetence or dishonesty. In several of the cases, conversion research uncovered failures to maintain and upgrade equipment, making commercial competitiveness difficult (Blaw-Knox) or outright corruption damaging the plant's reputation with the Pentagon (Quincy, Unisys).* Facilities involved were often subjects of recent mergers (Unisys) or buyouts (Blaw-Knox), and hypothesized to be of relatively minor importance to conglomerate managers who could reap tax benefits and "facility termination costs" from the government for closing them in any case. Some facilities, like Blaw-Knox, had been "milked" for years on profitable Pentagon contracts with no reinvestment.

Competent and honest managers may also have strong reasons for opposing joint conversion efforts, especially when initiated by workers or community groups. Companies in each case asserted their proprietary rights to plan, opposing the notion that they would have to open their books to joint committee members. Some companies have had historically bad labor relations that are difficult to transcend. Some oppose conversion out of fear of the unknown and unwillingness to invest in dark horses. Then, too, the general economic climate matters as well. Throughout most of the period we studied, defense outlays continued to rise, creating short-term sales for the companies involved and lessening their incentive to consider alternatives. For the most part, the companies stud-

---

*For a discussion of corruption allegations involving G. D. Quincy Yard managers see: Elizabeth Schuman, "Charting a New Course for Shipbuilding," *Plowshare Press* Jan.-Feb., 1984: 3, published by Mid-Peninsula Conversion Project: Mountain View, CA, vol 9, no. 1.

ied here disparaged conversion efforts and fought politically against legislation for mandatory alternative-use planning. Their stance is reminiscent of similar stands taken by business organizations against plant-closing legislation and environmental regulations, analogies that suggest that business opposition need not prevail.

The Need for Information: Early Warning and Disclosure

The cases taken together suggest that the longer the lead time, the better prepared and positioned the community/union coalitions are to cope with military cutbacks. Knowledge about company and Pentagon plans was essential to each strategy. In one case, the initiating group came upon crucial information only by chance (Blaw-Knox). In others, general information about product and weapons systems gave workers and locals a fairly clear signal about a facility's future. Where lead times were longer, as with Unisys, it was easier to complete coalition-building and preliminary studies. Where it was short, or where lags took place in response, facilities ended up being shuttered before planning could produce a reasonable alternative (Quincy, Blaw-Knox).

Access to company books and strategic plans also proved to be essential to the planning process. In general, this is proprietary turf, closely guarded by companies. Especially when a plant is just one of many facilities under a corporate umbrella, the profitability of existing operations is impossible to ascertain without access to the books. Also, while workers often suspected they were the subjects of slash-and-burn or milking tactics on the part of top financial managers, as at Blaw-Knox, this too was hard to prove without such disclosure. The cases suggest that companies will only share such information when required.

Technical Assistance

The case studies all reveal, in varying degrees, deficiencies in technical expertise available to community/union conversion initiators. In order to accomplish social cost accounting, new product assessment, marketing studies, financial feasibility, and business plans, coalitions had to turn to academics willing to do so for modest amounts of money or, if better endowed, to outside consultants. In some cases, insiders in plant management or engineers were supportive and willing to help anonymously. But even friendly managers are often at a loss in thinking about designing or marketing entirely new products. Although it is an appealing and probably correct notion that workers might have good ideas for new products and know the capabilities of their workplaces, in fact they too are not well equipped to tackle the entrepreneurial tasks of business restructuring.

In no case did a coalition come up with a complete business plan, or get as far as proposing a worker or community buyout, although over time groups demonstrate more awareness that this kind of design work is necessary. After ten years or more of massive plant closings in their industries, unions including the United Auto Workers and the United Steelworkers of America have learned that worker buy outs can be successful, although in every case outside professional help has been required, at a price. Financial resources to enable the purchase of these services must be found if such buy outs are to succeed. Alternatively, they could be provided by the state. The McDonnell Douglas case and the Unisys case both enjoyed capable third-party intervention from the state to work with both management and labor, with prospects for state aid if the joint efforts had succeeded. Technical assistance in a timely fashion is crucial because not all plants and facilities should be saved. Some are simply too old and without redeeming characteristics, or are too expensive to refurbish, or are polluted with chemicals, nuclear contaminants, or metals residues. Workers and communities hosting these plants should be able to get an assessment of their prospects as soon as possible, to avoid delays in retraining and other forms of adjustment assistance which will be necessary when employment evaporates.

The Next Steps: Social Cost Calculus and Public Policy

The cases together demonstrate the need for a social cost accounting framework to be applied to the conversion issue. In the case of Quincy Shipyards, for example, the state expenditure for the study of the shipyard and latter acquisition of the site could have been combined with the federal worker-training funding to reuse the facility. More research is needed to calculate the social costs of the closing compared with the public investment needed to convert to other productive uses. Other forms of public-sector intervention we recommend include technical assistance and early-warning programs (similar to those already existing in state and local economic-development operations), structural innovations like the Jobs Authority concept, and the extension of eminent domain powers to the industrial arena.

In some cases, the community or union initiative, if well organized, generated a set of legislative proposals that would pioneer new institutions to monitor military-related plant closings and to respond to them. Proposals for state conversion legislation have reflected the experience of local organizing efforts.[45] For example, the Pennsylvania bill mandates community-led alternative-use committees created by residents and/or workers, reminiscent of the composition of the League Island Development Corporation. The proposed Minnesota legislation mandates the creation of alternative-use committees at every defense-related facility, reflecting the needs articulated by the Unisys workers. While few states have passed effective conversion legislation, many states have conducted studies on military spending and/or conversion and are considering proposals. The state of Washington has combined proposals for alternative-use planning with a proposal for state economic diversification.[46] Historically state legislation has been a precursor for national legislation. For example, the national plant-closing legislation borrowed heavily from state legislation.[47] Inclusion of local alternative-use planning mechanisms within state legislation may lend authority to the Weiss conversion bill's effort to mandate alternative-use committees for all defense firms.

Overall—and despite some hope in the Unisys and Philadelphia Shipyard cases—we found that to date, none of the cases has been successful on the basis of the stricter criterion of maintaining jobs. Failure can be ascribed both to organizational difficulties and management resistance. However, the efforts have been successful in other ways. In each case they have helped to instruct peace-movement activists about the costs and difficulties of military shutdowns. Groups such as SANE/Freeze have added conversion to their agenda. Each case has involved the education of at least some workers into the rudiments of plant management and business planning. Efforts in Seattle, for example, led activists and workers to successfully create a worker buy-out of a maritime company. The cases, cumulatively, have contributed to a body of knowledge and practice about conversion planning that has proven helpful to new groups starting out.

We are guardedly optimistic because we view these cases as pilot projects. Any innovation goes through a period of frequent failures before it catches hold. Furthermore, these efforts all took place during a period of military buildup, and a majority of them foundered on management preference for short-term defense contracts over long-term, riskier alternative-use planning. If the military budget is indeed reduced, management at defense-dependent plants may not be as hostile to conversion.

It is too soon to tell whether or not the lessons of these cases can be applied to new and growing instances of military-related plant closings.[48] However, the progression in sophistication and cooperation among interested parties in the cases examined is heartening. Efforts around shipyards in Bath, Maine; nuclear facilities in Oak Ridge, Tennessee; a General Electric gatling gun producer in Burlington, Vermont; machine tool makers in western Massachusetts; aircraft plants in Long Island; and engine and machining factories in Connecticut are heartening signs of a growing interest in conversion. Groups in several cities and regions, including Boston, St. Louis, Seattle, Baltimore, the Naugatuck Valley (Connecticut), Orange County (California), and Cambridge (Mass.) have initiated public-sector or nonprofit conversion efforts designed to monitor, cajole, and act when military plant closings occur. All stand to benefit from the experience of these six pioneering efforts.

We recommend a number of strategies to encourage conversion. First, conversion activists must work diligently to secure management cooperation. However, planners and activists must expect antagonism, at least initially, from the contractor sector and be ready to consider regulation rather than relying on voluntary action. This is equivalent to the histories of environmental protection, worker health and safety laws, and early-warning notification in the case of plant closings.[49] In each case, behavioral norms had to be imposed on companies and monitored by the public sector. All such regulations were opposed by organized business interests, who sometimes succeeded in watering down but not defeating them. Most companies, however, have learned to live with them in the longer run.

Companies should be offered carrots as well as sticks to engage in conversion planning. Existing tax incentives that encourage companies to close facilities should be eliminated, and in their place, cost sharing for the planning stages as well as technical and financial assistance for new ventures should be provided. These should be equally available to old as well as new owners, whether private or public, and should require evidence of ongoing worker and community involvement to be awarded. Getting military contractors to face the new reality of shrinking budgets may not prove any more difficult than bringing auto and steel company managements into the modern era of international competition. A concerted public-sector program of education, incentives, and judicious regulation is the only hope, in our view.

Second, conversion efforts should focus on facilities but not necessarily on current management. New institutions should be built to operate as store fronts of "first resort" for military plants in trouble. Operating with the powers that local and regional authorities such as urban renewal or the Tennessee Valley Authority have in the past, Jobs Authorities encompassing both military and civilian plant closings could help a specific constituency survey its options. They could conduct pre-feasibility studies; package financial assistance for further product, marketing, and financial studies; exercise the power of eminent domain in the public interest to facilitate management turnover; and participate as an active party in plant restructuring, perhaps as landlord or as an equity partner. The Steel Valley Authority in the Pittsburgh area, an innovative new organization set up to perform these tasks, has been breaking new ground.

Third, site-based conversion planning will only work if the policies needed to support it become codified into law and exercised in the public domain. Legislation mandating alternative-use planning and providing financial assistance has been introduced in both national and state legislatures.

We also recommend state legislation that sets aside financial resources for conversion planning. This may play an important role in financing feasibility and marketing studies. State and local governments can also act as a catalyst for conversion by serving as a first market for new civilian products. Nevertheless, state legislation may not be sufficient to induce contractors to create alternative-use committees, nor can it channel enough financial resources to substitute for a national industrial and/or conversion policy. State and local legislation should work in tandem with federal policies.

These recommendations and the rationale for them return us to our theme of supply- and demand-side approaches to conversion. In general, dramatic shifts in the federal budget away from defense and toward social spending are not apt to happen, especially in an era of recession, without complementary initiatives on the supply side that will insure those with a stake in military production against the devastation of permanent job loss. However, the prospects for a purely supply-side approach will be much less effective if not accompanied by new commitments on the part of the federal government to expenditures on infrastructure, housing, the environment, and education. Many of the alternative products proposed at these six facilities—light rail at McDonnell Douglas, energy conversion plant/ship at Quincy, pollution-monitoring devices at Unisys—require a government-induced market either directly or through regulation. Prospects for orders for mass transit vehicles, multi-family housing, pollution-control equipment, or new solid-waste disposal technologies, for instance, would encourage some firms to make the costly transition from military production to commercial work.[50]

Overall, our conclusions are at odds with those who dismiss facilities-based planning in favor of conventional economic development planning on the supply side and the targeting of the national budget on the demand side.[51] The latter approach underestimates, in our view, the resistance that defense-dependent companies and communities can and have successfully put up to cuts in their programs without assurance of alternative livelihoods. It underestimates, too, the enthusiasm and knowledge that workers can bring to a conversion effort and the support that unions at the district and national level are willing to give to such initiatives. In the 1980s, in many other heavy industries, unions learned that their best bet may be something far more activist than adversarial collective bargaining—it may be assuming ownership of plants and running them themselves. Furthermore, the most powerful way of raising consciousness about national budgetary priorities may be the drama of tackling case-by-case military base closings, provoking creative thinking about what the local economy could be making instead.

Critics of facility conversion strategies suggest that they put supporters in an inherently marginal political position. We found that on the contrary, participation in such efforts proved to be empowering, broadening the political base for demilitarization and creating experiments and legislative innovations at the state and local level. Slowly, this entrepreneurial attitude is percolating up through political circles, helping to challenge the view that in the United States, the arms race originates and is sustained by decisions made in centralized bureaucracies in Washington impervious to public will. Unless attention is focused on displacement on a facility-by-facility basis, workers will be displaced and communities will face hardships. Fear of such a fate may feed into support for extending military spending and worse, into support for more militaristic forays around the globe. We cannot do better than to echo IBEW local 2047 member Claudette Munson of Unisys: "Peace shouldn't be a hardship for anyone!"[52]

Notes

1. Conversion efforts have been building throughout the 1980s, and a number of seminal books and articles have been written examining the case for conversion and suggesting how it might be done. See Greg Bischak, ed., *Toward a Peace Economy in the United States* (New York: St. Martin's Press, 1991); Michael Renner, *Swords Into Plowshares: Converting to a Peace Economy* (Washington, D.C.: Worldwatch Institute, 1990); Lloyd Dumas and Marek Thee, eds., *Making Peace Possible: The Promise of Economic Conversion* (Oxford: Pergamon Press, 1989); Seymour Melman,

The Demilitarized Society: Disarmament and Conversion (Montreal: Harvest House, 1988); John Lynch, ed., *Economic Adjustment and Conversion of Defense Industries* (Boulder, Colo., and London: Westview Press, 1987); Suzanne Gordon and Dave McFadden, eds., *Revitalizing America's Economy* (Cambridge, Mass.: Ballinger, 1984); and Philip Webre, *Jobs to People—Planning for Conversion to New Industries* (Washington, D.C.: Exploratory Project on Economic Alternatives, 1979).

2. Paul Quigley, "Arms Exports: The Stop-Gap Alternative to Pentagon Contracts," in *Making Peace Possible: The Promise of Economic Conversion,* ed. Lloyd Dumas and Marek Thee (Oxford: Pergamon Press: 1989), 84.

3. Ibid.

4. Ann Markusen and Joel Yudken, *Dismantling the Cold War Economy* (New York: Basic Books, 1992), chapters 3 and 4.

5. This is analogous to the case of commercial plant closings, where researchers have found that multi-plant, absentee-owned firms are more apt to close facilities than are single-plant, locally-owned firms. See for instance Bluestone and Harrison, 1982; The Calumet Project on Industrial Jobs, *Preventing Plant Closings in Northwest Indiana: A Public Policy Program for Action* (East Chicago, Ind.: 1989).

6. Michael Closson, "Economic Diversification: Opportunities and Problems" (speech for Roundtable Conference on Economic Diversification, City Hall, Irvine, Calif. 26 Feb. 1990), 4.

7. The federal government owns a considerable number of defense plants, some dating from World War II and others more recently built. Some of these, often the most critical nuclear facilities, are GOGOs—government-owned and government-operated—such as the Hanford nuclear weapons facility currently being dismantled. Others, including many aircraft plants, are government-owned, contractor-operated plants.

8. J. Lovering, "Militarism, Capitalism, and the Nation State: Toward a Realistic Synthesis," *Environment and Planning D: Society and Space* 5 (1987): 283–302.

9. A number of macroeconomists point out that in addition, military spending has been countercyclical. One Congressional Budget Office analyst stated in late 1990 that if a recession were to take place in 1991, military spending would be the most likely candidate in an effort to stimulate the economy. See Robert Hale, "The Outlook for the Peace Dividend," (paper presented at the Conference on Economic Issues of Disarmament, University of Notre Dame, November 30, 1990).

10. Markusen and Yudken, *Dismantling.*

11. Richard Stevenson, "Contractor Plans Cutback of 27,000 Jobs," *New York Times,* 2 May 1991: 1.

12. Massachusetts State Department of Employment and Training Field Research Services, *Defense Industry Profile* (Massachusetts: Dept. of Employment and Training Field Research Services, 1989).

13. M. Weidenbaum, "The Transferability of Defense Industry Resources to Civilian Uses," in *Convertability of Space and Defense Resources to Civilian Needs: A Search for New Employment Potentials, Subcommittee on Employment and Manpower,* reprinted in *The Economic Impact of the Cold War,* ed. James Clayton (New York: Harcourt, Brace & World: 1970).

14. R. DeGrasse, "Corporate Diversification and Conversion Experience," in *Economic Adjustment and Conversion of Defense Industries,* ed. J. Lynch. (Boulder, Colo. and London: Westview Press, 1987).

15. M. McNeilly, "Braving the New World," *Plowshare Press,* (Mountain View, Calif.) 15 (1990), no. 1: 1.

16. Markusen and Yudken, *Dismantling,* chapters 4 and 7.

17. President's Economic Adjustment Committee, Office of Economic Adjustment, *25 Years of Civilian Reuse: Summary of Completed Military Base Economic Adjustment Projects* (Washington, D.C.: Government Printing Office, 1986) and by the same committee/office, *Civilian Reuse of Former Military Bases* (Washington, D.C.: Government Printing Office, 1990).

18. J. Kulik and C. Fairchild, "Worker Assistance and Placement Experience," in Lynch, *Economic Adjustment.*

19. L. Wykle, W. Morehouse, and D. Dembo, *Worker Empowerment in a Changing Economy: Jobs, Military Production, and the Environment* (New York: Apex Press, 1991).

20. Ibid., 71.

21. Kulik and Fairchild, "Worker Assistance," 204.

22. K. Cooper, "Recruiting Among the Ex-Military," *Washington Post*, 6 Aug. 1990: A-9.

23. M. Howland, *Plant Closings and Worker Displacement: The Regional Issues*, (Kalamazoo, MI.: W. E. Upjohn Institute for Employment Research, 1988).

24. In Massachusetts, for example, annual earnings for workers in the seven defense-related industries taken together was approximately $33,000 in 1987, over 25 percent above the corresponding figure (roughly $26,000) in non-defense-related manufacturing and almost 60 percent above the average wage (approximately $21,000) in nonmanufacturing industries. See Massachusetts State Department of Employment and Training Field Research Services, *Defense Industry Profile*, June 1989, 8.

25. Melman, *The Demilitarized Society.*

26. Other communities where organizing for conversion has taken place include Savannah, S.C.; St. Louis, Mo.; Baltimore, Md., Chicago, Ill.; and San Diego, Calif. Generally these efforts have been community oriented rather than plant specific. E. Sherman and S. Meacham (for the South Shore Conversion Committee), "Conversion: New Hope for Shipbuilding?" testimony to the Massachusetts congressional delegation (16 April 1983), published in pamphlet form (Weymouth, Mass.: South Shore Conversion Committee, 1983).

27. Jon Brandow, former president of Local 5 Shipbuilders Union at Quincy, in an interview with the authors, Spring 1990.

28. Booz Allen & Hamilton, Inc. *Potential Reuse Study of the Quincy Shipyard*, (Bethesda, Md.: Booz Allen & Hamilton, Inc., 1986).

29. Phillip Primack, "Quincy Shipyard's Second Chance," *Boston Herald,* 1 Jan. 1990.

30. The Blaw-Knox case has been written up by the Calumet Project on Industrial Jobs, *Preventing Plant Closings in Northwest Indiana: A Public Policy Program for Action.* (East Chicago, Ind.: 1989); David Moberg, "Hooked on Tanks," *The Progressive,* September 1986: 30–32; Greg LeRoy and Lynn Feekin, "Converting Tanks in Indiana," *Labor Research Review* 7 (1985): 59–68; and Bruce Nissen, "Corporate Divestiture of a Calumet Region Foundry," chapter 3 in Charles Craypo and Bruce Nissen, eds., *Grand Designs: The Impact of Corporate Strategies on Workers, Unions, and Communities,* ILR Press, Cornell University Ithaca, New York. 1993. The following summary draws from all of these.

31. The Calumet Project, *Preventing Plant Closings.*

32. G. Lakey, "In the Liberty Bell's Shadow: Converting the Philadelphia Navy Yard," *Plowshare Press,* 1986.

33. Jobs With Peace, *League Island Development Corporation Mission Statement* (Philadelphia: Jobs With Peace, 1986).

34. J. Brandow, "The Philadelphia Story," *Plowshare Press,* Spring, 1987.

35. The bill, H.B. 697, would create an economic adjustment board within the State Department of Labor and Industry, consisting of representatives from business, labor, executive agencies, and the legislature. The board would be responsible for developing and monitoring an economic adjustment strategy and would fund local adjustment committees, which would identify alternative business activities that could maximize employment and minimize dislocation in the event of crisis. The bill proposes $2 million appropriation for the Economic Adjustment Board for its first year.

36. This section is based on personal interviews with Joel Yudken, Menlo Park, Calif., and Kate Squire, Berkeley, Calif. See also Joel Yudken "Conversion in the Aerospace Industry: The McDonnell Douglas Project," in Suzanne Gordon and Dave McFadden, eds., *Economic Conversion: Revitalizing America's Economy* (Cambridge, Mass.: Ballinger, 1984).

37. This section is based on an interview with Tom Croft, Steel Valley Authority, former director of the Seattle Worker Center, and documents from the Seattle Worker Center. See Puget Sound Shipyards Industrial Jobs Commission, *Recapturing Markets for Puget Sound Shipyards: Survey, Analysis, Recommendations* (Seattle: Seattle Worker Center, May 1989).

38. M. Duncan, "Local Planning in Minnesota," *Nuclear Times,* Summer 1990: 14; J. Markham and Associates with the Alternative Product Development Committee, *The Unisys Alternative Use Project, Parts I and II* (St. Paul, Minn: 1989).

39. W. Maki, R. Bolan, and H. Akhavi-Pour, *Forging a Peace Economy in Minnesota: A Report for the Minnesota Task Force on Economic Conversion* (St. Paul, Minn.: Department of Jobs and Training, 1991).

40. W. Maki, D. Bogenschultz, C. Evans, and M. Senese, *Military Production and the Minnesota Economy: A Report for the Minnesota Task Force on Economic Conversion* (St. Paul, Minn.: Department of Jobs and Training, 1989).

41. J. Ruzkowski, "Early Warning Network Model" (speech presented to the Labor and Business Working Group, Pennsylvania Economic Conversion Conference, Harrisburg, Penn., 4 Oct. 1990).

42. See the analysis of obstacles to organizing across such groups in Kevin Bean "Reconversion in Connecticut," *Social Policy,* Winter 1988: 46–49.

43. *The Union Advocate* Vol 93 no. 18 January 22, 1990 p 1 no author title "Perpich, Workers demand Unisys act to stop layoffs."

44. J. Yudken, "Conversion in the Aerospace Industry: The McDonnell Douglas Project," in *Economic Conversion: Revitalizing America's Economy,* eds. S. Gordon and D. McFadden (Cambridge, MA: Ballinger, 1984).

45. Catherine Hill, *State and Local Legislation on Conversion of a Military to a Civilian Economy* (Washington, D.C.: National Commission on Economic Conversion and Disarmament, 1991).

46. Department of Trade and Economic Development, 1988

47. R. Kerson and G. LeRoy, *State and Local Initiatives on Development Subsidies and Plant Closings* (Chicago: Federation for Industrial Retention and Renewal, 1989).

48. See Gregory A. Bischak, "Facing the Second Generation of the Nuclear Weapons Complex: Renewal of the Nuclear Production Base or Economic Conversion?" in Lloyd Dumas and Marek Thee, eds., *Making Peace Possible: The Promise of Economic Conversion* (Oxford: Pergamon Press, 1989) 111–136, for an analysis of conversion of government-owned facilities.

49. See the analysis and proposals in Tri-State Conference on Steel, *Industrial Renaissance: Building Support for National, Regional and Sectoral Reindustrialization.* (Pittsburgh, Penn.: Tri-State Conference, 1989).

50. Jeff Faux and Max Sawicky, *Investing the Peace Dividend: How to Break the Gramm-Rudman-Hollings Stalemate* (Washington, D.C.: Economic Policy Institute, 1990).

51. G. Adams, "Economic Conversion Misses the Point," *Bulletin of Atomic Scientists,* February 1986: 24–28.

52. Interview with Claudette Munson by the authors in Spring, 1990.

8

Building a Peace Economy from the Bottom Up

Michael Closson

During the Cold War era, few progressive ideas received as much discussion and as little action as economic conversion. But, with the crumbling of the Berlin Wall, the disintegration of the Warsaw Pact, and the demise of the "Evil Empire," the concept has gained new currency.

In the dramatically altered geo-political climate, it has become very difficult for all but the most strident hawks to justify continuing massive levels of weapons spending. Since the economic well-being of millions of workers, thousands of companies, and hundreds of communities depends upon Pentagon spending, as early as 1989 the mass media began to carry stories about the "economic threat of peace." In response to defense worker layoffs and base closings, concerned citizens and public officials alike commenced to seek out ways to transform the increasingly redundant military economy. Conversion, in one form or another, figured prominently in their deliberations.

Traditionally, conversion has been defined as the process of designing and implementing civilian economic plans for workers and facilities engaged in military-related activities. In classic conversion theory, its major elements include: advance planning to avoid dislocation, participation by workers and managers (and sometimes community members) in the planning process, reorienting managers and retraining workers as necessary, optimum use of existing facilities, and the production of socially useful goods and services. In recent years, the concept has been broadened to encompass the economic diversification of military-dependent cities and geographical areas.

Economic conversion has been linked to three objectives:

1. Avoiding economic dislocation caused by military cutbacks by enabling military-oriented workers, communities, and companies to make a smooth transition to civilian pursuits.
2. Undercutting the economic and political power of the Pentagon and allowing public officials to support weapons spending purely on its own merits and not as a giant, sacrosanct jobs program.
3. Setting in motion participatory economic planning processes that lead to the creation of sustainable peace-oriented economy.

Historically federal legislation was the primary vehicle selected to promote and achieve economic conversion. The first conversion bill was introduced by Senator George McGovern (D-SD) in 1964. His legislation would have established a national economic conversion commission to oversee a systematic and decentralized planning process for transforming military industry to civilian pursuits. Similar legislation was introduced in the ensuing years, most recently by Congressman Ted Weiss (D-NY). All of these efforts have gone down to defeat as a result of strenuous opposition from leaders of military industry, Pentagon officials, and their supporters in Congress.

But times have changed. In the autumn of 1990, with the Pentagon's budget slowly declining and layoffs underway across the country, Congress responded after months of debate by enacting modest economic adjustment legislation that set aside $200 million from the defense budget to assist workers and communities affected by contract terminations and base closures.

Although a step in the right direction, this legislation is clearly inadequate to the immense task of effecting a smooth transition for millions of defense workers. Moreover, the legislation does not address at all the needs of thousands of companies that are dependent upon Pentagon spending. And it provides only bare-bones economic support for the revitalization of the economies of hundreds of military-dependent communities across the land.

As a result of the widespread economic vulnerability spawned by Pentagon reductions and the demonstrated inability of Washington to address fully and systematically the problem through federal legislation, concerned citizens and local and state public officials across the country are taking matters into their own hands. This shift in the locus of conversion planning from federal to state and local initiative is to be welcomed. But as Bischack and Yudken point out in chapter 5, the federal government still has a critical role to play—especially altering national priorities and providing the substantial funds necessary to support systematic conversion planning. Congress and the president thus far are abnegating their responsibility in this regard. Therefore, local governments have moved, albeit reluctantly, into the breach. Fortunately, they have the potential to deal very creatively with the problems they face—even with the modest resources at their disposal.

To put the issue in its largest context, two forms of economic conversion are required at this critical point in history: first, a major shift from heavy levels of military spending to productive civilian activities and second, a transformation of our overall economy—nationally and globally—into patterns that are equitable and sustainable over the long term. Significant federal involvement in both of these great transitions obviously is critical. But, if an economy is to work well for the vast majority of people, individuals at the local level must have a lot of involvement in shaping it. Locally and regionally controlled conversion planning can provide just that opportunity. Not only can it generate creative alternatives to military dependency, it also can provide the stimulus and the context for people to rethink the ways in which their local economy works. This is the true, and untapped, potential of economic conversion planning.

At this early stage of conversion activity, that objective has not come close to being achieved. But one can hope that out of the confusing panoply of efforts that are underway will come increased levels of citizen involvement leading to strategies and practices that start to transform our overall economy.

To help sort out the array of current conversion-related activities, they are grouped here into four (overlapping) categories: military base reuse, military-dependent community diversification, defense plant conversion, and defense worker assistance.

Military Base Reuse

The Department of Defense owns 3,874 properties in the United States and its territories including 871 major military installations. Many of these now are redundant with the demise of the Soviet Union. In fact, for years military officials have desired to close a number of these bases. But, because of the facilities' local and regional economic importance, during most of the 1980s Congress thwarted the Pentagon's base-closure efforts.

The dam finally broke in 1989 when Congress, in an "all or nothing" package deal, succeeded in selecting 86 bases for closure. Two years later, Congress initiated another round of closures designed to target dozens more bases through 1995. Community response to this action has been predictable—howls of protest, followed by efforts to fight the closures, followed eventually by reluctant attempts to plan the installations' shift to civilian uses.

Despite the resistance to it, military base reuse is the one conversion-related area in which there is a significant and largely positive track record. During the 1960s and 1970s, several hundred military installations were closed and transformed, in whole or in part, to a wide variety of other uses: industrial parks, airports, shopping centers, housing developments, schools and colleges, governmental complexes, health-care facilities, prisons, recreational complexes, and open space. A study by the Pentagon's Office of Economic Adjustment (OEA), the federal agency charged with assisting communities affected by "defense realignments," documented a 50 percent increase in civilian employment at the reused bases.

A classic case in point is the former Raritan Arsenal in Edison, New Jersey. The facility, which employed 2,600 civilian workers when it was closed in 1965, was converted to a large business park of more than 200 buildings and 250 tenants including American Hospital Supply, B. F. Goodrich, Nestle, United Parcel Service, Michelin Tires, Ramada and Holiday inns, and Middlesex College. Currently over 13,000 people are employed on the site.

Another successful but less grandiose example of military base reuse is the former Laredo Air Force Base in Laredo, Texas, which closed in 1975. As a military installation it employed 700 civilian workers. Now 2,200 are employed on the site whose tenants include K-Mart, Tracor Aerospace, South Texas Private Industry Council, county and city government offices, and a municipal airport.

Not all bases have been converted successfully however. The exceptions to the rule are typically installations in rural areas without the population base to attract substantial new tenants. Two examples are Glasgow Air Force Base in Glasgow, Montana, and the Black Hills Army Depot in Edgemont, South Dakota. One of the rare urban failures is Hamilton Air Force Base in affluent Marin County north of San Francisco. After several conversion plans (including a solar village) were defeated at the polls, the community has chosen to let the facility sit largely idle rather than cope with the added traffic congestion and pollution that its full reuse is likely to bring. Other bases have been eventually converted but only after five to ten years of lag time during which the local economy foundered.

There is no one model for military base reuse planning. Some generalities do apply, however. Typically, public officials (a congressperson, county executive, city council, etc.) will convene a commission or task force composed of community leaders. That group will apply to the OEA for planning grants, solicit economic adjustment funding from the U.S. Departments of Commerce and Labor, hire paid staff, and set about exploring alternative uses for the installation. Mainstream citizen involvement will vary greatly depending upon the level of public concern and the openness of local officials to substantive public participation.

One of the most notable apparent success stories among the current round of closures is in Sacramento, California, home of Mather Air Force Base. When it was slated for closure in 1989, Mather was home to a wing of B-52 bombers and the headquarters of the Air Force's navigation school. Employing 1,900 civilian workers and 5,100 military personnel, the 5,900-acre facility, located just outside the city limits, was a key element of the greater Sacramento economy.

In response to the closure announcement, Congressman Robert Matsui (D-CA) appointed a commission, initially largely composed of members of a previous committee designed to fight the closure, to oversee Mather's reuse planning. Acting nearly as rapidly, a network of community activists organized the Peace, Environment, Justice Conversion Coalition to push for an open planning process that identified new civilian uses which met community needs. Potential community polarization was avoided when several of the coalition's leaders were subsequently appointed to slots on the official commission. After two years of work the commission came up with a plan for a mix of civilian activities centered around an airport devoted to air freight and general aviation. The plan also recommended the continued presence of Air Force Reserve, National Guard, and state and federal fire-fighting units at the facility plus converting base housing to civilian use and opening up its recreational facilities to the general public. Approved by the county's board of supervisors, the plan is now being implemented.

Three thousand miles to the east and light years away in public consciousness, the reuse planning for Pease Air Force Base in Portsmouth, New Hampshire, has not gone so smoothly. Located across the Piscataqua River from Maine, the closure of the 4,300-acre base was announced in 1989 during the same round as Mather Air Force Base. After that, its fortunes plunged. The state of New Hampshire took over the planning process, appointing the majority of the newly formed Pease Development Authority. That group, in turn, hired Bechtel Corporation to develop a comprehensive plan for the facility. Bechtel proposed an industrial airport scheme that has been blasted by local planners, environmentalists, business leaders, and citizen's groups in the area.

In addition, the Pease Development Authority has been accused of violating the state's open meeting law, its sensitivity to environmental concerns has been questioned, and it has been criticized for hiring two marketing firms without a public bidding process. Several environmental groups are challenging the conversion plan's environmental impact statement as well.

To make matters worse, Pease was the first among those bases selected for closure in 1989 to actually be vacated by the military. The rapid departure of 3,500 military families and the loss of 650 civilian jobs has the area's economy reeling. Thus far, only one interim tenant has been found for the vacant facility.

In dozens of other communities, military base reuse planning is also underway. Most planning processes appear to be proceeding quite well, certainly better than the debacle in New Hampshire. Because of numerous precedents and the fact that it is clearly a public domain issue, base reuse planning is largely the province of elected officials, professional planners, and other members of the establishment. Relatively few activists are involved in the nuts and bolts of base conversion planning and the issue is defined almost entirely in conventional economic development terms.

Military-Dependent Community Diversification

The economies of many cities, large and small, across the country depend heavily upon military spending. Some have a large defense plant or military base that dominates the local scene. Others have a number of smaller high-tech companies that depend to various degrees on the Pentagon dole.

Even when a city's economic vulnerability to military cuts is obvious, there is a tendency for public officials in those settings to deny their vulnerability or put off addressing it as long as possible. Some fear, especially in cases of base closure, that advance planning will encourage the Pentagon to make cuts in their area (either because it would appear that the community is not committed to the facility or that prior planning might lessen the economic impact of future cuts). For example, when Sacramento's mayor publicly announced her support for a conversion plan for Mather Air Force Base prior to the official closure announcement, she was roundly criticized by the local business community. Other local officials would rather fight than switch, often losing valuable time opposing a base closure even after it has been announced or lobbying for new Pentagon contracts for a declining defense plant.

The fear of economic dislocation resulting from military cuts reflects a widespread, if unacknowledged, realization that market forces alone cannot bring about a timely adjustment to civilian pursuits. Indeed, in the case of defense firms, the exigencies of the market exacerbate the problem by spurring many companies to "downsize" even before substantial contract cuts occur. Possibly, in a healthy economy over the long term—five to ten years—the economies of many military-dependent communities could rejuvenate on their own through largely private-sector initiative. But the current economy is anything but healthy. And most people do not want to endure years of dislocation and stagnation. Hence, it is not surprising that, when substantial cuts occur, even the most ardent free marketeers rapidly turn to federal sources of assistance, when they exist.

Given the paucity of economic development resources available in smaller cities, it is not surprising that when the need for planning is acknowledged, it is the large military-dependent cities that lead the way in the community diversification arena. For example, one of the hardest-hit areas is St. Louis and its environs. In 1991, with $4 billion in Pentagon contracts, McDonnell Douglas Corporation was the state of Missouri's largest employer even though it had laid off 8,000 defense workers during the previous year. Those cuts precipitated a wave of layoffs and closures among the area's 2,000 smaller defense firms. Sparked by the layoffs and pressure from activists associated with the St. Louis Economic Conversion Project, local officials established a regional Economic Adjustment and Diversification Committee. The EADC applied for and received two federal planning grants (from the OEA and the Department of Commerce's Economic Development Administration) and set about designing a plan to respond to the cuts. Not yet implemented, the plan has six components: import/export assistance, job training/employee enhancement, financing strategies, technology transfer/management assistance, business development programs, and research and planning.

Although not as dramatic as the situation in St. Louis, Pentagon cuts also have damaged San Diego's heavily military-dependent economy.

Responding to the prospect of continuing cuts and pressure from activists associated with the San Diego Economic Conversion Council (SDECC), in 1990 the San Diego City Council formed an Economic Conversion Subcommittee. That body's purpose was to prepare plans for the "orderly and smooth transition of the San Diego economy to a peace-based economy." In 1991 the Subcommittee's work was taken over by the Economic Conversion Advisory Group of the city's Economic Development Task Force and the SDECC was asked to serve on that body. The group's charge is to develop a city-wide economic conversion program that will address the problems faced by both defense workers and their companies.

One hundred miles up the Pacific coast, companies in Los Angeles County receive nearly ten percent of the entire nation's defense contracts. Predictably, the entire Los Angeles basin is heavily affected by Pentagon cuts. Between January 1990 and October 1991, L.A. County's aerospace industry employment declined by 38,000 jobs and some estimates predict that 25 percent of all defense companies in southern California will go under by 1994! In the midst of this massive downturn, in July of 1990 the County Board of Supervisors directed the County's Economic Development Corporation to create an Aerospace Task Force to address the burgeoning problem. The task force is divided into five committees: a steering committee that acts as policy coordinator, an alternative business committee that identifies new business opportunities (foreign and domestic), a training/retraining committee, a community impacts committee, and a public awareness/clearinghouse committee. Recently the task force was awarded $90,000 in federal "Sudden and Severe Economic Dislocation" funds to aid its work. It is premature to determine the effectiveness of the task force's efforts but it faces an enormous challenge, even in Los Angeles' giant regional economy.

Smaller communities also are attempting to tackle the problem of Pentagon cuts. City officials in Burlington, Vermont, have tried for several years to convince managers and workers at the local General Electric plant, the area's largest employer, to explore conversion planning. Both groups have remained resistant to the overtures even though layoffs at the gattling-gun plant occur regularly and some fear its eventual closure. As an alternative, local officials are exploring the recruitment of companies able to make use of G.E.'s highly skilled workforce.

In Maine, with the assistance of activists associated with the Peace Economy Project, the Bath-Brunswick Conversion Task Force has developed into a model community-based planning committee representing a variety of stakeholders. Confronted by the possible closure of the Brunswick Naval Air Station and substantial layoffs at the Bath Iron Works (BIW, a major shipbuilder for the Navy and the state's largest employer) the task force is developing contingency reuse plans for the base and has held discussions with BIW's management, encouraging them to undertake a systematic conversion planning process.

Defense Plant Conversion

Unlike military base re-use planning, the conversion of military production facilities has not been, for the most part, an arena of public involvement. This is in spite of the fact that there are many more companies than bases that are in trouble as a result of Pentagon cutbacks. Their problems can wreak just as much economic havoc upon a community as a military base closure. The discrepancy in the level of public involvement between the two areas is due largely to the nature of ownership. Bases are governmental facilities with a long history of close ties to the communities in which they are located. Defense plants, on the other hand, are run by private companies—although some of the largest facilities, such as shipyards and aerospace plants, are owned by the federal government and operated by private contractors. Private companies traditionally assert, and zealously guard, their independence and community members tend to accept their view of management's prerogatives.

It is important in this context to make distinctions among the thousands of businesses that receive prime contracts and subcontracts from the Department of Defense (DoD). They range from giant corporations like Boeing and General Dynamics, which employ tens of thousands of workers, to tiny "mom-and-pop" machine shops, design firms, and software companies. Some of these companies depend entirely upon military contracts for survival while others have only minimal involvement in the field. Obviously, the nature and extent of a company's military-related production will have a great impact upon its ability to make the transition to the civilian marketplace.

Most discussions of defense industry conversion concentrate upon the aerospace behemoths. They are large and very visible. But for various reasons, they may well be the most difficult companies to transform. Many of the largest—e.g. General Dynamics, Lockheed, Northrup, and Grumman—make over 80 percent of their sales to the DoD. These companies have had little success designing, producing, and marketing products for the civilian sector. Their arcane technologies, batch-production processes, "old-boy" marketing procedures, hierarchical organizational structures, and authoritarian and secretive corporate cultures make it very difficult for them to adjust rapidly to a very different environment.

As a result, the small and medium-sized contractors may be the best candidates for conversion, especially if they are innovative and can change rapidly. However, because of their limited financial and technical resources, thousands of the smaller firms have gone out of business in recent years as Pentagon spending declined.

There is a long history of antipathy to conversion planning on the part of executives in charge of major defense companies, bulwarked by a number of failures when the shift to civilian production has been attempted. Proposed federal legislation mandating conversion planning especially has aroused the ire of defense industry leaders. They maintain that required conversion planning, particularly that involving worker participation in the planning process, would infringe upon traditional managerial prerogatives to make product and employment decisions. (For a more extensive development of this point, see chapter 5.) In addition, they recognize that, if conversion plans are in place, their ability to pressure Congress for continuing high levels of military spending would be diminished. Appealing for public support on the basis of jobs generated by weapons contracts, a practice characterized by detractors as "job blackmail," is a familiar ploy of military-serving companies large and small. For example, in September of 1991 when the B-2 Stealth Bomber was being considered for continued funding by Congress, its prime contractor, Northrop Corporation, placed large advertisements in newspapers throughout California stating that each year for the next ten, the B-2 program would keep 35,000 jobs in California.

Typically conversion, even on a voluntary basis, is the last option considered by defense firms confronted by Pentagon contract cuts. Instead, when threatened, large defense companies will pursue several other not mutually exclusive alternatives to conversion planning.

First and foremost is lobbying Congress (directly and indirectly through hostage workers and local elected officials) for the continued funding of weapons systems on which they work. A closely related strategy is pursuing alternative markets for their military products. These alternative markets increasingly take the form of arms sales to foreign countries, a practice that snowballed after the Gulf War. Both of the above strategies are frequently accompanied by "downsizing"—laying off workers and sometimes closing facilities or transferring them to other (more politically influential and/or less expensive) states such as Georgia.

Another defense industry business adjustment strategy is diversification. It should not be confused with conversion but sometimes it is. Diversification involves a company changing its product mix or field of investment by acquiring or merging with one or more (nondefense) firms. It may be a very smart business strategy for maintaining profits but it does little to insulate a company's defense work force from layoffs or its hometown from serious economic dislocation unless workers are retained and happen to be shifted to new projects in the same community.

True corporate economic conversion up to now has been seriously pursued in only a small number of instances and then with limited success. One of the few success stories to date involves the recent transformation of a small Long Island, New York, company named Frisby Airborn Hydraulics. In 1985 the 100-person company was 90 percent military oriented, depending primarily upon sales of airframe hydraulic equipment to nearby Grumman Corp. Facing flat sales and Grumman's uncertain future, the two Frisby brothers decided to move their company into the commercial sector. Even though its technology had dual-use applications the shift was a daunting endeavor. To accomplish it, several middle-level managers were phased out, the workers were organized into teams that identified cost savings and more efficient production processes, a profit-sharing program was established, monthly financial reviews were initiated, commercial aircraft marketing consultants were hired, and profits were redirected to the conversion process. By 1990 the company's profits were higher than ever and less than one-quarter of its sales were military-related.

Frisby's remarkable success in making the transition to civilian production was due in no small part to the transferability of its technology. But, there is little doubt that the total commitment to conversion on the part of its top managers was the other major factor in the company's successful shift. The two owners effectively stimulated their workers' enthusiasm and creativity by providing them with opportunities for meaningful involvement. In addition, they invested in the future, preparing for and enduring several lean years during the transition period. (The fact that Frisby is a privately owned company and does not have publicly traded stock greatly contributed to its success.) In short, the primary lesson to be learned from the Frisby experience is that managerial leadership is central to conversion success.

Despite the serious obstacles confronting most defense industry conversion, some activists continue to organize local campaigns around it. Perhaps the most notable example of this is the ongoing effort by trade unionists and community activists to promote conversion planning at Unisys Corporation's plant in St. Paul, Minnesota. In this instance, Local 2047 of the International Brotherhood of Electrical Workers attempted unsuccessfully to write conversion planning into their collective bargaining agreement with the company. Rebuffed, they hired a consultant who assessed the workers' skills and the plant's productive capabilities and identified a range of alternative civilian products including: system control computers for high-speed rail vehicles, bar-code readers and page-scanners for the visually handicapped, low-power lighting ballasts, and ground-level sensor networks for "smart" irrigation systems. The activists also publicly pressured the company to undertake conversion planning, enlisting the involvement of public officials including the governor, congresspeople, and state legislators. All of this effort thus far has been to no avail. The company refuses to discuss seriously with the union the idea of converting to civilian production. Layoffs continue at the facility.

Another union-supported industrial defense conversion effort perhaps holds more promise for success. In 1990, the Naugatuck Valley Project (a coalition of sixty-eight community organizations) and Local 1010 of the United Auto Workers jointly approached the management of Textron-Lycoming's Stratford, Connecticut, plant with a proposal intended to save jobs at the defense facility. Faced with impending reductions in manufacturing orders for their AGT 1500 gas turbine engine that powers the M-1 battle tank, company management responded favorably to the proposal. The upshot was the formation of an "optimum use committee" composed of managers, workers, and community members. Several meetings have been held with the emphasis upon identifying new commercial production opportunities that can push the plant's civilian sales well beyond its current 40 percent level.

Both of these labor/community-initiated conversion efforts demonstrate labor's slowly growing openness to conversion planning. But they also show the immense power that management wields in such situations. Unless management plays ball, the plant conversion game cannot take place. Both the Unisys and Textron-Lycoming facilities are parts of larger corporate conglomerates. Their local plant managers only will agree to explore conversion planning if they have direction from corporate headquarters. This appears to be forthcoming in the case of Textron-Lycoming but not with Unisys. Such efforts would be aided greatly by federal legislation that provides inducements to corporations to engage in advance conversion planning.

The States Respond

State governments also are increasingly involved in helping companies move beyond the military orbit. Three states—New York, Washington, and Connecticut—have already undertaken programs. Texas and Massachusetts are a short step behind. And others are seriously considering entering the arena.

In New York, Governor Mario Cuomo established a Defense Advisory Panel to recommend a course of action. In response, the state Departments of Economic Development and Labor both have initiated programs to help military-dependent companies adjust to Pentagon cuts. These efforts include:

- A $170 thousand grant to help Grumman Corp. on Long Island bid for a $500 million superconducting super collider contract.
- Hosting a meeting between representatives of 243 military aerospace suppliers and buyers from Boeing's commercial division.
- Providing "Small Business Innovation Research" matching grants to firms seeking commercial applications for their military-related research.
- Providing a $7 million financial package to Hazeltine, another large Long Island defense company, to help it build an electromagnetic technology center.
- Providing state grants to a consortium of companies to enhance their ability to produce a Maglev transportation system in the state.

In Washington state, following significant pressure from peace activists in SANE/Freeze, the legislature created and funded the Community Diversification Program to address the problem of economic vulnerability caused by heavy military spending in certain sections of the state. Part of the program's charge is to "assist military-dependent firms by providing information and assistance needed to introduce new products or processes." The program is just getting underway but it plans to:

- Establish flexible manufacturing networks of small and medium-sized defense firms, helping them share technical knowledge and cooperate on training programs, purchasing, and marketing.
- Provide financial incentives and assistance to military-serving companies—e.g. tax deferrals, gap financing, and grants and loans for feasibility studies.

- Apply to defense companies the expertise of the Washington Marketplace Program, which matches buyers and sellers of local products within the state.
- Expand the focus of the Washington Technology Center to include technical assistance to smaller defense companies.
- Establish a plot conversion project with a selected group of interested small and medium-sized military contractors.

In New England, Connecticut Innovations Inc., a quasi-public agency designed to help businesses become more competitive, is devoting an increasing proportion of its efforts to assisting defense companies in its state. Its activities include:

- Developing a $500 thousand financing package to help Reedville Tool and Manufacturing Co. diversify its production beyond hydraulic motors for submarines.
- Working with the state Department of Economic Development to identify diversification strategies for the state's largest military contractors such as Electric Boat, Pratt and Whitney, and Sikorsky.

Also in Connecticut, the state Product Development Corporation gives priority to proposals from defense firms to convert to nondefense production. The Department of Economic Development provides property tax exemptions to businesses severely affected by Pentagon cuts. And, loans and loan guarantees are available from the Connecticut Development Authority.

Other states are also getting into the act. On his last day in office, former Governor Michael Dukakis signed a Massachusetts bill into law that established an advisory board to implement and nurture economic diversification efforts in defense industry. Although no funds were appropriated, the state will provide technical, financial, and training resources to assist defense firms to move in nonmilitary directions. Similarly, in July of 1991, Texas Governor Ann Richards established the Task Force on Economic Transitions to promote diversification planning in the "Lone Star" state. States such as Maine, California, Maryland, Minnesota, Virginia, and Pennsylvania are all in the process of considering conversion-related legislation.

Defense Worker Assistance

Workers in defense companies and military bases are the first to feel the effects of Pentagon cutbacks. Despite their obvious vulnerability, rank-

and-file trade union members in defense industry and their local leaders have not flocked to the banner of economic conversion planning. This has been the case even when high-level union officials, such as the leadership of the International Association of Machinists and Aerospace Workers, actively promote conversion. The ambivalence of defense workers toward conversion planning stems from a combination of factors: a lack of tradition in the United States of workers challenging production authority, a realization that conversion planning is unlikely to be successful in many defense firms, a recognition that comparable jobs in the civilian sector are hard to come by, and a general resistance to change. Hence, aside from the two instances at Textron-Lycoming and Unisys mentioned above, in most cases workers have chosen to roll with the punches, even when confronted by significant layoffs. Sometimes, as with the machinist union local at FMC Corporation in San Jose, California, workers have actively supported conversion planning for a time, only to pull back from it when the military contract picture brightens (in that case, an order for Bradley Fighting Vehicles from Saudi Arabia).

Once substantial layoffs do occur, however, public officials eventually see the light. For example, after the Pentagon's cancellation of the A-12 fighter jet at McDonnell Douglas in St. Louis in January of 1991, local officials helped the company to establish a job-finding program, they worked with local community colleges to set up retraining and entrepreneurial development programs, and they funded studies of future job growth in the region. (Their study found that all but three of the fifteen fields projecting job growth were low-pay, low-skill service-sector jobs.) Chastened by the difficulties defense workers were experiencing in finding decent work, the St. Louis Economic Adjustment and Diversification Committee developed plans for a Job Training and Employee Enhancement Program carrying a hefty $43 million price tag.

Something similar occurred in California. There the state Employment Development Department established a computer job-matching program designed to enable laid-off defense workers to land jobs elsewhere in defense industry throughout the state. But, unlike the early and mid 1980s, when job hopping was a common phenomenon for defense workers in California, the early 1990s proved to be much less conducive to the practice. The program was abolished after eight months, overwhelmed by a glut of 20,000 aerospace job seekers but few job openings.

As an alternative, entrepreneurship training programs for skilled defense workers are also being explored in several settings. They, however, can only apply to individuals having the requisite skills, capital, and self-confidence. And, even then, a failure rate of 90 percent of the resultant small businesses is to be expected, perhaps even higher in these difficult economic times. In St. Louis, for example, 300 workers participated in an entrepreneurship program sponsored by McDonnell Douglas but only 30 attempted to start new businesses.

Ultimately, a smooth transition of defense workers to comparable civilian economic activity is most likely to happen when the economy itself is stimulated. A case in point occurred in the tri-cities area of Washington state—the location of the Hanford (nuclear) Reservation—where for nearly fifty years the federal government produced plutonium for nuclear weapons. Now that Hanford's reactors have been shut down, a massive cleanup campaign has begun on the highly contaminated site. The cleanup program together with an ambitious regional economic diversification planning process has resulted in the creation of thousands of new jobs, many of which are appropriate to the skills of the former nuclear workers.

In a similar vein, Congress recently passed legislation with a component introduced by Congressman Howard Berman (D-CA) that will provide seed funding for the development of nonpolluting transit systems and electric vehicles. It supports the formation of a manufacturing consortium to explore a range of innovative technologies. And special emphasis will be placed on the participation in the consortium of defense and aerospace suppliers and manufacturers. Such demand-side conversion, if seriously pursued, has a lot of potential to reemploy former defense workers, albeit with a good deal of retraining in many cases.

In summary, around the United States and increasing amount of local and state-level economic conversion-related activity is taking place—largely motivated by current and threatened military budget cuts. The situation is messy and unpredictable. It is not at all the path the conversion theorists envisioned and promoted during recent decades. Nevertheless, it is a significant phenomenon with interesting potential.

One way to assess this potential is to examine these activities in the context of the three goals of economic conversion listed at the outset.

Avoiding economic dislocation and enabling a smooth transition. This is the one rationale for conversion that is broadly supported by most of society. Some people oppose advance planning as an inappropriate form of government intervention but the great majority appear to support after-the-fact adjustment assistance—especially for workers. And that is exactly what has taken place to date. Because nearly all of the activity described above is reactive, it has not been able to avoid substantial direct and indirect job loss. (Even with advance planning, the hope of avoiding economic dislocation after cuts of this magnitude was probably a false promise of the conversion movement.) Yet progress is being made helping workers to transition in cities such as St. Louis. One major concern is the poor prospects for skilled defense workers—even with significant retraining—to find similar work at comparable pay levels, especially in the near term. A continuing slump in the overall economy could exacerbate the overall transition problem.

Despite the obstacles, state assistance to small defense firms holds a good deal of promise because many of those companies are prepared to change and are flexible enough to do so. What they need is targeted financial and technical assistance. Increasingly savvy local and state officials are recognizing this need. They are confronting the challenge of economic dislocation head-on—seeing it not only as a threat but also as an opportunity to pursue creative economic revitalization strategies.

Undercutting the economic and political power of the Pentagon. Although the military-industrial coalition continues to wield enormous economic, political, and psychological power in the United States, military spending has fallen in constant dollars each year since the peak year of the Reagan administration's massive buildup in 1986. This decline, thus far rather modest, is not due to the emergence of economic alternatives to military dependency but rather the evaporation of the Soviet military threat and the host of other pressures on the federal budget. Even conflicts in the Third World such as the Gulf War do not appear capable of sustaining giant levels of U.S. military spending, especially in the face of so many other critical demands upon the federal purse. However, continued pressure to cut military spending and reallocate resources along with additional progress on the economic adjustment front is critical since the still-massive level of Pentagon spending remains an attractive pork barrel to members of Congress, liberals as well as conservatives, even as it diverts vital resources from other areas of critical need.

Promoting planning for a sustainable peace-oriented economy. Although this goal may have been implicit in the idea of alternative-use planning within the defense industry, its explicit articulation is of relatively recent vintage. It emerged as a significant agenda item in the late 1980s as conversion advocates began to realize that ending the military economy was a necessary but not sufficient objective to pursue. The nature and shape of the post-military economy is obviously of critical importance to people concerned about positive social change. Its configuration and processes cannot be left solely to the determination of "market forces" nor, as is more likely, to the manipulation of transnational corporations. After all, a nonmilitary economy still could be highly problematic. It could foster vast disparities of wealth and high unemployment. Its workers could be treated badly. It could tolerate environmentally destructive production practices, reward the creation of shoddy products, and encourage the conspicuous consumption of goods and services that meet largely cosmetic needs. Therefore, at every level of economic transformation the ultimate question is "Conversion to what?"

It is clear that our current economy, nationally and globally, has a number of structural problems that lead not only to major income inequities and inadequate work opportunities but also to serious environmental degradation. More and more people are coming to recognize that our current modes of production and consumption cannot long endure without wreaking massive environmental havoc. This is where the concept of sustainability enters the picture. A truly peace-oriented economy must meet critical human needs and nurture the earth, our only home and most basic resource, in the short and long term. It can only be attained through practices that promote sustainable economic development—locally, nationally, and globally.

With the issue of sustainable economic development as a frame of reference, the third goal takes on significant importance for conversion advocates. It is not enough to simply reduce the power of the Pentagon or help defense workers find alternative civilian employment, as daunting as those tasks are. The real challenge for conversion-related efforts is to set in motion processes that contribute to the redirection of our economy onto a sustainable path.

Movement in the direction of a sustainable economy requires action at all levels of government and society. While federal action will carry the most political and financial clout, states cannot and should not depend upon the federal government to carry the ball on this critical issue. It is imperative that affected states continue and expand their adjustment efforts—increasingly tying them to long-term sustainable economic development strategies. If states continue to do so, they will not only help themselves but can break new ground with creative models of economic development. In addition to more conventional economic development strategies, state officials can start to:

- Establish and support pilot projects that promote broad-based participatory diversification planning in military-dependent areas.

- Facilitate worker and community buy-outs of defense firms in transition.
- Promote demand-side conversion by linking defense industry transformation with programs in key need areas such as renewable energy development, mass transit, and pollution control and cleanup.
- Work with educational institutions to create defense worker retraining programs targeted toward emerging areas of critical need and technological development.

While activists and concerned citizens can serve very effectively as lobbyists for federal and state conversion efforts, the venue of community-based conversion and diversification planning (including military base reuse) offers distinct possibilities for more in-depth and ongoing citizen participation. Areas confronting military cutbacks are often a focal point for other potential allies such as environmental, housing, and transportation advocates—all of whom have an interest in sustainable economic development. There are usually opportunities for people of knowledge and commitment to become involved in these settings. A well-organized coalition of concerned citizens can promote the institutionalization of conversion planning, involve itself in the planning process once it is established, and provide guidance to public officials in the form of information on other efforts around the country and a continuing stress on long-term sustainable development.

In such situations, concerned citizens can promote conversion planning not only as an adjustment strategy to mitigate economic dislocation but also as a catalyst to:

- Address critical local and regional needs—e.g. affordable housing, mass transit, urban renewal, health care, open space, and recreation.
- Empower citizens to envision and start to move the local economy onto a sustainable path.
- Stimulate participatory planning practices that can be emulated elsewhere.
- Make the connections between local needs and national policy, thus strengthening efforts to establish new federal budget priorities.

Let's take one possible setting in which such citizen involvement in sustainable economic development could be pursued: Monterey, California. The area is home to a major military base, Fort Ord, which was selected for closure in the 1991 round of base closings. This giant, 28,000-acre facility sits on prime real estate on the shore of Monterey Bay. When closure was announced its work force numbered 13,000 military personnel and 4,000 civilians. About one-third of the total economic activity in the neighboring cities of Marina and Seaside was dependent upon business generated by the base, its personnel, and their dependents. The installation is contaminated with toxic wastes, and much of its acreage is littered with unexploded ordnance.

The challenge to the citizens of Monterey County is to put together a viable plan for the facilities' conversion, a plan that will enhance the area's long-term economic vitality and quality of life. This will demand a good deal of creativity on the part of the official local planning task force and its seven committees (in areas such as: economic development, housing, environmental cleanup, and land use). They are considering a number of optional uses for the site including an industrial park, a college campus, an international airport, an amusement park, a low-income and senior housing project, and a coastal state park. The danger is that, in their haste to overcome the substantial economic impacts of the base's closure, the planners will focus on economic activity with short-term growth potential (e.g. an amusement park and hotel complex on the beach) rather than on sustainable development over the long term.

Members of the local political establishment are in charge of the planning process in Monterey but there are entry points for activists and other concerned citizens to get involved. It is to be hoped that they will do so and, in the process, raise important questions about the types and mix of future jobs, the emphasis upon attracting outside businesses versus stimulating local ones, the environmental impacts of the various development alternatives, and the compatibility of various options with current life styles in the area. Most importantly, the reuse planning process provides an opportunity for members of the community to envision the kind of economy they want to see in the region in the year 2020 and to determine how transforming the base can move them in that direction.

The jury is still out on the question of significant citizen involvement in the conversion planning process in Monterey and a number of other similarly affected communities. And it is also an open question whether conversion-related activities can be used to exert leverage on the planning process to advance economic sustainability across the country. In fact, if that goal is to be achieved, a number of obstacles must be overcome.

Traditionally, conversion activists, and peace activists in general, have viewed conversion largely in the context of its first two goals—smoothing the transition and undercutting the Pentagon's power—not as a vehicle for an overall economic transformation. As a result, most activists have concentrated upon public education and enacting federal legislation. Only recently have they turned toward getting conversion and diversification planning institutionalized. And they have given little attention to their roles once that objective is attained. Since, by definition, they tend to be action oriented, quite a few have become frustrated by the slow progress and conservative orientation of official planning processes. Also, they are often discouraged by public officials from getting involved or shunted aside after limited involvement, especially if they start to raise the tough questions about sustainability and equity noted above. Even when activists understand conversion planning's possibilities as an instrument of economic transformation and have the patience to pursue it, they often have inadequate grounding in economics and economic development to formulate a coherent program of action.

In spite of substantial obstacles, local and state economic conversion-related planning remains a field ripe with potential for substantive social and economic change even though it is relatively unexplored to date. Growing numbers of state and local officials are actively pursuing economic adjustment strategies and that in itself is a significant advance. But our economic problems require much more than tinkering around the margins with adjustment strategies primarily geared toward reducing dislocation through short-term growth.

In the new economic and political climate, the challenges for conversion advocates are to educate ourselves about the structural flaws in our economy, develop positive visions of a sustainable economy—locally and nationally—and use conversion planning, writ broadly, as a vehicle to help us move in that direction.

Since healthy communities, cities, and states are critical to the vitality of our overall national economy, work in them has more than just local relevance. In fact, it can stimulate the development of creative models that can be emulated elsewhere across the country and raise the horizons of the nation. If concerned citizens can devote their creative energies to local conversion planning, it may prove to be the embryo from which a dramatically different economy can be born.

9

Post-Soviet Conversion: Problems and Prospects

David W. McFadden

The summer and fall of 1991 may loom as important for the future of the transformation of the Cold War world as the revolutions of 1989. Nearly lost in the aftermath of the failed Soviet coup and the disintegration of the Soviet Union itself has been the breaking of the logjam holding back serious nuclear and conventional disarmament, and the rapid acceleration of forces for the transformation of Soviet and American military economies to civilian production. Even the signing of an unprecedented START agreement between Gorbachev and Bush has now been overtaken by other events. Bush's tactical nuclear weapons cutbacks, and corresponding reciprocal action by Mikhail Gorbachev have initiated a process (really begun by Gorbachev in 1988) for a new kind of disarmament: unilateral initiatives, disarmament by example and response, something long advocated by many in the international community, but long resisted by the superpowers. The speed with which Gorbachev and the leaders of the republics were able to reach agreement on responses to the Bush initiatives shows that the key republics of Ukraine, Russia, and Kazakhstan still

Grateful acknowledgment to Kevin Cassidy, Michael Closson and Susan Strong of the Center for Economic Conversion, Alexei Izyumov, and Seymour Melman for their helpful suggestions.

desire central nuclear control in the process of disarmament and dissolution of the union. This process itself helped lead to quick action between Boris Yeltsin and Bush on a follow-on treaty between the Russian Republic and the United States for the complete destruction of all land-based multiple-warhead missiles, and the reduction of warheads on both sides to the lowest level since the MIRV revolution of the late 1960s.[1]

We are now at an unprecedented juncture in history. The United States Department of Defense is now engaged, for the first time since the Grand Alliance in World War II, in technical and organizational assistance for Soviet armed forces and defense industries. Only this time, instead of assistance for the purposes of war, the assistance is for the reorganization of a shrinking military in a changed world, and the conversion of post-Soviet weapons factories into civilian production and entry into competitive world markets.[2]

Moreover, the bungled attempt to oust Soviet President Mikhail Gorbachev by Soviet hardliners, including head of Soviet defense industry Oleg Boklanov, has led to the humiliation of all the forces most resistant to rapid reform in Soviet society, particularly elements of the KGB, the military, and the Communist Party. It also greatly accelerated the breakup of the Soviet Union and strengthened the power of Yeltsin and Leonid Kravchuk, the leaders of the major nuclear weapons states. This is true regardless of the staying power of the Commonwealth of Independent States, initiated by Yeltsin as a way to keep Russia and Ukraine in some kind of cooperative relationship. All of these breathtaking developments should give added impetus to the process of breakup of the military-industrial complex of the former Soviet Union and the possibility—if not the necessity—for conversion of this complex to civilian production. Yet the same revolutionary and centrifugal forces raise obstacles to the efforts of any republic or commonwealth planners and reformers for a smooth transition of this gigantic complex to a positive, constructive role in a new democratic Russian, Ukrainian, Belarusan, or Kazakh society.[3]

But even moves toward the breakup of the Union can support the conversion process. In Ukraine, for example, the movement toward independence has accelerated the efforts toward a nuclear-free Ukraine. And the preferred way that many Ukrainians see of ridding themselves of nuclear weapons and weapons systems is not to send them back to Russia, but rather to dismantle them and convert the factories to civilian production.[4]

And in Russia, the strong moves in the Russian Parliament to support Yeltsin's drive for more drastic economic reform have not met a total backlash among managers of military enterprises. Rather, many of them see the only hope for their firms in *accelerated* privatization. In October, 1991, a large group of aircraft manufacturers petitioned the Russian Parliament to speed up privatization not only of the economy as a whole, but of the military-industrial sector.[5]

Still, the rapid collapse of the former Soviet defense industry has led recently to concerns, both in the West and among Yeltsin's advisors, that only the acceleration of worldwide arms sales by Russian defense firms can stave off disaster. A great fear remains that, without substantial infusion of investment, the tremendous pool of talent, skill, equipment, and plant space will not be available for the future needs of Russia's economy.[6]

General Konstantin Kobets, Russia's defense minister, has stated recently his own belief that the best way to smooth the transition for Russia's military complex is to speed its privatization while at the same time investing as much money as possible in its technological upgrading and civilian development.[7] Only such a double emphasis can prevent its total collapse and the real dangers associated with it, including the sale of nuclear and military brainpower to the highest bidder.[8] Vladimir Sidorovich, a key conversion planner of the former USSR Military-Industrial Commission and now an advisor to Yeltsin, agrees with this approach.[9] The only way to combine these two aims would seem to be an infusion of western assistance, both money and technology, through such efforts as Dean Le Baron's Batterymarch Financial Management of Boston.

Perhaps the most ambitious joint effort for Soviet defense conversion to date, Batterymarch is a massive effort to gather investments from U.S. firms to the tune of from $500 million to $1 billion to sink into Soviet defense giants and convert them to civilian technological development. Possible investment targets include Tyupelev Aircraft design bureau and other massive aerospace conglomerates in both Russia and the Ukraine. Potential conversion fields include civilian aircraft, space, environmental technology, communications, optics, and shipbuilding.[10]

The coup and its collapse seem not to have interfered with the Batterymarch efforts. Meetings were actually held during the coup attempt in Moscow, St. Petersburg, and other cities, and the relationships established with military enterprises have survived the political upheaval. Much of the money for the Batterymarch investments are being provided by U.S. pension funds, including those of labor unions and churches.[11]

A closer look at the effort to convert Soviet defense industry to civilian production in the Gorbachev era may help illuminate the complex issues involved. These include the transition from command to market economy, decentralization of power to the republics and enterprises, and the technical and social obstacles and opportunities of the conversion process. Closer examination also may provide an interesting contrast to the conversion process in the United States in the wake of the end of the Cold War and the pressures to end the arms race.

On the positive side, commitment to economic conversion at the level of government planning, both in the Gorbachev government and now in the Russian Republic, has never been higher. Ever since the announcement of a commitment to major reductions in military spending and conversion by Gorbachev at his seminal address to the United Nations in December, 1988, economic conversion has been a top government priority among economic planners and political leaders in both the former Soviet and Russian governments. These leaders are determined to shift increasing portions of the redundant factories, equipment and skilled technical and scientific work force currently tied up in the defense industry to address urgent problems of health, environment, and consumer goods. Even the weakening of central government authority occasioned by the collapse of the coup should not alter this resolve. More than 70 percent of Soviet military industry is concentrated in the Russian Republic, and Boris Yeltsin's ascendancy should strengthen efforts to transform this albatross into useful, productive work.

The nature and character of the conversion process, however, may be significantly altered by events. The central government conversion effort launched by Gorbachev, Gosplan (the former Soviet State Planning Committee), and other central planning authorities has at times run at cross purposes with the decentralization and dismantling of the Soviet command economy. Efforts to demand "self-accounting" and independent marketing and decision making for individual firms run counter to the defense complex's habits of priority supply, unlimited costs, and central distribution and decision. Much more pertinent to the future of conversion now may be an acceleration of two segments of economic perestroika that seemed to show some promise, even under Gorbachev's reluctant pace: the explosion of cooperatives and entrepreneurs. At every level of society, even manufacturing and research in such areas as pollution cleanup, smaller-scale energy development, information services, and medical technology, coops and entrepreneurs are beginning to play a critical role. This is truly conversion from the grass-roots. Many of these enterprises remain tied closely to democratic progressive reformers in local governments throughout the Russian Republic, the Baltic states, and Ukraine.

Equally integral to any conversion effort are international efforts at what the Council on Economic Priorities has called "co-conversion," the infusion of Western capital and technology in innovative joint projects to transform portions of the defense economy. These efforts, quite tentative and rudimentary prior to 1989, have received a major boost with the failure of the coup, the rise of Yeltsin, and the breakup of the Soviet structures of power.

In any event, the Soviet military economy is in the midst of breathtaking change toward diversification, decentralization, marketization, and conversion. A look at these issues and this process may help illuminate the need, the complexities, and the interaction with Western efforts at conversion.

The Need and the Opportunity: A Look at the Beginnings

The defense burden on the Soviet economy is enormous. Although official estimates of Soviet military spending show roughly 9 percent of the annual gross national product devoted to defense, even central government economists admit that this understates the situation, due to the fact that foreign military aid, the military space program, much research and development, the republic militias, and the KGB forces are excluded from this budget. CIA estimates are in the 15–17 percent range, while some independent Soviet economists, such as Oleg Bogomolev and Yuri Ryzhov put the figure at 25 percent, and some Western economists go as high as 40 percent.[12] Whatever the true figure, it dwarfs U.S. spending (6 percent), and far exceeds Western European (3 percent) and Japanese (1 percent) spending.

Even more important than the burden on the gross national product is the fact that a huge number—probably between 35 and 40 percent—of all Soviet industrial workers are employed in defense-related industry. These include an even greater percentage of highly skilled and highly paid workers, technicians, engineers, and scientists. Defense workers in the former USSR now total at least 4 million and probably more than 7 million individuals.[13] Clearly, any major economic reform program would have to take account of the huge dependence of these workers and their families on the defense industry. By the same token, no military budget reductions or arms agreements could succeed without somehow shifting the resources—monetary, technical, and human—from this sector of the economy into some new areas of production. Gorbachev was determined to avoid Khrushchev's mistake of making major reductions in the size and scope of the military in the mid 1950s with absolutely no plans for alternative employment, production, or housing.

The very nature of the defense industry, with its concentration on mammoth industrial complexes, heavy industry, and machine building, can be seen as an asset for its transformation. Moreover, some 25 to 40 percent of the capacity of the major Soviet military-industrial complexes is already devoted to civilian production. These complexes are responsible for the manufacture of the highest quality civilian durables, such as washing machines, vacuum cleaners, and televisions, as well as civilian industrial machinery. As modern defense technology worldwide moves increasingly in the direction of microelectronics, computers, and high-tech research, it appears likely that civilian technological developments, both in the former Soviet states and the West, will have far more relevance to defense production in the future than in the past. This can facilitate a reversal of the dependency and encourage Soviet defense industrial managers to strengthen their civilian sectors.[14]

Even the centrally controlled and highly specialized nature of the defense industry could be seen as a short-term asset for the transition, assuring priority delivery of supplies and helping cushion the blows as enterprises began the painful entry into a competitive, highly uncertain civilian market. Government orders for civilian technological and industrial goods could be substituted for government military orders. As the military orders declined, more money could be pumped into the ministries of health, agriculture, or environment for replacement contracts.

The recent flurry of serious interest in the problems and prospects of conversion of Soviet defense industry had earlier antecedents in the mid 1980s, stimulated in large part by Seymour Melman, professor emeritus of industrial and management engineering at Columbia University, and probably the preeminent scholar and proponent of economic conversion in the world. Melman first organized an exchange of American and Soviet scholars on the question of economic conversion in 1984, even before Gorbachev came to power. This two-week seminar in Moscow, co-sponsored by the USSR Academy of Sciences and the American Council of Learned Societies, brought together economists, engineers, planners, and technicians from the U.S. and the USSR to explore problems in the military economies of the two countries and to examine the possibilities and potentialities for conversion.

At this first seminar, despite the inclusion on the Soviet side of economists from the Institute of World Economy and International Relations, the Soviet Institute of Economics, and the Institute of U.S. and Canada Studies (such as Ivan Ivanov, later Gorbachev's Minister of Foreign Trade), the American side found it very difficult to get their Soviet counterparts to begin serious work on the problems of conversion. Despite the much freer admission of the weaknesses of the Soviet economy, and the ready acknowledgement of the myriad ways in which the Soviet economy would benefit from a reduction in military spending—making possible a range of civilian infrastructure investments, including energy efficiency, housing, and transportation—the Soviets continued to insist that the USSR economy could make a successful and relatively easy transition from a military to a civilian basis, once the political decisions calling for reductions in defense expenditure were made. When the American specialists pointed out concrete difficulties in conversion requiring careful planning, including retraining, reallocation of the work force, and the overdesign and overpricing of civilian goods produced by military plants, the Soviets obliquely acknowledged the difficulties, but were reluctant or unable to pursue them in depth. Significantly, no representatives of Gosplan or defense managers were present at this initial symposium.[15]

But events and approaches began to change rapidly in 1987 and 1988. In late 1987, following the U.S.-Soviet Intermediate Nuclear Forces (INF) agreement, necessitating the dismantling of Soviet intermediate-range missiles and the suspension of further production, most civilian light industry was put under the authority of the Soviet defense industry. And in August 1988, the Soviet Council of Ministers specifically designated increases in Soviet consumer durables and entrusted the defense complex to produce them.

The announcements of unilateral reductions in the size of the Soviet military budget (14 percent) and defense production (1.95 percent) announced by Gorbachev in late 1988 were accompanied by a planned determination to increase the share of civilian production in military plants from their current 25–40 percent share to 60 percent over a period of five years, and to nearly triple the civilian output.

These changes saw corresponding reflections in international consultations and meetings. In late 1987, Melman and others found renewed interest in the necessity for conversion planning in meetings with officials at IMEMO (the Institute of World Economy and International Relations) and various government scientific, technical, and economic advisors.[16]

With Gorbachev's speech at the United Nations in December, 1988, the floodgates began to open. Gorbachev himself followed up his initial appeal with a speech at Stanford University following the U.S.-Soviet June 1990 Summit in which he publicly praised Stanford University scientists and economists for ground-breaking work in the field of contacts with Soviet counterparts on conversion planning. This was an oblique reference to Stanford engineering professor Bernard Roth and representatives of the Center for Economic Conversion, who had brought some of these ideas to the attention of Ivan Ivanov, Georgy Arbatov, and others in meetings in 1984 and 1985.[17] Gorbachev followed this up with a direct and explicit appeal to the members of the Group of Seven industrialized nations in July 1991 for international financial assistance for the conversion of Soviet defense industry.[18]

International meetings of experts, with major participation from the Soviet Union and support from the highest levels of the Soviet government, began to be scheduled, and two public commissions were formed in the USSR to push for conversion and to produce papers and send experts to international meetings. The most significant of these commissions, the National Commission for the Promotion of Conversion, was organized by trade union leadership and the Academy of Sciences. This commission included for the first time representatives from Gosplan, the defense-related industrial ministries, academic experts from the universities, and the Academy of Sciences. They have focused their energies on drafting a long-term comprehensive conversion program, a program overtaken by the demise of the Soviet Union but now revived by the advisers to Yeltsin and Kravchuk.[19]

Gosplan, the former Soviet State Planning Committee, produced a 1990 program for converting the defense industry. In this program, it assigned to each of the twelve defense production ministries one of the priority areas of civilian production, including consumer durables, farm machinery, light industry equipment, medical technology, communications, and electronics. In 1990 alone, Gosplan announced, civilian goods produced by the military complex would be increased by nearly 22 percent, while defense output would drop 15 percent. The Draft State Conversions Program of Gosplan saw the future civilian work of the defense complex eventually focused in three areas: (1) durable consumer goods, health, and the environment; (2) accelerated research and development in electronics, computer technology, and communication to try to leap forward in the information revolution; and (3) upgrading machinery and technology for all civilian industries. The hope was palpable that military budget cutbacks and civilian production increases could proceed in tandem, strengthening the entire economic reform process and even putting more and better consumer goods in the stores within months.[20]

The belief in the efficiency, quality, and productivity of this defense industrial base for civilian use was so strong, in fact, that a number of weak and inefficient civilian ministries, such as The Ministry of Machine Building for Light and Food Industry and Household Appliances, were transferred to the supervision of defense production managers in 1989 and 1990.[21]

The Gorbachev economic leadership also realized that the shifting over of portions of the military complex to civilian production would not occur without difficulty, and would require some subsidies to smooth the way. The 1990 Gosplan program allocated some 4 billion rubles for retooling and creating additional civilian capacity in existing defense plants, an amount expected to rise to 40 billion rubles by 1995.[22]

From the beginning of Soviet plans and attempts at conversion in the late 1980s, human and social concerns in the process have been paramount. Maintenance of jobs at commensurate rates of pay utilizing workers' skills, preservation of special pensions for hazardous work, funds for retraining and relocation—all of these were included in the Draft Law on Conversion, which attempted to maintain social protections for those affected by any defense cutbacks or conversion of enterprises. In addition, policy and economic planners have consistently stressed a conversion labor policy, promising that no one would suffer as a result of the transformation of industry. Both the Military Industrial Commission and the Supreme Soviet Defense Committee have stressed the importance of maintaining labor guarantees, and the government established a special fund to help make up the difference in salaries and bonuses for workers.[23]

Yet major social problems remain. Skilled Soviet defense workers are leaving their jobs in large numbers, estimated as high as 500,000 in 1990, lured by higher pay in cooperatives, joint ventures, and other entrepreneurial opportunities. Remaining workers are watching their prerogatives and status diminish as plants struggle with the transition. And the recent nuclear cutbacks raise the specter of thousands of nuclear engineers and scientists made suddenly expendable.[24]

Obstacles

Soviet steps in the direction of conversion in the late 1980s, however, were met with tremendous resistance on the part of the managers of the various enterprises and all those who stood to lose from the reductions in military budget and defense production priorities. The chiefs of defense enterprises resisted their orders to shift production, forty-six of them signing an open letter to *Pravda* claiming that Gorbachev was trying to destroy Soviet national security. Gorbachev capitulated, stepping back from the radical economic reform plan and reassuring the military and defense chiefs that he would not undermine them.

Not only was the Soviet military able to reverse the 1990 budget cutbacks in planning for 1991, but the ambitious plans for conversion have largely remained just that: plans. By all accounts, less than 10 percent of defense plants have increased their mix of civilian production in the two years since these plans were announced, and those managers who have made the effort, either because of military cutbacks or out of a desire to expand a civilian product line, have run into numerous technical, economic, social, and political obstacles. Richard Parker, an economist at the University of Texas, reported recently that of the $40 billion allocated by Gosplan for conversion, less than $4 billion had been spent by October 1991, and of 125 defense plants in the process of conversion, only 4 had been converted.[25] Most of the highly publicized examples of "conversion" of Soviet defense plants have actually been expansion of civilian output already under way, or use of auxiliary space and extra personnel to enhance the production of goods that can be used either for military or civilian production. Little retooling or transformation of defense production lines has yet taken place.[26]

There are a number of major obstacles that Soviet conversion efforts have run into in the last several years since these plans and programs have been announced. The first might be called the bureaucratic obstacle—perhaps the most pervasive and intractable roadblock to all reform in the Soviet system. In this case, the natural resistance of plant managers to any change is compounded by the fact that it remains far easier for them to fight for continued military orders than to expand civilian production with the uncertainty of markets and the developing competition among enterprises, even with Gosplan shifting a portion of funding into the civilian ministries. Few of the enterprise mangers have taken any initiative to market their civilian goods, preferring instead to devote fully 100 percent of their production to the fulfillment of state orders. Almost no incentives exist for saving resources or for keeping prices low or quality high. Even the fulfillment of state orders is fraught with more difficulties than military production. For example, military hardware can always be stockpiled if overfulfilled, while an inexact amount of a civilian order will do nothing to stimulate an already stagnant economy.[27]

Structural problems add even greater difficulty. Although many enterprises have both civilian and military production, isolating or separating the two productive capacities may be difficult, unlike corresponding situations in the West where military and civilian divisions of a plant are almost always completely separated. Moreover, the scientific and technological interaction between high-quality, high-tech military industry and civilian technological development is practically nonexistent. Virtually no high-quality civilian technological infrastructure exists, and civilian consumer production is low-quality and outdated in raw materials, equipment, and products. So-called spinoff or transfer of military technology to civilian industry, so well known in the West, occurs in Soviet industry only in equipment or technology somehow unacceptable to the military. On the other hand, Soviet military specialists often expropriate any good technology available on the civilian side, whether domestic or foreign, without any compensation, further widening the gap between the two technologies.[28]

All of these structural problems are exacerbated by the sheer size of the Soviet military production complex, and the extreme secrecy pervading every aspect of its work. Many enterprises are gigantic in themselves, and many more individual enterprises depend totally or almost totally on the defense ministry for their very existence. Secrecy prevents both an accurate assessment of the problem, and a detailed assessment of plant technology product mix, labor skills, machine and research availability. Although Gosplan called for conversion, details were almost entirely left up to the managers of the defense plants themselves, with little assistance or pressure from the civilian economic managers. No specific enterprise-level plans for conversion could be prepared without data on jobs, military hardware costs and prices, or technological capacity. Sometimes this has led to total absurdities, such as the report that one missile-production facility will soon start making chocolate truffles, or the danger of a massive oversupply of heavy construction trucks from converted tank production lines.[29]

Efforts to overcome these structural and bureaucratic obstacles hinge on the success of two approaches to conversion: decentralized market reform, and international financial and technical assistance.

Market Reform and Conversion

On first glance, it might seem that the further acceleration of the breakup of the command economy and the new moves toward the "free" market in Russia and Ukraine in the wake of the coup would run at cross purposes to the conversion and diversification of the military industry already underway. Yet it comes at a time already full of debate about the best way to deal with the Soviet defense sector. Many argue that the best means of converting Soviet defense industry is its rapid breakup: the devolution of central responsibility to the republic level; the independent responsibility for marketing, production, and profitably at the plant level; and the simultaneous development and growth of civilian research, technology, and production. Perhaps the most extreme version of this view is held by a senior Bush administration official quoted in *Business Week* who said, "Our idea of defense conversion is to take the Soviet plant, shut the door, and build another one next door to produce civilian goods."[30] A recent article in *Foreign Affairs* echoes this belief, arguing bluntly that "defense conversion should not be viewed as 'conversion' at all. Rather it is the result of two independent and parallel actions: shedding many elements of the defense sector; and absorbing those assets into a new entrepreneurial consumer sector."[31] But such a draconian approach ignores the very real transitional problems of a post-Soviet economy and buys into the first great myth of conversion, "that normal economic growth can deal with the economic disruption of a major reduction in military spending," as Bischak and Yudken have pointed out in chapter 5 above.[32]

Russian economists and planners, while accepting the very real need to shift in a free market direction, have instead placed their focus on micro-planning in the strategies for transition. Alexei Izyumov of the Russian Academy of Sciences has urged much greater attention in the conversion debate to the assistance of cities, republics, "inter-regional or inter-ministry associations and the reliance of individual enterprises themselves to develop data banks, financing, technical assistance, and marketing." This might lead directly to the development of all of the civilian sides of defense plants into independent corporations or self-financing subsidiaries.[33] Even a huge plant like Uralmash, the gigantic machine-building conglomerate in the Urals now employing 45,000 workers, might be broken up into smaller divisions and made independent, then able to compete for new business or foreign contracts.[34] And Yuri Andreev, Secretary of the Russian Commission for Promotion of Conversion, argues that the key problem for Yeltsin is planning at the regional and factory level.[35]

Although it is far too early to judge the impact of the Commonwealth of Independent States, it seems sure to speed the privatization of all parts of the economies of the Russian Federation, Belarus, Ukraine, and Kazakhstan, at the very least. And even before this latest political development, the cooperatives were already the most successful part of the economic reform process, despite their difficulties and the political obstacles that were often put in their way.

The Russian "kooperatsiia" is often misunderstood. Established by Gorbachev at the height of economic reform in 1987 as a way of revitalizing socialism via market relations, the "ko-ops" were a legal way to begin private enterprises. The property and profits of the cooperatives belonged to those who owned them, subject only to taxation. But there had to be more than one owner, and all owners technically had to work in the business—thus the "cooperative" rather than a "shareholder" or private business.[36]

The cooperative movement had already grown, by the spring of 1991, into the most dynamic part of the economy, accounting for between 15 and 20 percent of the output of the economy. This sector is a strange hybrid of state development and private enterprise, often with involvement of the republics, former state enterprises, or local governments. Reformist politicians such as Anatoly Sobchak, the mayor of St. Petersburg, have not only encouraged cooperative development, but have put the resources and political clout of the local government behind them. Despite major problems of supply and resources, the cooperative/private sector continues to grow, bringing in more and more public resources from state businesses, former party resources, and the republics.[37]

The co-ops have also organized to help and protect each other, by forming the Organization of the Association of Cooperatives and the Union of Amalgamated Cooperatives, to work on behalf of political changes at the local and republic level that will facilitate their growth and development. Yet they may be reaching their limit on growth without further infusion of resources, especially from abroad, or the total breakup of state property, which Yeltsin has so far refrained from doing.[38]

Reform economist Abel Aganbegyan saw the growth of cooperatives nearly as important as joint ventures in furthering a different kind of foreign trade for the reformed Soviet economy. He particularly hoped that cooperatives in services, such as engineering and computer technology, will become heavily involved in foreign trade with the West.[39]

"Co-Conversion": Foreign Trade, Investment, and the Conversion Process

Foreign cooperation in the Soviet conversion efforts, since the explicit request of Mikhail Gorbachev at the Group of Seven Summit in July 1991 for major Western aid in the conversion process, has received enhanced attention, but has been underway for a number of years. In fact, it provides some of the major success stories and projects in process in Soviet conversion. Soviet interest in Western investment in the conversion process is quite understandable. Such efforts allow for risk sharing, provision of technological expertise, marketing assistance, and the tie-in to sophisticated Western specialists of all kinds. Before detailing some of these successes and failures, some background on joint ventures, foreign trade, and the evolution of economic reform over the last several years is necessary.

Aganbegyan, one of the more far-seeing of Gorbachev's early economic advisors and a recent aide to Yeltsin, has stressed the importance of high technology and capital assistance from the West. He has repeatedly denied that self-sufficiency, as sometimes hinted at by Gorbachev, was possible "in a time of rapid scientific and technological development, when demands concerning quality change rapidly and new products and technologies appear all the time."[40] Aganbegyan also has placed a greater emphasis on the reforms in the foreign trade mechanisms currently in force. He believes that joint ventures, cooperatives, and the decentralization of the control of foreign trade can transform its very nature by the turn of the century so that a majority of both imports and exports will be composed of high-tech and machine-building products and services.[41]

The emphasis on reforms in foreign trade was enhanced by the appointment of Ivan Ivanov as Deputy Chairman of the Soviet State Foreign Economic Commission, the agency of the Council of Ministers established in 1988 to take over and open up the tight monopoly on foreign trade formerly exercised by the Ministry of Foreign Trade. Ivanov formerly served in a variety of capacities both in the academic world and in the United Nations, most recently as a key staff person in IMEMO (the Institute of World Economy and International Relations), perhaps the USSR's most prestigious think tank, and a research institute highly valued by Gorbachev. Ivanov has specialized in technology transfer, international economic order, foreign trade policy, and export promotion. He also has been visibly involved in international seminars, such as one in 1984 on the economics and technology of defense spending and alternatives with U.S. specialists.

Ivanov has emphasized the important role of foreign trade in the formation of a more open, intensive economy in the USSR, and has helped to supervise the reform legislation pushed through the Council of Ministers. In writing about the importance of these reforms, he has stressed the need of joint ventures with the West and the increasing necessity for foreign capital. When criticized for this on ideological grounds, he was likely to remind his readers that Lenin always emphasized two criteria for any assessment, particularly in foreign relations: good sense and "practical results."[42]

The foreign trade reform that former Prime Minister Nikolai Rhyzhkov and Gorbachev pushed through the Council of Ministers and that Ivanov helped to oversee has been developed in stages since 1986. The monopoly of the Ministry of Foreign Trade has been broken by putting the ministry under a new superministry, the State Foreign Economic Commission, and giving the right to engage directly in importing and exporting activities to associations, regional ministries, and some selected enterprises. In addition, in the legislation establishing joint ventures and expanding the rights of cooperatives, foreign partners are permitted and even encouraged in both. In order to facilitate all of the foregoing activity, a cautious plan for phasing in the convertibility of the ruble has been outlined.[43]

Although the original 1986 decree was rudimentary and lacking in much detail concerning contemplated changes, it did accomplish the most important action: elimination of the monopoly that the Foreign Trade Ministry has had on foreign trade since 1918. Decentralization of functions was at least outlined, which opened the way for the subsequent emphasis on associations, enterprises, cooperatives, and joint ventures that has since accelerated the process. Cooperatives and joint ventures with Western companies now play an important role, and the Ministry of Foreign Trade is struggling to control or keep up with a variety of activity.[44]

The decrees creating the possibility of joint ventures, first adopted in January, 1987, were but a modest step and still maintained many Soviet controls on such ventures. But they opened the door for joint ventures and were later followed by further relaxation of controls. Most observers feel that eventually, once the currency becomes convertible, joint ventures hold great promise for significant foreign involvement in the Russian economy or that of other republics. Ivanov, in his discussion of joint ventures, stresses the importance of technology transfer and management experience, the buildup of capital, and the hoped-for outcome of greatly improving the exports of the USSR.[45]

A number of intriguing developments are now underway linking Western companies—Swedish, French, German, and American—with Russian firms, both defense firms interested in conversion and cooperatives engaged in alternative economic projects. These include a joint venture with Siemens for manufacture of digital telephone exchanges and the joint production of fiber-optical cable; a Soviet-West German joint venture in Odessa, transforming SS-20 mobile missile transport vehicles into mobile cranes; and a joint venture between the U.S. firm Gulfstream Aerospace Corporation and the Sukhol Design Bureau for passenger jetliners and executive aircraft.[46]

One of the most successful of such ventures is a Swedish-Russian enterprise now known as Tetra Pak-Luch, the conversion of the Luch Experimental Works in Podolsk, just south of Moscow. A former manufacturer of parts for nuclear reactors and metal optics for advanced weapons systems, Tetra Pak-Luch now makes cardboard containers for milk and fruit juice. The new venture has made a successful technical conversion, and has even begun to turn the corner economically, impeded only by the at-times-erratic orders for the cartons from milk and juice producers who have seen their supplies of foodstuffs shrink.[47]

Intensive efforts to expand the range of joint ventures have been made in the last two years. In April 1990 in Munich the Soviet government sponsored an exhibition, "Conversion 90," which tried to stimulate interest in foreign investment in the conversion process by highlighting creative civilian technical ideas that could be accomplished by Soviet defense firms. These included sample products, designs, and blueprints. While publicizing various possibilities, and highlighting the technical potential, most of these ideas had no immediate practical consequences. New discussions with foreign partners have, however, been stepped up.[48]

Soviet Ministry of Aviation executives visited U.S. firms such as Interturbine (a Texas jet engine manufacturer and repairer), United Technologies' Pratt and Whitney Group, Raytheon's Beech Aircraft Corporation, Occidental Chemical, Kaiser Aluminum, and other U.S. firms in an intensive three-week trip in the spring of 1990. These officials spent some intensive days in management training and exploration of the questions of quality control, process improvement, marketing, and export, and in preliminary discussions with all of the firms regarding joint ventures.[49]

Stanford University's Center for International Security and Arms Control has established a long-term project to facilitate meetings of managers of Soviet defense industries with U.S. counterparts in a further effort to expand the possibilities for cooperative ventures in conversion. Two delegations of Soviet managers visited U.S. firms and management, technical, and economic specialists in the United States in 1991. These included managers of such Soviet firms as Scientific Production Amalgamation Machinostoenie and Krunichev, both large aerospace research and production facilities involved in military aircraft, rockets, and satellites as well as civilian space, food-processing equipment, robots, machine tools, and ships. In meetings arranged by Stanford, these Soviets and some Soviet government representatives met with representatives of Lockheed, TRW, FMC Corporation, and Boeing. Out of these meetings came a number of possible joint ventures or cooperative possibilities for future discussion including joint design and production of equipment to deal with hazardous waste, international use of Soviet space production and launching facilities, and Soviet production of American-designed equipment.[50]

All of these discussions and fledgling attempts at international assistance for conversion of Soviet defense firms have been accompanied by a barrage of international meetings, discussions, and production of technical, scientific, and economic papers, exemplified not only by the Stanford project, but also by two 1990 events: a high-level conference organized by the Council on Economic Priorities and a United Nations gathering in Moscow.

International discussions on these questions culminated recently at the United Nations conference, "Conversion: Economic Adjustment in an Era of Arms Reduction," held in Moscow in August 1990. Although the conference considered the conversion problem worldwide, special attention was focused on Eastern Europe and the Soviet Union, and the conference revealed not only the seriousness with which conversion was being undertaken in the former USSR, but also the magnitude of the problems faced and the terms of the developing debate concerning the best approaches to take. Stark contrasts were apparent between Gosplan's Victor Kotov and independent researchers such as Alexei Izyumov. Kotov continued to insist upon the need for centralized control of the process and the substitution of state civilian orders for military ones. Izyumov, as we have already seen, not only sees the problems much more clearly, but essentially comes down on the side of decentralization, a breakup of the massive defense complex, the need to do careful market research and skills assessment, and create a fit between the burgeoning cooperative sector and the skilled work force available in the collapsing defense complex.[51]

The concerns and questions raised by Izyumov were underscored at the Council on Economic Priorities academic conference on conversion in Moscow in November 1990. Izyumov and others, agreeing with many American specialists, argued that the USSR conversion plan was far too centralized and "rigidly deterministic," and that conversion should be encouraged at the local and enterprise level, to better dovetail with market economic reforms.[52]

Future Prospects

The collapse of the coup and the resulting demise of the Soviet Union may yet make this debate irrelevant, particularly if the movement toward a market economy and local economic decision making continues unabated. But the fact that most of the major defense industry complexes are located in the Russian Federation and Ukraine, with the great majority in the major cities of Moscow, St. Petersburg, Novosibirsk, Sverdlovsk, Chelyabinsk, Tula, and Gorky, the Ural Mountains, and the Ukrainian Donbass region makes clear that the problems of conversion in the former Soviet Union will not go away simply because of a shift of decision making from the center to the republics.[53] There is increasing evidence that local officials are well aware of the problem, and are determined to connect conversion with decentralization. In Nizhny Novgorod, for example, Gennady Hodryrev (chairman of the NN Regional Council) recently discussed the relationship between defense conversion in his region and the stimulation (with regional council support) of consumer-goods machinery production and formation of cooperatives. While concerned about economic losses and calling for some degree of central government income support, Hodryev remained committed to local economic initiatives in the transition.[54]

The concern in both Moscow and the West to maintain some degree of central control over nuclear weapons and weapons facilities and the military command structure may yet bring back the need for coordinated efforts at the transformation of the military complex in the former Soviet Union. If that is true, perhaps more attention needs to be paid to the sober assessment of Evgenii Kuznetsov and Felix Shirokov, who called as long ago as 1989 for a two-stage conversion process. In Kuznetsov and Shirokov's view, the barriers between civilian and military production in the same plant must first be eliminated and then the infusion of civilian technological investment would begin to transform not only the military side of production, but the antiquated civilian side as well. Only then, in their view, would conversion be serious and relate to the overall needs of the economy.[55]

Arthur J. Alexander of RAND Corporation said at the United Nations conference, despite all the problems and difficulties facing the conversion process in the former Soviet Union, "real resources are being allocated. Competent technical and production people have been given new responsibilities; they are struggling to find the right products and searching for the real users. As usual, the Soviet manager has been given an impossible task, and with intelligence, energy, and native wit they are marching forward. . . ."[56]

But, in view of the overwhelming problems that have developed since that time, Alexei Izyumov's more cautious approach might ring more true to the current situation: "Taking into account the delicate nature of conversion processes, . . . so much depends upon the political will and mutual understanding of the participants. . . ."[57] It remains to be seen whether such cooperation, political will, and understanding can yet be summoned to convert an enormous resource for the benefit of post-Soviet societies.

Notes

1. For details and commentary on this agreement, see *New York Times,* 15 June 1992.

2. Eric Schmitt, "U.S. Weighs Aid to the Soviet Military," *New York Times,* Sept. 16, 1991. In the U.S. Defense Budget for FY 1992, $500 million was included to aid the former Soviet Union, with economic and technical assistance for conversion, particularly in the dismantling of nuclear weapons (*New York Times,* 3 Nov. 1991). On the Soviet response to Bush, see Igor Malashenko, "Behind Gorbachev's Arms Cutback," *New York Times,* 18 Oct. 1991.

3. Alexei Izyumov points out that four of the eight members of the junta had direct roles in the Soviet military-industrial complex. Alexei Izyumov, *Defense Conversion in the Former Soviet Union: The Difficult Path Ahead* (Middlebury, Vermont: Geonomics Institute, 1992).

4. *New York Times,* 18 Oct. 1991, 30 Oct. 1991.

5. *Izvestia,* 7 Sept. 1991. See also Mikhail Zaraev (deputy editor of *Ogonyok*), "An Insider's Guide to the New Russia," *World Monitor,* November 1991.

6. See *Krasnaya Zvezda,* 19 March 1992; *Rossiiskaya gazeta.* 14 Feb. 1992; *Izvestia,* 3 March 1992; and Steven Greenhouse, "Post-Soviet Arms Industry is Collapsing," *New York Times,* 9 June 1992.

7. Boris Rumer, "Beating Swords into . . . Refrigerators?" *World Monitor,* January 1992.

8. For discussion of this fear, based on a classified report recently prepared by the CIA, see *New York Times,* 1 Jan. 1992.

9. *Izvestia,* 17 Oct. 1991; Vladimir Faltsman, "The Price of Conversion and Who'll Pay for It," *Independent Newspaper from Russia,* December 1991.

10. *New York Times,* 26 Aug. 1991; McNeil-Leherer Newshour transcript, 9 July 1991; Center for Economic Conversion, *Positive Alternatives* (Fall 1990).

11. National Public Radio Report, 22 Nov. 1991; Steven Greenhouse, "Seeking to Give a New Life to a Dying Soviet Industry, *New York Times,* 23 Dec. 1991.

12. Izyumov, *Conversion of Ex-USSR,* 7, points out that both the last Gorbachev budget and Yeltsin's both accepted a figure closer to 25 percent.

13. Michael G. Renner, "Is the Soviet Union Prepared for Peace?" *World Watch* (September–October 1990); "Moscow's Hungry Monster," *Time,* 13 May 1991; *New Times* no. 10 (1990), 27; Sophie Quinn-Judge, "Financial Crunch Puts Generals on the Defensive," *Far Eastern Economic Review,* 27 June 1991; Izyumov, *Conversion of Ex-USSR,* 8. The best overall summary of the former Soviet Defense industry is Julian Cooper, *The Soviet Defence Industry* (New York: Council on Foreign Relations Press, 1991).

14. Russell Bova, "The Soviet Military and Economic Reform," *Soviet Studies* (1988) 40:385–405; Arthur J. Alexander, "The Conversion of Soviet Defense Industry, RAND Paper P 7620 (January 1990).

15. Unpublished papers and author's notes on Joint U.S.-Soviet symposium on conversion of military to civilian economy, July 1984. See also, Seymour Melman, "Readying Conversion," *New York Times,* 27 July 1984.

16. *Science,* 6 March 1987 and Seymour Melman, "Soviet Swords and Plowshares," *New York Times,* 21 March 1987.

17. Mikhail Gorbachev, speech at Stanford University, 5 June 1990, in *San Jose Mercury News,* 6 June 1990.

18. Mikhail Gorbachev, speech at Group of Seven, in *New York Times,* 22 July 1991. Also *Washington Post,* 29 July 1991.

19. Vsevolod Avduevsky, "Conversion and Perestroika," (paper presented at UN Conference on Conversion, August 13–17, 1990).

20. Alexei Izyumov, Soviet Academy of Sciences, in testimony to the UN Conference on Conversion, August 13–17, 1990; Arthur Alexander, "National Experiences in the field of Conversion: a Comparative Analysis," (paper presented at UN Conference on Conversion, August 13–17, 1990); Valentin Smyslov, "State Program for Conversion of Defense Industry," (paper presented at UN Conference on Conversion, August 13–17, 1990).

21. Izyumov UN testimony, 9; Alexander, "National Experiences," 34.

22. Alexander, "National Experiences," 35.

23. Smyslov, 89; Alexander, "State Program," "National Experiences," 44; Vladimir Salo, "Conversion Problems in Production Sphere in USSR," (paper presented at UN Conference on Conversion, August 13–17, 1990).

24. Alexander, "National Experiences," 43; Smyslov, "State Program," 86. For an interesting survey of military engineers in the former Soviet Union, the majority of whom support conversion despite the job threat, see "Conversion to Peace Time: the Social Cost," *Independent Newspaper from Russia,* 2, no. 8–9 (October 1991).

25. As quoted on National Public Radio, Morning Edition, October 1, 1991. Both Izyumov and Yuri Andreev, Secretary of the Russian Commission for the Promotion of Conversion, fault Gorbachev for not

providing the funds to make conversion a reality. (Izyumov, *Conversion of Ex-USSR,* 17; Andreev, interview, *Positive Alternatives,* Spring 1992.

26. Greenhouse, "Seeking to Give"; D. Khrapovitsky, "Who Needs This Conversion?" *Izvestia,* 17 Oct. 1991; Izyumov, *Conversion of Ex-USSR,* 17–18.

27. Vsevolod Avduevsky, "Conversion to Perestroika," in testimony to the UN Conference on Conversion, August 13–17, 1990. Evgenii Kuznetzov and Felix Shirokov, "Problems of Conversion of Soviet Defense Industries," *Kommunist,* July 1989.

28. Izyumov, UN testimony, pp. 12–13; "Swords into Chocolate Truffles," *New Scientist,* 11 Nov. 1989; Michael Dobbs, "Gorbachev Aides Target Military-Industrial Complex," *Washington Post,* 29 July 1991.

29. *Business Week,* 29 July 1991. Izyumov, *Conversion of Ex-USSR,* particularly stresses the importance of detailed micro-data.

30. *Business Week,* 29 July 1991.

31. Kenneth L. Adelman and Norman R. Augustine, "Defense Conversion," *Foreign Affairs,* Spring 1992, 41.

32. See p. 169, this volume.

33. Izyumov, UN Testimony; Anthony Jones, "Coops: the Rebirth of Entrepreneurship in the Soviet Union," (paper presented at the New England Slavic Association meeting, Framingham, Mass., April 1991). And See Anthony Jones and William Moskoff, *Ko-ops: the Rebirth of Entrepreneurship in the Soviet Union* (Bloomington: Indiana University Press, 1991).

34. Bill Keller, *New York Times,* 6 Jan. 1991.

35. Andreev interview, *Positive Alternatives,* Spring, 1992.

36. Jones and Moskoff, *Koops,* xv–xvi.

37. Jones, "Co-ops."

38. Jones and Moskoff, *Koops,* 110–120.

39. Abel Aganbegyan, *Inside Perestroika* (New York: Harper and Row, 1988).

40. Ibid., 176. See also Anders Aslund, "Gorbachev's Economic Advisors," *Soviet Economy* 3 (1987): 246–69.

41. Aganbegyan, *Inside,* 187.

42. Ivan Ivanov, "The State Monopoly of Foreign Trade: Today's Forms and Problems," *Foreign Trade* [Moscow] 14 (1988): 4–7. See also Ivan Ivanov, "Perestroika and Foreign Economic Relations," in *Perestroika 1989* (New York: Macmillan, 1988), 148–49, 159, and interview with Ivanov, "On a Businesslike Basis: There will be Joint Enterprises," *Trud,* 4 Feb. 1987, as published in FBIS-SU, 12 Feb. 1987, 51–54.

43. Ivanov, *Perestroika,* 159–160. See also D. Blagutin, "The Technological Spectrum of Joint Venture on Soviet Territory," *Foreign Trade* [Moscow] 4 (1989): 25–28 and Mikhail Ryshkov, "Joint Ventures as a Channel for Transferring Technology," *Foreign Trade* [Moscow] (1989):12–15.

44. Ivanov, *Perestroika,* 159–60.

45. *Ibid.,* 159.

46. Valentin Smyslov, "State Program for Conversion of Defense Industry," U.N. Conference Papers on Conversion, August 13–17, 1990, 92; Izyumov, UN testimony, 15.

47. *New York Times,* 27 July 1991.

48. Smyslov, "State Program," 92; Vasily Petrov, "Guns for Butter: Changing Production," *Soviet Life* (March 1990).

49. *Aviation Week and Space Technology,* 26 Feb. 1990.

50. David Bernstein and Catherine Smith, "Collaborative Project on Soviet Defense Conversion," Center for International Security and Arms Control, Stanford University, May 1991.

51. Various UN Conference Papers (including Izyumov, Smyslov).

52. Council on Economic Priorities, *Soviet Conversion* (1991). Izyumov expands on this concern in his most recent work, *Conversion of Ex-USSR*.

53. *Ekonomika y Zhizn* no. 19 (1991).

54. *Ibid.*

55. Kuznetsov and Shirokov, "Problems of Conversion."

56. Alexander, "National Experiences," 48.

57. Izyumov, *Conversion of Ex-USSR*, 38.

10

Conclusion: Real Security, Real Democracy

Kevin J. Cassidy

In the summer of 1991 the world watched breathlessly as a coup d'etat was attempted in the rapidly disintegrating Soviet Union. Americans tuning into CNN saw columns of tanks and garrisons of soldiers arrayed against their countrymen who openly defied the military. Thanks in part to the worldwide coverage, the defiance by these irregulars prevailed over the power of the military and the Communist Party. The Party has for all practical purposes ceased to exist and the impact of the military on national life has been substantially reduced.

Many Americans watched all this with a sense of smug satisfaction that their nation was not controlled by the forces of tyranny and domination. Yet there is an increasing awareness, as the above chapters have made clear, that the impact of the military, and the economic and political institutions related to it, have a disproportionate influence on the United States and the formulation of its policies. Resistance to this military-industrial complex or "military corporatism," as Gregory Bischak refers to it in chapter four, is becoming more organized and also more sophisticated in the alternatives that it proposes to current national security policy. The Russians might interpret this as perestroika, the term used by Gorbachev as he attempted to change the basic, fundamental structures of the former Soviet Union. Conversion advocates recognize that what they propose is really part of a larger package that does indeed include a new vision of the United States and its role in the world. Yet conversion might also be seen as part of an American glasnost as well because conversion has the potential of bringing a new openness and new voices to the policy-making processes of the government.

The idea of broader, more democratic participation in policy making is discussed in this chapter. The first section describes the unique scale and power of the national security apparatus and especially its fundamentally undemocratic character. Conversion is then considered as an opportunity to reduce the power of this system. The second part of the chapter continues the theme of participation by reviewing local conversion efforts as examples of democratic planning and politics. Finally, conversion planning—whether on the local, state, or national level—raises the issue of public planning and its relationship to the private sector. This theme, long a controversial one in American life, is discussed within the context of democratic political theory.

The Undemocratic National Security Apparatus

Bischak's analysis of military corporatism in chapter four provided an economic explanation for the influence exerted over national security policy making by military-related groups in the economic and political sectors. E. P. Thompson has pointed out that the scale of this "iron triangle," as Gordon Adams has called it, is far larger than anything in the civilian economy. Thompson argues that it is really a social system in its own right. It has its own

> distinctive hierarchies of command, rules of secrecy, prior access to resources and skills, and high levels of policing and discipline: a distinctive organization of production, which, while militarist in character, employs and is supported by great numbers of civilians (civil servants, scientists, academics) who are subordinated to its discipline and rules.[1]

One of the points made by the authors in this volume, as well as by Thompson, is that this social system operates in a manner that is largely independent of the democratic values and institutions of society and it wields political pressure that is extraordinary even by the standards of

Washington lobbyists. Its influence, as Thompson argues, is "more inexorable than can be explained by recourse to notions of an 'arms lobby' or a 'military interest.'" Weapons seem "to grow of their own accord, as if possessed by an independent will."[2] As a result the United States is now involved in large-scale preparation for wars of all sizes. We have become a warfare state or a permanent war economy, where military production is now counted as ordinary economic goods and the national economy is heavily dependent on this type of manufacturing.[3]

What has disappeared with the coming of military corporatism is the traditional distinction between war and peace. Historically, a weapons buildup was understood as a response to the aggressive actions of an adversary who had either invaded one's borders or engaged in threatening actions that appeared to make war imminent. The conflict began on one's borders and then was brought to the center of society where decisions could be made on how to meet the threat. Now the situation has been reversed. With a whole social system devoted to weaponry the arms race is really generated at the center of society, i.e., by the different parts of this social system. It has a logic and autonomy of its own and it functions outside of the ebb and flow of international diplomacy.

Moreover, this social system stamps its own priorities on the nation as a whole because, as the authors in this volume have demonstrated, it determines which social needs can be met, what types of goods and services will be available. The weaponry system also employs its own ideological constructs to bring about citizen acquiescence to the militarist version of national priorities. In sum, it is possible to argue that the United States does not *have* a military-industrial complex; rather it *is* such a complex.[4] "The warfare state is no longer an ideological abstraction," Seymour Melman argues, "but an increasingly accurate portrait of American society."[5]

Overlooked in this development is the cost to democracy. Militarism, and especially nuclearism, have brought with them a huge secret police network, the official management of news, a classification system so rigid that access to policy documents is limited to a tiny elite, and the casting of those citizens morally concerned about all this as "fools, at best, or if they persist so as to obtain a hearing, as enemies of the state."[6] The legitimacy of democratic participation is severely compromised as political life is more and more restricted. Wartime conditions, including the continual preparation for wars of all kinds, inevitably concentrate power in the hands of a few and threaten the first principle of democracy itself: the normal accountability between government and its citizens.[7]

What conversion offers is the possibility of having a *structural* impact on the institutions of this warfare state, an impact fundamentally different than what the peace movement has ever achieved in the United States. By confining itself to short-term efforts to stop this or that weapon system, the peace movement has left intact the structures responsible for the military buildup. The same is true for arms control, which reduces the number of older weapons systems so that new ones can be more readily financed. Again, the power of the arms manufacturers and their allies in the military and civilian bureaucracies and in Congress is unaffected. Only conversion and disarmament treaties can touch on the power of these institutions and, in the process, offer hope of altering the warfare state and the permanent war economy.[8]

Converting excess defense production to civilian manufacturing could reduce the dependence of defense contractors on weapons production, thereby reducing as well the pressure that these firms and their employees bring for bigger military budgets. With scaled-down weapons outlays, the influence of military corporatism on national security policy might also be curtailed. This in turn could make it easier for the concept of common security, outlined above in chapter 1, as well as other alternative ideas on America's role in the world, to get a hearing in Washington. Conversion then is not merely about finding jobs for defense workers; it is also about democratizing policy making by reducing the impact of war-making institutions on the policy process.

However, as this book has argued throughout, national security policy cannot be limited to traditional questions of defense policy. Environmental integrity and economic development are also critical and in the rethinking of these two areas it is again military corporatism that has proven to be the major obstacle. As Michael Renner has demonstrated in chapter 3, military considerations have precluded the development and enforcement of adequate environmental policy. Concerns for the environment, like those for common security, have been put in a secondary position behind the goals of the military, especially the building and testing of new weapons systems. Military production, even apart from war itself, is by far the greatest source of environmental degradation and the end of the Cold War will leave massive sources of pollution to be cleaned up at extraordinary expense.

Economic development policy, as Joel Yudken has argued in chapter 2, has faced a similar fate. The enormous investment the United States has made in military production has been substantially responsible for its inability to develop a civilian industrial policy. The nation *has* had an industrial policy for many years but it has masqueraded as defense policy and therefore never been properly evaluated. Accordingly, few have appreciated until recently how much of the nation's resources have been committed to the military rather than to the civilian sector. This has been especially true in the scientific and engineering fields where the United States has had difficulty maintaining a stable position in the new international marketplace.

Both Yudken and Renner indicate that there is no shortage of groups and professionals espousing progressive ideas in the fields of environment and industrial policy. Indeed, a major new area in public policy is an attempt to synthesize the concerns of both sectors in what is called "sustainable development." Again, the problem is that these voices have not been heard because of the dominance of military corporatism in these two critical areas of national security. The same has been true for Congress's attempts to develop conversion policy. In chapter 6 Maggie Bierwirth has described Congress's timid efforts, which have not addressed the enormity of the problem. Yet members of Congress, as she clearly points out, have so far been unwilling to do more in the context of the defense budget because, in the words of one congressperson, they see it as "the Pentagon's money." So in this case, as with the previous issues of common security, industrial policy and environmental protection, there has not been a lack of new ideas; the real obstacle is the power of military-related institutions to prevent serious consideration of these ideas in the policy process.

Democracy in Local Conversion Efforts

In his chapter, "Building a Peace Economy from the Bottom Up," Michael Closson shares the concern of the other authors over the undemocratic impact of the Pentagon in public policy. He argues, however, that if the federal government—and the Congress in particular—has abnegated its responsibility on this issue, the efforts taking place on the state and local levels may offer more promise and may eventually have a positive impact on the federal level. Closson, together with Hill, Dietrick and Markusen in chapter 7, chronicles a wide variety of undertakings including community responses to both the closing of military bases and the termination of contracts at local defense plants. In many of these cases the communities involved did diversify their economies, i.e., made them less defense-dependent.

What is particularly striking in these cases is their democratic character. If federal policy suffers from a lack of participation by different groups, the local efforts at diversification and conversion are consistently democratic. They have provided a diverse group of citizens in each community with a voice in the economic development process. This democratic element is rare in economic development and seems to result from the community's recognition that its defense-dependency is a condition affecting all in the community and therefore should be addressed by the entire community. These efforts have frequently been initiated by labor and/or peace groups in coalition with church and small business organizations lobbying elected officials to make a peace economy part of the public agenda. Moreover, the democratic makeup of these efforts has provided them with a legitimacy that has permitted them to begin to work effectively within their communities or states. It is not coincidental that these democratic planning efforts give some promise of creating policies that will benefit more than a few vested interests. In both respects, democratic makeup and democratic benefits, these efforts provide a prototype for what national industrial policy-making efforts could strive for.

Closson echoes the argument of Yudken and Renner that conversion must not only be geared to reducing the economic impact of the Pentagon and helping defense workers find alternative employment. As daunting as those tasks are, conversion and community diversification must also be focused on the development of an environmentally sustainable economy. Again, democratic participation is essential; local and state voices must be heard if the policy developed is to be responsive to citizens' needs and be supported by their communities.

This trend is also apparent in the former Soviet Union. David McFadden explains in chapter 9 that one of the most important forces in democratizing the Soviet economy and moving it away from dominance by the military are the new cooperatives. These are free-enterprise organizations on the local level and they exist largely independently of the centralized government. While they are not conversion-specific they offer hope for the development of the economy away from the immense impact that military production has had in the former Soviet Union. Indeed, despite the extraordinary conversion efforts by the Gorbachev government, the military-industrial complex in the former Soviet Union was largely effective in thwarting these policies. It now appears, as McFadden points out, that the most promising prospect for renewing the economy is also the most democratic, i.e., the cooperatives.

The democratic efforts at community diversification described by Closson might also be understood as examples of what Alvin Toffler refers to as "anticipatory democracy." Toffler argues that unless citizens have the power to plan the circumstances of their future, including their workplace future, they will have ceded power over their lives to the technocratic elites who shape corporate policy and public policy generally.[9] Having a share in the economic planning of the community is often the only guarantee its members have of the future direction of the community. This type of insecurity has long been felt in defense plants because of the boom-and-bust cycle of defense contracting, and also because of the increasingly high-tech nature of weapons production that has left large numbers of defense workers without jobs, even during the eighties when the number of weapons contracts increased. Workers and defense-dependent communities have had no control over these factors and defense contractors have made few structural efforts to promote job security and limit unemployment among workers. Community diversification planning, with its democratic participation, is an alternative to this position of powerlessness.

The potential of democratic participation to create a true peace economy and, in the process, a more progressive national security policy, is also evident in the efforts at site conversion documented in chapter 7 by Catherine Hill, Sabina Dietrick, and Ann Markusen. The cases cited in their study make it clear that real progress is being made toward the conversion of individual defense plants, and that the expertise and worker interest are there. The real obstacle has been the opposition of management to worker participation in the planning decisions of the company. Indeed, where site conversion has succeeded, as Closson and Yudken point out as well, the workers were completely integrated into the process and played an important role in it. Moreover, site conversion could have succeeded in a number of instances, e.g., the Unisys effort in Minneapolis among others, if workers' plans had been given serious consideration by management. While Hill, Dietrick, and Markusen suggest a variety of carrots to entice management into conversion and while they also recognize the crucial role to be played in that regard by government, they conclude by pointing out that workers may have to consider assuming ownership in those instances where management would rather sell off a plant than consider converting it.

Direct worker involvement in conversion planning has been suggested by the late Congressman Ted Weiss (D-NY) in his bill proposing that alternative-use committees consisting of workers, management, and representatives of the local community be set up at defense plants. To date this approach has been unsuccessful in Congress, Maggie Bierwirth has pointed out, as corporate management has strongly opposed it. If adopted it would be an example of what is often referred to as "work place democracy." This form of worker participation is substantially more than a choice of jobs since that choice itself could be limited to the performance of relatively mechanical tasks. Instead, the idea of work place democracy, as Edward Greenberg and other democratic theorists have pointed out, is to eliminate the hierarchical structure of the work process and especially the distinction between planning and execution of production plans.[10] In short, the goal is to provide all the workers in an enterprise with the opportunity to exercise self-governing capacities in the workplace itself. Workplace democracy seeks to reorganize the production environment to empower workers in controlling the decisions that are made about production and the final deployment of the product. It is precisely that empowerment that has held real potential in some conversion attempts but is so strongly opposed by management. As a result, the prospects for site conversion are not good, at least apart from a substantial effort by government or through the type of comprehensive national needs planning advocated by Yudken, Bischak, and Bierwirth.

Behind both site conversion and community diversification is a view of human nature that is especially participative and democratic. People are seen as capable of involving themselves in the decisions of their workplace or community and rightfully doing so. This is in the spirit of classical democratic thinkers including J. S. Mill and Rousseau. Democracy for these thinkers is about citizens having autonomy over their own lives in society.

However, not all democratic thinkers share this confidence in direct participation. A more skeptical approach is taken by theorists such as Schumpeter and Sartori, who see democracy as little more than competition among rival elites for the power to determine government policy. Democracy in this view is only a set of procedural principles for determining the selection of ruling elites; it does not permit any extensive participation by citizens in industrial policy making.

Peter Bachrach, one of many critics of this view, argues that it is based on two faulty assumptions: "first, that the masses are inherently incompetent and, second, that they are, at best, pliable, inert stuff or, at worst, aroused, unruly creatures possessing an insatiable proclivity to undermine both culture and liberty."[11] For conversion and diversification advocates there is a particular irony to these characterizations of the "masses." Certainly the studies recorded by Hill, Dietrick, and Markusen, as well as the examples cited by Closson and the co-ops in Russia described by McFadden, indicate that when workers and community groups have been involved, efforts to save a defense plant have been thoughtful and well planned and movements to diversify defense-dependent economies have made real strides. Moreover, this type of participation has been successfully used in the civilian sector, particularly in a number of flexible specialization industries.[12]

Moreover, the conversion proposals presented to Congress have often been the expression of defense workers' concerns as articulated to planners and legislators. The same is even more true at the level of state government. The examples described earlier in this volume by Closson represent the efforts of individual legislatures and state agencies to respond to the expressed concerns of defense workers or public policy groups who have involved themselves directly with these workers. While workers themselves may not always have the technical expertise to plan for conversion, it is clear that through their unions, local community groups, and individual professionals interested in the issue, the concerns of workers have been translated into real policy proposals.

At stake in efforts at public planning, as Robert Reich has pointed out, is really the question of community: "What does it mean to be a member of a community within a business enterprise? To be a member of an economic community within a nation? For whom does the business enterprise exist?"[13] In short, site conversion and community diversification are ultimately about social membership, about who really belongs and to what degree. Site conversion, by directly involving workers in the decision process, invests them with a full-fledged membership in the business enterprise. Community diversification operates in a more indirect manner as it seeks to organize the civic community to control its own economy and to do so by directing government toward specific goals. This is less threatening to management even though those promoting community diversification are no less committed to the activist use of government to promote economic planning. The goal is to establish within the community, through government and public organizations, direct responsibility for the economic good of the community.

These grass-roots planning processes can also serve as antidotes to the political lethargy afflicting American democracy today. Americans exhibit a profound disillusionment with politics and its ability to respond to their real concerns. The need, as Frances Moore Lappé has argued, may not be for a convincing program as much as it is for a process through which people can create that program: "a politics of practical problem solving."[14] Diversification planning and site conversion hint at what a truly responsive economics and politics might look like.

Public Planning and the Private Sector

Traditionally the issue of public direction of the economy has been a controversial one. There is a populist strain in American political tradition that insists on seeing economic and political relationships as necessarily adversarial. Part of this is the notion that government is always inefficient—a bad rap, as Gar Alperovitz and Jeff Faux have argued, that is the result of the fishbowl existence of public institutions. Their inefficiencies are much more visible than those of private institutions whose operations are less open to public scrutiny. Alperovitz and Faux also point out that in the United States we have generally limited government to those endeavors that are not profitable or to those in which the private sector has failed. Therefore, "*by definition* we have declared the public sector inefficient."[15]

Reich also laments that Americans have chosen to divide their national life into the two separate realms of government-politics and business-economics. Issues of justice, including participation, equality of opportunity, civil rights, social security, pollution, and crime, are restricted to the first realm, that of government-politics. On the other hand, we have generally limited our concerns about prosperity, including production, economic growth, inflation, savings, investment, and trade to the second realm, that of business-economics.[16] This separation of civic values on the one hand and business values on the other is outdated because, as Joel Yudken has pointed out in chapter 2, it has prevented our mounting a coordinated, comprehensive response to the fundamentally new problems facing the American economy. This has put the United States at a disadvantage with respect to those nations having policies of national economic planning. Meeting the new mercantilist challenge of the world economy requires an adaptation of the American system that would allow the two sectors of society, otherwise understood by Americans as separate if not adversarial, to be more closely connected in a new political-economic, government-business mode. This argument ultimately goes back to the Hamiltonian attitude of being willing to restrict the freewheeling individualism of American practice in favor of a more focused approach to economic development. It represents the use of strong, assertive government to transcend group conflict and establish a national common good.

The advocates of economic conversion, whether site conversion or community diversification, share this commitment to national planning but they insist on a consciously democratic approach to it. Their outlook is similar to that of Carol Pateman, who argues that "the industrial sector is a political system in its own right" because it has a power to determine citizens' lives comparable to the power of government itself.[17] A truly democratic society therefore must provide its citizens with the public means to exercise control over that industrial sector. Democracy must extend to the economic realm, not just to the political; the public must have control over both realms because both shape its life. Economic conversion is one way of exerting that control.

Pateman's position is stated in similar terms by Alan Cawson who argues that, because of concentration and centralization within corporate capitalism, large corporations now have a social impact that gives them a public character and public purpose.[18] Certainly this is the case within military corporatism, as Bischak has pointed out in chapter 4. The issue is how to control these companies in such a way as to underwrite rather than undermine democracy. As Cawson sees it, the point then is "how to extend democratic control over the corporate sector of the political economy whilst at the same time preserving and extending those features of liberal democracy, such as civil liberties and freedom of association. . . ."[19]

The point of claiming this control, of demanding this participation, is to be able to create a humane, secure society. This is the other major component of contemporary democratic thought. David Harris speaks for this position in arguing that democracy is not only about participation in decision making but also about ensuring "material outcomes" that are in the interest of all in society.[20] This is Yudken's goal when he stresses in chapter 2 that conversion strategy should have three priorities: economic stability, the environment, and health. These are fundamental to meeting the basic needs of citizens. Fulfilling these needs is necessary if citizens are to enjoy the personal autonomy required for participation in the social deliberation that is the heart of democratic life.

This is the "real security" in this volume's title. Each of the authors in the book understands conversion planning as a means to this end. While they differ in the terms they use—new national priorities, a new economic agenda, sustainable development, a new industrial policy—all of these authors envision democratic conversion planning as a means of redirecting the economy to meet the fundamental human concerns of our society. All of them agree that the existence of military corporatism, and the conventional "national security" policies that are expressions of it, stand in the way of establishing the democratic society outlined here by Harris, Pateman, and others. Real security means building this kind of society. Economic conversion is a major step toward that end and, done democratically, it *is* that end in the process of becoming.

Notes

1. E. P. Thompson, "Notes on Exterminism, the Last Stage of Civilization," *New Left Review,* 121 (London, 1980): 7, 8.

2. Ibid.

3. Seymour Melman, *The Permanent War Economy* (New York: Simon & Schuster, 1974).

4. Thompson, "Notes," 23. The same point is made in the classic article by Marc Pilisuk and Thomas Hayden, "Is There a Military-Industrial Complex That Prevents Peace?" *Journal of Social Issues,* July 1965: 98–9.

5. Seymour Melman, *The Demilitarized Society* (Montreal: Harvest Books, 1988), 57.

6. Robert Jay Lifton and Richard Falk, *Indefensible Weapons* (New York: Basic Books, 1982), 138.

7. Ibid., 193. The importance of relying on democratic participation in the formulation of national security policy is articulated as early as Thucydides when Pericles states in the funeral oration, "our city is open to the world, and we have no periodical deportations in order to prevent people observing or finding out secrets which might be of military advantage to the enemy. This is because we rely, not on secret weapons, but on our own real courage and loyalty." (Thucydides, *History of the Peloponnesian War,* trans. Rex Warner, [Baltimore: Penguin Books, 1968], 118.)

8. This point is developed throughout Melman, *The Demilitarized Society.*

9. Alvin Toffler, "What Is Anticipatory Democracy?" in Clement Bezold, ed., *Anticipating Democracy: People in the Politics of the Future,* (New York: Random House, Vintage Books, 1978), 361–365.

10. Edward Greenberg, *Workplace Democracy* (Ithaca: Cornell University Press, 1986). See also Michael Margolis, *Viable Democracy* (New York: St. Martin's Press, 1979) and Benjamin Barber, *Strong Democracy* (Berkeley: University of California Press, 1984).

11. Peter Bachrach, *The Theory of Democratic Elitism* (Washington: University Press of America, 1980), 2.

12. Michael J. Piore and Charles F. Sabel, *The Second Industrial Divide* (New York: Basic Books, 1984), 17. See also C. Richard Hatch, "Reviving Local Manufacturing, Italian Style," in *Conversion and Reindustrialization* (proceedings of a one-day conference at Columbia University, Department of Industrial Engineering, June 1987).

13. Robert B. Reich, *The Next American Frontier* (New York: Times Books, 1983), 267. The question of individualism and the priority of the community has been examined at length by Alasdair MacIntyre, in his *After Virtue: A Study in Moral Theory* (South Bend: University of Notre Dame Press, 1984) and in his *Whose Justice? Which Rationality?* (South Bend: University of Notre Dame Press, 1989).

14. Frances Moore Lappé, *Rediscovering America's Values* (New York: Ballantine Books, 1989). In addition, see her statement in the forum "Building a Living Democracy: responses to an economic vision beyond socialism and capitalism," *Sojourners,* October 1990: 17–18.

15. Gar Alperovitz and Jeff Faux, *Rebuilding America* (New York: Pantheon, 1984), 247. Emphasis is that of Alperovitz and Faux.

16. The philosophical problems of applying any single concept of justice to all areas is also discussed at length in Michael Walzer, *Spheres of Justice: A Defense of Pluralism and Equality* (New York: Basic Books, 1984).

17. Carole Pateman, *Participation and Democratic Theory* (New York: Cambridge University Press, 1973), 106.

18. Alan Cawson, “Functional Representation and Democratic Politics,” in *Democratic Theory and Practice,* ed. Graeme Duncan (New York: Cambridge University Press, 1983).

19. Ibid., 180.

20. David Harris, “Returning the Social to Democracy,” in Duncan, *Democratic Theory,* 222.

Appendix

President Clinton's 1993 Conversion Program

Gregory A. Bischak

President Clinton's first defense budget calls for spending $263 billion in 1994, for a reduction in real spending by 18 percent over five years. Its timidity reflects the enduring influence of the military-industrial interests over the defense budget. While Defense Secretary Aspin would have us believe that this budget is shaped by the threats from Iraq, North Korea, Iran, and worldwide terrroism, the facts speak to the contrary. Continued funding of SDI, the C-17 jet cargo transport, the advanced tactical fighter, and other weapons cannot be justified by the military capabilities of these villified nations.

Yet, even these modest defense cuts imply large-scale economic dislocation. The proposed Clinton defense cuts, coupled with those already in the pipeline under the Bush plan, mean that more than 1 million defense industry workers will be laid off during the 1994–98 period. Another 700,000 uniformed and non-uniformed workers will also be cut.

Representative Ron Dellums, Chairman of the House Armed Services Committee, has moved the defense budget debate squarely back onto the issue of conversion, arguing that a conversion program "should not just provide money or training as people are being ushered out the door, but should be a real and effective bridge from their present position to one in a full-employment economy." It is in this light that the President's newly unveiled conversion program must be judged.

The President's Conversion Program

President Clinton recently said his administration would "continue to reduce defense, as we must, but we're trying to plan for the future of those people and those incredible resources" being released from the defense sectors. Indeed, the commitment of nearly $20 billion over the next five years for the *Defense Reinvestment and Conversion Initiative* establishes clear federal leadership in helping workers and communities adjust to defense cuts.

Yet it would be a mistake to conclude that the job of conversion is now being adequately addressed, thereby allowing the nation to focus its attention and energies elsewhere. Many daunting problems remain for defense-dependent industries, workers and communities that are not addressed by the Clinton plan. Over 150,000 defense industry workers were laid off in 1992, and forecasts indicate 1.3 million more will be laid off over the next several years. The closing of more military bases will compound the impact.

The Clinton Administration took the architecture for much of its conversion program from last year's $1.7 billion initiative in the Defense Authorization Act and added about $18 billion to be spent over the 1994–97 period. These programs provide over $3.2 billion in transition and training benefits for laid-off military personnel and civilian workers, over $1.5 billion for retraining displaced defense industry workers, nearly $300 million in economic adjustment assistance to defense-dependent communities, and $4.7 billion for defense industry and technology programs. Most of the conversion and adjustment functions are to be managed by the Department of Defense or the Veterans Administration. The exceptions are the community economic development assistance which will continue to be managed by Commerce Department's Economic Development Administration, the manufacturing extension programs which will be managed by the National Institute of Standards and Technology, and the retraining program which will be administered by the Department of Labor.

New federal investments in high-technology and manufacturing extension programs are also part of the Clinton program, with nearly $10 billion being targeted to create conversion opportunities for defense firms and communities.

Defense Reinvestment and Economic Growth Initiatives, President Bill Clinton

	Budget Authority ($s in Millions)				
Program	1994	1995	1996	1997	Total
DoD Personnel Assistance/ Community Support	697	697	697	697	2,788
DoE Personnel Assistance	100	—	—	—	100
Displaced Worker Training	300	400	400	400	1,500
EDA Community Assistance	33	55	55	55	198
DoD Dual-Use Technology	964	964	964	964	3,856
Conversion-related High Technology Initiatives	1,206	2,329	2,758	3,175	9,468
Grand Total:	3,300	4,445	4,874	5,291	17,910

Clinton's Budget and the Job Gap

Delivering on the promise of job creation through reinvesting defense savings will be the major challenge for the administration. This is true especially since Clinton is planning to cut $118 billion more from the defense budget on top of the $48 billion the Bush Administration had proposed for the 1994–97 period. But as the Office of Management and Budget has found, many of the cuts proposed by Bush were not specific, forcing the Clinton Administration to scramble to tie them down. Yet, the Clinton Administration faces a similar problem itself, since its defense budget has no details beyond 1994. This vagueness will more than likely be filled in by big cuts in procurement and research and development over the 1995–98 period.

Meanwhile, of the $160 billion in the administration's investment package, only $48 billion is being reinvested in high-tech industry, civilian Research and Development, and infrastructure. Thus, it is doubtful that this reinvestment will offset the magnitude of the defense cuts for manufacturing sectors and industrial workers, especially in those high-tech, high-skill, high-wage occupations that President Clinton hopes to retain. Thus, the central challenge for the Administration and the nation is to find the means by which job bridges can be built between declining defense-dependent industries and occupations and those that are to be stimulated by the civilian reinvestment initiative.

Building Job Bridges

New industries in high-speed rail, electric vehicles, environmental technologies, and other fields will take time to ramp-up, thus creating a timing problem for reemploying dislocated defense workers. This situation is being compounded by the commercial restructuring currently underway in aerospace and other fields. To span the gap between the rapidly accelerating defense cuts and the slowly developing civilian jobs in high-tech commercial work, reinvestment must be linked to the retraining and redevelopment programs. In order to bridge this job gap, six pillars will have to be built.

First, new high-tech job incubators must be created through spin-off enterprises and new business incubators that can exploit new technological opportunities emerging from each area of civilian investment. Spin-off enterprises provide one solution when large prime contractors choose to lay off workers and shut down plants, rather than convert. These enterprises can create job incubators, like the CALSTART initiative in California, to retain a critical skills base being released by defense industries and help to maintain high-wage jobs in manufacturing. Such job incubators could also provide a foothold for union membership in new and emerging occupations.

Second, defense firms may be able to move into some of these emerging new technology markets if they begin planning now to develop new products, retool, reorganize production, develop marketing capabilities and retrain their managements, engineers, and workforce for commercial work. But it is evident that some economic incentives such as an investment tax credit will have to be targeted to promote advance planning and job retention. However, such incentives should be geared to converting existing capacity and reemploying defense workers in civilian work.

Third, the retraining programs currently being revamped by Secretary of Labor Robert Reich should include income support and relocation benefits for displaced workers of all kinds in order to ensure that where it is required they can receive the long-term training necessary to get high-wage jobs. This is especially important if the administration and the nation is committed to retaining high-skill, high-wage jobs in manufacturing. Such a program should go beyond mere extensions of Unemployment Insurance and improve on the performance of the current Trade Adjustment programs.

Fourth, linking reinvestment with retraining and redevelopment efforts will require an interagency coordinating and planning body, preferably housed in the Commerce or Labor Departments to carry out this program. Such a body is necessary to coordinate the various programs and to streamline procedures in order to speed access and assistance. In addition, having a civilian-oriented agency take the lead in interagency coordination would place the proper emphasis on conversion to civilian production and serve to counterbalance undue influence from the DoD in its role of maintaining the defense industrial base. Finally, this body could examine the regional, industrial, and occupational issues stemming from the large scale shift of resources and help states and localities adjust to these changes.

Fifth, given the shortfall of the reinvestment initiative and the inevitable mismatch between the skill requirements of jobs being lost and those being created, there will be a need for expanding educational assistance. Educational grants for university-industry consortia could be used for the retraining of engineers and managers for work in the civilian sector, particularly in the newly emerging technology fields. In addition, educational loans should be provided for production workers who may wish to qualify for emerging opportunities in high-tech occupations or to pursue higher education.

Finally, new sources of finance for enterprise development will be needed to assist in the development of innovative enterprises, including employee ownership, middle management buyouts, and community redevelopment projects. The Clinton plan puts very little money in community redevelopment assistance and provides little for financing new business development. These are some of the issues which must be addressed if the conversion process is to create new jobs.

As the nation embarks on a broad initiative to convert the Cold War military system, it will be essential to ensure that the conversion process meets the goals of generating new jobs, equitably distributing the benefits of the conversion, ensuring the participation of all the major stakeholders and safeguarding against large-scale waste of public monies. If we fail in this effort, the nation will lose the opportunity to revitalize the civilian economy and create the basis for sustainable economic development. Moreover, failure to successfully convert will create resistance to further reducing our military budgets and block the chance to develop a more enduring basis for international peace and security.

Contributors

MAGGIE BIERWIRTH is a senior legislative assistant to U.S. Congressman Sam Gejdenson of Connecticut. She was an active participant in the development of the 1990 economic conversion legislation, which provided the first substantial federal funding to defense-dependent communities. A former executive director of the Connecticut Campaign for a U.S.–U.S.S.R. Nuclear Arms Freeze, she is the author of numerous articles on nuclear arms control. In addition to her duties on Capitol Hill, she is a student at Georgetown University Law Center.

GREGORY BISCHAK is the executive director of the National Commission for Economic Conversion and Disarmament in Washington, D.C., and the executive editor of *The New Economy*, an international periodical published four times a year on economic conversion and disarmament issues. He received his doctorate in economics from the New School for Social Research in New York, and has taught as an assistant professor of economics. He is author and co-author of numerous articles and chapters in books on industrial and military economics, energy issues, and economic conversion and is contributing editor of *Toward A Peace Economy in the U.S.* (St. Martin's Press, 1991).

KEVIN J. CASSIDY is professor of political science at Fairfield University in Connecticut, where he is also the director of the academic program in peace and justice studies. His research on the alternative use of defense production has appeared in the *Journal for Peace and Justice Studies, Social Policy, Science, Technology and Human Values, Policy Studies Review, The Social Science Journal, Peace and Change, Thought,* and *Commonweal*. Professor Cassidy has been a member of both the Connecticut state legislature's

Task Force on Manufacturing as well as the Defense Advisory Group of Connecticut Innovations, Inc. which have formulated responses to the defense-dependency of the state. He received his doctorate in political science from the Graduate Center of the City University of New York.

MICHAEL CLOSSON has been executive director of the Center for Economic Conversion since 1982. In this position, he consults with local, state, and national officials on strategies to overcome military dependency and build healthy peace-oriented economies. He assists in planning and the conversion of military bases and defense plants, helps activists develop local conversion strategies, and lectures widely on military economics, conversion planning, and sustainable economic development. He received his doctorate from Cornell University in 1971. His articles have appeared in a number of publications including *Multinational Monitor, Earth Island Journal, Bulletin of Municipal Foreign Policy, Building Economic Alternatives,* and *Creation*. He is a peer of the Elmwood Institute and serves on the advisory boards of *New Options, Peace Review,* The Other Economic Summit—Americas, the Twenty-First Century Project, and the General Electric Stockholders' Alliance. He also serves on the Advisory Board of the Council on Economic Priorities.

SABINA DEITRICK is an assistant professor of public and international affairs at University of Pittsburgh, and co-author of *The Rise of the Gunbelt* with Ann Markusen, Scott Campbell, and Peter Hall (New York: Oxford University Press, 1991).

CATHERINE HILL is a doctoral candidate in the Department of Urban Planning and Policy Development at Rutgers University. She recently co-authored a study with Ann Markusen, *Converting the Cold War Economy: Prospects for Industries, Workers and Communities* (Washington, D.C.: Economic Policy Institute, 1992).

DAVID W. MCFADDEN is assistant professor of history at Fairfield University in Connecticut, specializing in Soviet-American relations. He received his doctorate from the University of California at Berkeley in 1990. Dr. McFadden was the founder and co-director of the Center for Economic Conversion in California, 1975–1983, and co-edited with Suzanne Gordon, *Economic Conversion: Revitalizing America's Economy* (Cambridge, Mass.: Ballinger, 1984). His latest book, *Alternative Paths: Soviets and Americans, 1917–1920* will be published by Oxford University Press in 1993.

ANN MARKUSEN is director of Project on Regional and Industrial Economics at Rutgers University, where she is also professor of Urban Planning and Policy Development. She is the author and coauthor of several books on high technology and American economic development, including *Dismantling the Cold War Economy* (Basic Books 1992), *The Rise of the Gunbelt* (Oxford 1991), *Regions: the Economics and Politics of Territory* (Rowman and Allenheld 1987), *High Tech America* (Unwin Hyman 1986) and *Profit Cycles, Oligopoly and Regional Development* (MIT Press 1985). Professor Markusen received a Bachelor's Degree in Foreign Service at Georgetown University and her M.A. and Ph.D. in Economics at Michigan State University, and has held faculty positions at the University of Colorado, University of California Berkeley, Northwestern University, and Rutgers. She has served as a Brookings public policy fellow and as an advisor to the cities of Chicago, Cleveland, and Pittsburgh, and the states of Michigan, California, and Ohio. She is presently serving on review panels for the National Science Foundation and the Office of Technology Assessment. Her recent research is on the impact of military spending on American industry and regions, and a comparative study of new industrial districts in Japan, Korea, Brazil, and the United States.

MICHAEL RENNER is a senior researcher at the Worldwatch Institute, a non-profit research organization in Washington, D.C. He was a Corliss Lamont Fellow in Economic Conversion at Columbia University from 1986 to 1987, and a research associate at the World Policy Institute in New York from 1984 to 1986. He has been a contributing editor of *The New Economy* since its inception in 1989. Mr. Renner is the author of *Economic Adjustments after the Cold War: Strategies for Conversion,* (1992) by Dartmouth Publishing Co. in Britain for the United Nations Institute for Disarmament Research (UNIDIR). He has published four Worldwatch Papers: *Rethinking the Role of the Automobile* (no. 84, June 1988), *National Security: The Economic and Environmental Dimensions* (no. 89, May 1989), *Swords Into Plowshares: Converting to a Peace Economy* (no. 96, June 1990), *Jobs in a Sustainable Economy* (no. 104, September 1991). Mr. Renner holds degrees in international relations and political science from the Universities of Amsterdam, the Netherlands, and Konstanz, Germany.

JOEL YUDKEN has been a postdoctoral research fellow at the Project on Regional and Industrial Economics at Rutgers University since 1990. In 1989–90 he was Fellow of the National Science Foundation's Science, Technology, and Society Program. From 1979–86 he was Director for Programs at the Center for Economic Conversion in California, and served on the California state senate's Industrial Competitiveness Task Force. A former engineer in aerospace industry, he holds a bachelor's in electrical engineering from Rensselaer Polytechnic Institute, a masters in engineering-economic systems, and a doctorate in technology and society from Stanford University. He has consulted, written, and spoken extensively on science and technology policy, industrial policy, and economic conversion. He is co-author (with Michael Black) of "Targeting National Needs: A New Direction for Science and Technology," *World Policy Journal* (Spring 1990), and co-author with Ann Markusen of *Dismantling the Cold War Economy* (New York: Basic Books, 1992).

INDEX